Health Care Ethics for Psychologists

Health Care Ethics for Psychologists

A CASEBOOK

Stephanie L. Hanson
Thomas R. Kerkhoff
Shane S. Bush

AMERICAN PSYCHOLOGICAL ASSOCIATION
WASHINGTON, DC

Published by
American Psychological Association
750 First Street, NE
Washington, DC 20002
www.apa.org

To order
APA Order Department
P.O. Box 92984
Washington, DC 20090-2984
Tel: (800) 374-2721; Direct: (202) 336-5510
Fax: (202) 336-5502; TDD/TTY: (202) 336-6123
Online: www.apa.org/books/
E-mail: order@apa.org

In the U.K., Europe, Africa, and the Middle East, copies may be ordered from
American Psychological Association
3 Henrietta Street
Covent Garden, London
WC2E 8LU England

Typeset in Goudy by Stephen McDougal, Mechanicsville, MD

Printer: United Book Press, Inc., Baltimore, MD
Cover Designer: Berg Design, Albany, NY
Technical/Production Editor: Gail B. Munroe

The opinions and statements published are the responsibility of the authors, and such opinions and statements do not necessarily represent the policies of the American Psychological Association.

Library of Congress Cataloging-in-Publication Data

Hanson, Stephanie L.
  Health care ethics for psychologists : a casebook / Stephanie L. Hanson, Thomas R. Kerkhoff, Shane S. Bush.—1st ed.
    p. cm.
  Includes bibliographical references and index.
  ISBN 1-59147-152-4
  1. Medical ethics—Case studies. 2. Medical care—Decision making—Moral and ethical aspects—Case studies. 3. Psychologists—Professional ethics—Case studies. I. Kerkhoff, Thomas R. II. Bush, Shane S., 1965- III. Title.

  R724H234   2004
  174.2—dc22
                                                 2004003104

British Library Cataloguing-in-Publication Data
A CIP record is available from the British Library.

Printed in the United States of America
First Edition

United Book Press, Inc., Baltimore, MD

CONTENTS

ACKNOWLEDGMENTS

We believe no one is ever successful without the support of others. We would like to thank our families, friends, and colleagues who encouraged us to pursue this text. They tolerated us when we felt the weight of the task and supported us with the time and freedom to devote substantial energy to the creative process whose end result is an ethics casebook of which we are very proud.

We also would like to acknowledge the exceptional thinkers (and even some above-average ones) who have contributed to the field of ethics and laid the foundation of ideas that gave birth to our own work.

INTRODUCTION: VALUES AND THE PRACTICE OF PSYCHOLOGY

Mention the word ethics in a crowd of professionals and the reactions are varied, spanning the continuum from intense interest through anxiety and loathing to self-righteousness. Yet, negative emotional valence and misgivings regarding the utility of ethics codes need not be their calling card. As psychologists, we make decisions every day that incorporate our fundamental beliefs and values regarding what is appropriate in our interactions with patients, health care professionals, and institutions. Psychology's global view of practice is grounded in the American Psychological Association's (APA, 2002) Ethics Code (http://www.apa.org/ethics/). The "Ethical Principles of Psychologists and Code of Conduct" provides overarching principles and standards that guide the actions of psychologists vis-à-vis our clients, their families and communities, and our colleagues. Further, these principles and standards affect our professional roles as advocates for social change.

In general, professional codes of ethics represent systems of thought, bolstered by a combination of cultural values, professional experience and philosophical underpinnings (American Medical Association, 1997; American Psychological Association, 2002; Beauchamp & Childress, 2001). These ethics-based systems of thought are concretized when they incorporate enforceable ethical health care practice standards. The APA Ethics Code provides an overarching structure that sets the stage for evaluating and enforcing adherence to what is and is not acceptable psychology practice within our current sociocultural climate. It is important that the APA Ethics Code is directly linked to everyday professional actions of the APA membership and presents a time-tested model of enforceable practice standards. The APA Ethics Code provides such enforceability for psychologists who are APA members and in states in which the Ethics Code has been adopted as part of professional practice guidelines.

However, considering the APA Ethics Code simply as a set of post hoc sanctions on our professional behavior fails to embody an important facet of the ethical decision-making process. We argue for the aspirational nature of ethics, a developmental and preventative approach that sets an expectation of accountability for our needs and those of the persons and institutions we serve in *anticipation* of implementing an action plan; it provides a global methodology for optimizing our professional behavior. However, this aspirational aspect of the Ethics Code is somewhat abstract. The utility of the Ethics Code is primarily validated in its applicability—how effectively it can concretely guide proactive decision making for resolving difficult real-life challenges, rather than relying on post hoc consequences. It is the applicability of the APA Ethics Code to real-life concerns that we directly address in our volume. This casebook is designed to offer guidance on how to approach ethical issues in diverse health care settings consistent with the ethical principles and standards under which we practice.

PSYCHOLOGISTS IN THE HEALTH CARE SYSTEM

Beauchamp and Childress (2001) presented a cogent and balanced summary of issues in contemporary ethics theory regarding the complexities of the health care system in the United States. Disparate theories exist among proposed health care models, yet each seeks to develop an ethically defensible health care delivery system. The health care system and the professionals who practice within it must strive to achieve a reasonable balance across the broad ethical principles of respect for autonomy, beneficence, nonmaleficence, and justice. These same principles represent the core of the APA Ethics Code.

The profession of psychology has been attentive to the need for refinement of guiding ethical principles and standards as each new generation of discovery has brought with it unanticipated ethical complexities. This process of refinement is evidenced in the evolutionary development of the APA Ethics Code from 1953 to its present iteration (Hanson, Guenther, Kerkhoff, & Liss, 2000). The profession must remain vigilant in its evaluation of psychology's contributions to ethical thought and assess the appropriateness of the APA principles and standards to the practical realities of everyday decisions in the constantly evolving sociocultural fabric. In addition, psychologists have used and continue to develop unique pathways in professional training that afford a comprehensive, integrated view of clinical and societal challenges. Refining critical thinking skills along these innovative pathways will contribute to both the processes of ethical debate and policy formation. Psychologists must continue to be active in the broader societal arena in order for the profession to thrive.

Training the next generation of psychologists practicing in health care settings to embrace and use sound ethical practice will require increased attention to cultural shifts already underway. For example, few would argue against the need for major health care reform in the United States, but the early stages of such a reform will likely impact resource allocation for the elderly more directly than the younger, healthier segment of the populace (Beauchamp & Childress, 2001). This is partly because, as the population ages, the percentage of individuals with chronic health conditions who disproportionately require health care resources also rises (Frank & Elliott, 2000b). Unfortunately, low- and middle-income elderly cannot afford to cover the costs of services needed. For example, Medicare currently covers only 50% of outpatient mental health costs. In general, older adults underutilize mental health services, which, if accessed, could actually help reduce general medical costs (Frank, Hagglund, & Farmer, 2004; Haley, 2004). The costs of health care resources will only increase as the mean population age increases across the next few decades (Beauchamp & Childress, 2001) and as the social and personal values of the "boomer" generation take stronger hold on routine expectations for health care provision (e.g., health care security, entitlement, preventative care, cosmetic improvement, attendant care). These value-based expectations will challenge the social zeitgeist underpinning the current health care system. Historically, societal needs have ultimately dictated the timeframe for such systematic transformation within health care. Psychologists can play a vital role in both developing and using innovative methods for delivery of psychological care as this transformation unfolds. We must also champion reimbursement revisions and vigilantly monitor regulatory changes affecting coverage of psychological services in the diverse settings in which we practice. We must admit that the political risk attending the championing of needed reform early in a cycle of change may impede progress, but that risk cannot derail the inexorable evolutionary process.

To respond to changing health care models, as psychologists we are just beginning to incorporate into our identity the role of primary care provider. In such a capacity, we can contribute to cost reductions by preventing unnecessary medical care and reducing future strain on limited resources through early and accurate diagnosis, intervention, and consultation (Bray, Frank, McDaniel, & Heldring, 2004). In addition, we can contribute more fully to ethical decision making through application of our unique skills in understanding and integrating emotional, behavioral, and interpersonal aspects of a patient's and family's situation affecting potential ethical challenges and resolutions.

As psychologists, we are ethically mandated to both assist and advocate on behalf of our patients. Although psychologists face some harsh realities in responding to that mandate in the current health care enterprise, by virtue of our broad-based training in health issues, we can offer an across-the-spectrum approach to evaluation and intervention that embraces the primary care model. Psychologists possess unique skills to enhance the health care process in complex delivery systems. We need to continue to press for change that embodies this wealth of psychological knowledge that serves as the foundation for our clinical decisions and broader advocacy for the benefit of our patients and the profession. In these endeavors, we must remain cognizant of the importance of incorporating the ethical principles and standards.

GENERAL ORGANIZATION OF THE CASEBOOK

The ethical analyses of the cases presented in this book illustrate the authors' basic premise that ethical principles and standards serve as guideposts in the often murky process of clinical decision making. We do not purport to have the final answer regarding these case examples, but we make use of the APA ethical principles and standards in such a way as to offer structure within which individual and societal needs can be constructively addressed. It is in considering both the strengths and the failings of our cast of characters that the complexities of the ethical decision-making process play out.

The goals of this casebook are to create a text that is interesting and useful to the clinician in everyday practice and that enhances the educational process of psychologists and students. The casebook is organized around the health care continuum, with each chapter presenting a particular type of health care environment, ranging from crisis care to long-term care. Although the reader may be selectively interested in chapters dealing with the situational dynamics of a specific work setting, each chapter contains ethical issues relevant to the general field. Therefore, the reader may find cross-application of pertinent concerns and discussion relevant to a setting in chapters representing other areas. We attempt to highlight this by taking a patient who sustained severe burns across the continuum of care from acute medical care to outpatient therapy (see chaps. 2–4, this volume). These varied clinical settings and their narratives possess common threads that reflect the interwoven ethical principles underlying the APA Ethics Code, on which this volume relies for guidance. With the adoption of the latest APA (2002) Ethics Code, we have the opportunity to incorporate up-to-date ethical considerations in structuring the entire text.

Each chapter is organized in the same manner. The initial section presents introductory comments regarding the professional practice setting, including the psychologist's responsibilities and roles, the social dynamics at work, and common ethical challenges.

The initial section is followed by a series of cases with analysis. The cases selected are founded in real-life situations experienced by the authors. However, they have been altered to protect patient and organizational confidentiality and to facilitate explication of the relevant principles and standards.

Following each case description, relevant APA (2002) ethical principles and standards are presented to demonstrate the direct applicability of the Ethics Code to the specific clinical situation. Principles and standards have been selected for their unique contribution to the case. Therefore, not all applicable principles and standards are presented (i.e., typically we did not include overlapping or secondary principles and standards). Throughout the text, we attempt to demonstrate how the Ethics Code provides both proactive guidance and clarity of thought in resolving situational challenges in an ethically acceptable manner.

This section is followed by brief commentary on institutional and legal concepts relevant to the scenario. It is important to ground clinical issues confronted in organizational and legal, as well as ethical, constructs early in the decision-making process because legal mandates may directly affect the chosen decision-making path. We caution the reader that the legal section is not meant to substitute for legal advice. Legal issues clearly vary by state and by the individual clinical circumstances. Psychologists should seek legal assistance if faced with legal concerns in their practice.

The next section of each case presents contextual information and key stakeholders. No case occurs independently of chronological events that trigger the issue or dilemma or impact its unveiling. Therefore, this section is designed to give the reader a view of the clinician's considerations as each case evolves. Included are descriptions of major stakeholders and their roles and contributions to the situation as it develops. We then move to case resolution in which we lay out steps taken by the psychologist with various parties to address the ethical challenges faced. These steps commonly incorporate negotiation and acquisition of commitment from various parties toward a mutually agreed-on action plan.

The final section of each chapter describes the eventual outcome of the case. Additional commentary is routinely provided to discuss continuing concerns regarding case resolution, additional ethical considerations, and to provide reference material.

The approach we have taken is based on several years of experience in various professional instructional settings. Its expressed purpose is to make the ethical decision-making process both meaningful and user friendly. Although this casebook leaves many issues untouched (e.g., minors in health care and restraints), we hope students and professionals find the casebook useful in enhancing sensitivity to ethical concerns and current levels of decision-making knowledge. The casebook is meant to reflect ethical pragmatism, that is, to demonstrate sound ethical decisions that are reasonable to implement in applied clinical settings. We hope the cases and commentary provided are both broad based and specific enough to be applicable to other situations practitioners encounter. To the extent that we effectively apply the ethical decision-making process to issues pertinent to practicing psychologists, this casebook will have succeeded.

1

CRISIS AND EMERGENCY CARE

A standard part of psychological training is learning how to appropriately respond to patient emergencies. Psychological interventions sometimes can make the difference between life and death for patients in crisis. As psychology consultation and liaison services have expanded their roots in health care centers, psychologists are increasingly consulted to assist emergency personnel dealing with patient and family crises. Rozensky, Sweet, and Tovian (1997) offered a comprehensive overview of common assessment areas and useful tools for psychologists practicing in the emergency room (ER).

However, crisis intervention by psychologists is not limited by the walls of the ER. Psychologists in private practice or other community-based settings who have partnerships with primary care physicians create a common point of entry for evaluating psychological and medical factors requiring immediate intervention (Bray, Enright, & Easling, 2004; Haley et al., 2004; Ruddy & Schroeder, 2004). In addition, psychologists often are recruited as members of crisis response teams to deal with the aftermath of natural disasters such as hurricanes and fires and man-made disasters such as bioterrorism. (Please see Case 1.1 for specific disaster citations.) Finally, psychologists not part of an organized response may address emergency situations simply because they are available through independent consultation or on their own initiative based on a sense of moral responsibility to help others given their

9

background in psychology. The American Psychological Association (APA) 2002 Ethics Code specifically allows for this latter situation. Standard 2.02 states that psychologists may go beyond their current level of expertise and competency to benefit a person in need during an emergency. The psychologist is then obligated to relinquish responsibility to someone better qualified once he or she arrives on the scene. In addition, most states provide protection from undue liability to those assisting in emergencies through "Good Samaritan" legislation. (The Medical Reserve Corps, 2003, Web site lists Good Samaritan statutes by state.) This proactive and reactive approach to society's needs encourages psychologists' involvement in social as well as individual crisis situations that can benefit from psychologists' unique professional training.

Situational dynamics related to crisis intervention are broad because of the diversity of emergency settings in which psychologists work. As noted previously, these range from the sole practitioner making an emergency referral to the psychologist working in consultation with psychiatry, nursing, and medicine in the ER to having to coordinate actions in the context of a broader and extensive response effort. Anticipated ethical issues include, but are not limited to, conflicts between patients and families regarding the patient's presenting symptoms, conflicts among providers regarding role definitions and discharge placements, and conflicts between providers and patients and families regarding decisional capacity and commitment.

Regardless of setting, conflicts facing psychologists may involve differing moral obligations based on the APA Ethics Code, organizational procedures, or legal mandates for reporting and documenting situations resulting in the need for emergency care. Having a long time to deliberate the ethical considerations of each person's situation is inconsistent with the dynamics and nature of the emergency environment. Psychologists must be able to analyze ethical concerns and moral and legal obligations quickly. Therefore, an acute awareness of state and national policies as well as local influences affecting emergency response (e.g., abuse reports and commitment procedures) is critical before finding oneself in an emergency situation. Public policy preparedness and flexibility in the face of the ever-shifting structure of the emergency process are key to successful integration of psychologists in emergency care. Psychologists are ethically obligated to avoid harming patients (Standard 3.04) and to protect each patient's safety and welfare during periods of high stress, consistent with psychology's ethical principles.

CASE 1.1
DO THE RULES STILL APPLY? CRISIS RESPONSE TO 9/11

Ben Fissent, PhD, entered Mrs. Jones's hospital room Tuesday morning to assess the patient's emotional status after she had undergone an unexpected hysterectomy. Mrs. Jones's television displayed the unbelievable scene of a jumbo jet crashing into the World Trade Center in New York City. The camera panned back to reveal black smoke billowing from both towers. The morning, of course, was September 11, 2001. The events were unfolding just 50 miles away as Mrs. Jones slept.

The health care providers and patients were experiencing a range of thoughts and emotions—disbelief, grief, anger, apprehension. Both staff and patients had family or friends in nearby Manhattan. Everyone hoped for the best, feared the worst, and waited in emotional agony for word from their loved ones. In the initial hours following the attack, Dr. Fissent and the rest of the mental health team provided emotional support to patients and staff while attempting to remain informed of the evolving events and manage their own emotions.

A captain in the Army Reserves with training in disaster response, Dr. Fissent felt a strong pull, as a psychologist, a military officer, and a human being, to go to the site of the crisis to help. He attempted to contact his reserve center, located in New York City, but the phones were out. He had outpatients scheduled in the afternoon and was torn between staying to provide support in the hospital and outpatient clinic or going to Manhattan. Knowing that other mental health professionals were available to assist on the inpatient unit, he contacted his outpatients and gave them the choice of being seen or rescheduling. They all rescheduled. Dr. Fissent decided to go to the site of the tragedy.

Dr. Fissent stopped at home to change into his military uniform and tell his family of his plan. His wife, noting the potential danger for those responding to the tragedy, asked him not to go, to think instead of their two young children. She asked why he felt compelled to go, a question to which he could provide no specific answer. Instead, he shared a feeling of duty and a desire to fight back. If anything went wrong, he believed his children would understand. At around 10:00 a.m., he left for Manhattan.

The expressway to Manhattan was closed to all but emergency vehicles. Because of his military credentials, Dr. Fissent was granted access. The drive to Manhattan was an eerie experience. Typically crowded, the expressway was now deserted. Columns of smoke rose into a cloudless blue sky over lower Manhattan; sirens from an occasional ambulance or fire truck sounded as they passed; and armed checkpoints blocked the expressway every few miles. Questions about what he would find ran through Dr. Fissent's mind. Thoughts of unseen dangers, such as another attack or biologic warfare, added to his concern. As he neared Manhattan, the expressway, streets, and bridges leaving the city were choked with people escaping the attack. It felt strange to Dr. Fissent to be heading into a place that millions of people were fleeing.

The scene in Manhattan was equally bizarre. Having parked in midtown, Dr. Fissent walked the 30 blocks to Ground Zero. Along the way, many people seemed to be enjoying a beautiful fall day as if nothing had happened.

People sat in parks and outdoor cafes, laughing and smiling. Dr. Fissent wondered if it was possible that some people did not know what was happening downtown. However, as he neared Ground Zero, the scene began to change quickly. Some people walked swiftly away; some stood at roadblocks trying to talk their way through; and many just stood staring into the smoke and dust.

Having passed the checkpoints into Soho, Dr. Fissent continued walking down West Broadway. Minutes later, dozens of people came running toward him, followed by a loud rumbling and a large cloud of smoke. Building 7 of the World Trade Center had just fallen. The reality of the scene merged with disbelief, becoming surreal. He then crossed over to West Street and continued walking south on that main route to Ground Zero. Stores went from being open to closed to destroyed. Emergency vehicles with lights and sirens lined the street. Emergency workers walked to and from the most forward position, a staging area at a local high school just a few feet from the fallen buildings. Beyond that point, which was closely guarded by police, only select units of firefighters were allowed. The firefighters marched in columns into the rubble, passing other weary, dust-covered firefighters returning from the rubble. Fires could be seen burning in the upper stories of nearby buildings.

Exhausted firefighters sat in groups along walls or beside their fire trucks, and police officers stood or sat along the street. Volunteer workers handed out water while other volunteers passed by with protective equipment, such as facemasks, gloves, and hard hats. The smoke and dust were so thick that visibility was measured in feet. Debris covered the ground. Flattened cars and fire trucks dotted the street. Most people wore an expression of blank disbelief and resolute purpose. Some talked about what they knew about the attack. Others cried.

Dr. Fissent checked in at the staging area in the high school. Medical sections were being established, including a small area for mental health services. Two counselors were sitting at a table, but here, as in the medical units, there were no patients. An occasional firefighter was treated for smoke inhalation or blisters, but otherwise personnel just waited. Dr. Fissent thought he would have more to offer by going back to the street among the emergency personnel.

He saw two firefighters in their 20s, faces streaked with gray soot, leaning against a building; one was crying. Dr. Fissent approached the firefighters and identified himself, "Hello, I'm Dr. Ben Fissent, a psychologist. What can I do to help you?" The firefighter who was not crying looked at the military-attired psychologist, nodded toward his buddy, and walked away. His voice choked with tears, the remaining firefighter immediately started describing his experiences from earlier in the day, "Doc, I was working at the base of the north tower. The upper floors were burning and billowing smoke. All I could do was watch helplessly as people jumped out of windows and hit the ground near me." He paused, tears flowing more freely, "It was . . . horrible."

Ben Fissent stood near, just listening to the unbelievable tale, "Many of the guys were still in the building when it came down . . . folding in on itself . . . at first it seemed like slow motion, then the concrete pulverized in a sooty gray cloud . . . it roared, exploded . . . covering everything!"

The young man looked pleadingly at the psychologist, "Forgive me doc, but I had to get out from underneath the wreckage . . . didn't know what else to do. I had my mask on, but couldn't see anything." The firefighter paused, then tearfully recounted the horrific images in vivid detail while Dr. Fissent continued to listen.

Almost as abruptly as he had begun speaking, the young man stopped. He looked Ben Fissent in the eye for a long minute. He had stopped crying. He said he had to get back to his unit, struggled back into his heavy coat, and held out his hand. Dr. Fissent shook his hand, feeling the connection. The firefighter then turned back toward his unit and walked into the haze of smoke and dust.

Relevant Ethical Principles and Standards

Principle A: Beneficence and Nonmaleficence

Dr. Fissent must consider potential harm to his patients if he is unavailable to help them process their reactions to the terrorist attack and resulting changes in their health status. He also must evaluate the possibility that he influenced his outpatients' decisions not to attend their scheduled visits for his own personal gain. Finally, he must consider the potential for harm through his individual efforts to help, which could prove more detrimental than helpful to organized relief efforts.

Principle B: Fidelity and Responsibility

Dr. Fissent is trying to balance his patient responsibilities with what he believes is his broader obligation to society. He has made a commitment to his country to assist in times of national conflict, and he believes this commitment is particularly important in situations in which others may have limited access or training. However, Dr. Fissent needs to consider whose needs are being met by going to Ground Zero, society's, his patients', or his own. Is going to the disaster site and using his military credentials to gain access responsible or irresponsible given the uniqueness and gravity of the disaster? Although not all psychologists possess the military and disaster training Dr. Fissent possesses, he may still be reacting to the events independently of his professional background. Is the strong pull to go to Ground Zero because of a well-meaning but misguided desire to help? Dr. Fissent needs to identify his motives and the roles he serves in such a chaotic situation. He also must consider his obligation to other team members and his employer, both of whom might benefit from his crisis expertise. He is obligated to make decisions responsibly for providing care.

Standard 2.01, Boundaries of Competence

Many psychologists experience a strong desire to help others in times of crisis. However, not all psychologists who want to assist have training commensurate with their desire. Standard 2.01, Boundaries of Competence, mandates that "Psychologists provide services . . . with populations and in areas only within the boundaries of their competence, based on their education, training, supervised experience, consultation, study, or professional experience" (APA, 2002, p. 1063). In this case, Dr. Fissent has received such training through his service in the Army Reserves. However, the psychological trauma encountered by military personnel in combat and the methods used to treat it may not parallel civilian trauma. Furthermore, had he not had training in crisis intervention, would his basic clinical training have been sufficient given the apparent paucity of psychologists at Ground Zero on September 11?

Standard 2.02, Providing Services in Emergencies

Psychologists may provide emergency services "to individuals for whom other mental health services are not available" (APA, 2002, p. 1064). Specific organizations like the American Red Cross typically coordinate services during disasters. However, does the makeshift mental health area with two counselors qualify as making services available to the extent needed? If not, is Dr. Fissent justified in attempting to provide services while organizational efforts are being more fully developed given that he has checked in at the staging area?

Standard 3.04, Avoiding Harm

In addition to considering the foreseeable risk to his patients and organization if he leaves the hospital unit to which he is assigned, Dr. Fissent must consider the potential risk to firefighters in discussing the events at Ground Zero while still on duty.

Standard 3.10, Informed Consent

Is consent required in a disaster and, if so, how is this consent acquired and defined (e.g., the level of detail necessary)?

Standard 4.02, Discussing the Limits of Confidentiality

In general, limits of confidentiality are discussed at the beginning of a therapeutic relationship. However, this standard allows for some flexibility (i.e., "unless it is not feasible or is contraindicated" [APA, 2002, p. 1066]). Perhaps this flexibility can be applied in a disaster to waive discussion of the limits of confidentiality. However, what are the implications of this if someone reveals unprotected information (e.g., suicidal ideation or abuse)?

Standard 6.01, Documentation of Professional and Scientific Work and Maintenance of Records

One purpose of record keeping is to facilitate the provision of additional services. Dr. Fissent did not attempt to acquire information to allow reasonable documentation. He did not even ask the firefighter his name. Does this place Dr. Fissent at ethical and legal risk?

Standard 10.01, Informed Consent to Therapy

The psychologist must clarify whether this type of interaction is considered therapy and, if so, his professional obligations regarding consent.

Institutional and Legal Concepts That May Apply

The APA Ethics Code allows psychologists to provide emergency care even if not trained to do so. However, the psychologist's actions might still raise concerns regarding scope of practice if he ignores readily available knowledge about how to offer services during disasters or bypasses his state psychological association's organized response efforts if he is a member of such an organization.

Relevant Context and Key Stakeholders

The terrorist attack on September 11, 2001 was an unpredictable and catastrophic event whose emotional impact resonated with the entire country. The psychologist possessing both military and disaster training felt a need to assist. However, if he chose to do so, he was clearly making a decision to relinquish temporarily his responsibilities on a hospital unit whose patients were being affected by these same events in addition to their already challenging health concerns. The need to weigh the possibility of harm to those patients, the benefit of staying and helping them or attempting to help at Ground Zero, and the obligations to patients versus the country are at issue.

His patients, the hospital, and society were important parties in Dr. Fissent's deliberations.

The Psychologist

Dr. Ben Fissent's initial reaction to the events of September 11 is not unlike what might be expected of many psychologists, that is, a strong desire to help. However, Dr. Fissent needs to be clear about the rationale for his decision to leave his more immediate responsibilities to his employer and established patients. He acknowledges his patient obligations, sees some of his inpatients, and offers to see his outpatients. He believes he is acting in the best interest of his country to go to Ground Zero to make a small contribution toward recovery from disaster. He attempts to coordinate his offer to help at Ground Zero with his commanding officer, who is not reachable. Dr. Fissent, therefore, uses his military credentials to gain access to Ground Zero and checks in at the staging area. He identifies himself as a psychologist to the firefighters but offers no other information common to a more stable initial therapeutic contact. He does not discuss confidentiality and establishes no treatment parameters or follow-up services.

Inpatient Team and the Organization

Dr. Fissent has a clear obligation to his employer and to the team with whom he serves. Although the team is capable of managing each patient's treatment plan, the psychologist's unavailability may delay implementation of plans and potential discharge, costing the organization money and inconveniencing the team. The extent to which these events occur needs to be considered in making a decision regarding who is best served and by whom. Through appropriate coverage and rescheduling, financial loss may be minimal.

Patients

Dr. Fissent's inpatients and outpatients are reacting to the same tragic events as he is. It could be argued that at least some of these patients might be in greater need of psychological services on September 11 or shortly thereafter. Dr. Fissent does attempt to arrange appropriate coverage, but he cannot predict his patients' needs. Perhaps he can provide the greatest good by remaining at the hospital and giving support to patients and their families. On the other hand, his inpatients are in a fairly protected environment in which other psychological support is available. Although not their primary care provider, other psychologists could offer coverage to allow Dr. Fissent the opportunity to offer services in a situation where few others could.

People in Need at Ground Zero

The individuals at Ground Zero have experienced a horrific trauma. Their rights need to be protected under these circumstances while they receive the help they need. Dr. Fissent, who has no prior relationship with anyone at Ground Zero, assumes substantial risk in offering to assist and then not being able to follow up with individuals who may find open but limited discussion to be traumatic or distressing rather than initially helpful.

Emergency Response Team

The emergency response team has organized mental health services as part of their broader efforts to respond to the terrorist attack. However, these efforts are still being developed in response to the evolving events when Dr. Fissent offers his assistance. Dr. Fissent checks in at the staging area where two other mental health professionals are located. No other mental health services are apparent, and the staging area has not been well used; most of the people in potential need of services are out on the street.

Case Resolution

Explore Motives for Going to Ground Zero

Dr. Fissent initially experienced a conflict between the principles of beneficence and justice. Sensitive to the potential benefits of having psychological services immediately available, he wanted to go to the site of the tragedy to offer his assistance to those in need (beneficence). However, justice, the equitable distribution of services, required him to consider whether remaining at the hospital unit with other mental health professionals to provide support to patients, their families, and staff members or going to Ground Zero where trauma was high and the availability of mental health services unknown would be the best way to assist the greatest number of people (i.e., a just decision). As the APA ethical principles of beneficence and nonmaleficence suggest, "When conflicts occur among psychologists' obligations or concerns, they attempt to resolve these conflicts in a responsible fashion that avoids or minimizes harm" (APA, 2002, p. 1062). Dr. Fissent had to consider the possibility that he wanted to go to Ground Zero given his general humanity and not because of his professional role. This may be a difficult distinction to make. He acknowledged that he might be using his credentials manipulatively to satisfy his own need to help; however, he did not believe this was at the expense of losing focus on his patients. He believed his primary rationale and drive for going to Ground Zero were based on the rare skills he possesses.

Evaluate Risks and Benefits of Decision to Go to Ground Zero

Dr. Fissent reasoned that there would be very few mental health professionals who would want to go to or be able to gain access to Ground Zero in the initial hours when the tragedy was still unfolding, whereas other mental health staff were available to assist those where he worked. In fact, it was unlikely Dr. Fissent would have gained access if he did not present his military credentials. Therefore, he reasoned that he had leverage and training that were fairly specialized. Although this training also would have been applicable to helping hospital staff and patients, the relative risk in not offering his services on a specific day was low relative to the potential benefit of being in the immediate disaster area in which mental health services were warranted but possibly insufficient (given the lack of warning and magnitude). Furthermore, the ethical principle of fidelity and responsibility states that psychologists consider their professional "responsibilities to society and to the specific communities in which they work" (APA, 2002, p. 1062). Therefore, Dr. Fissent felt it was ethically defensible for him to go to Ground

Zero. Given the rapidly unfolding events, he did not think about the potential risk of harm to others in his being at Ground Zero.

Arrange Appropriate Coverage

Dr. Fissent did not relinquish his obligation to his patients when the disaster occurred. He arranged coverage consistent with any circumstance under which he would be unavailable. He spoke with the other psychologist on the unit and discussed both his decision and coverage needs. He also informed the team of his decision to go to Ground Zero but chose not to inform his patients of his decision. He instead requested that the other psychologist simply state that he was unavailable today and would return tomorrow. He did not want to escalate patients' anxiety related to the disaster and danger still present. Dr. Fissent rescheduled all outpatients given the extraordinary circumstances. This met the ethical obligation of appropriate coverage. What remained unpredictable were the personal reactions to an event of such great magnitude that affects so many. Although it did not happen in this case, Dr. Fissent could, for example, have arranged impromptu crisis training or a grief session the same week to help staff process their feelings, if indicated.

Evaluate Appropriate Role at Disaster Site and Implement Accordingly

Once at Ground Zero it was apparent psychological services were sparse. However, similar to medical services, these services were underutilized. Dr. Fissent surmised he could be more effective by going into the disaster area itself and offering his assistance to those at or near the site of impact. Although only one interaction was described, Dr. Fissent had many similar interactions throughout the day. That is, Dr. Fissent introduced himself as a psychologist, and the firefighter or whomever else he was speaking to voluntarily began describing his or her experiences. There was no discussion of issues such as limits to confidentiality. In fact, the degree to which the interaction was a therapeutic contact could be debated. No treatment parameters were established; no history was obtained (the firefighter's name was not even known); Dr. Fissent said almost nothing throughout the interaction; and there were no plans for follow-up services. Nevertheless, it was a professional interaction. Had the firefighter stated that he could no longer live with the day's experiences and planned to take his life, Dr. Fissent would have had to respond without having informed the firefighter of the psychologist's professional responsibility to prevent foreseeable harm. Dr. Fissent was aware of these issues and chose not to interrupt the firefighter as he tearfully described his experiences. Can the clinical and ethical needs be separated in such a situation? Although clinical interactions performed in the staging area's mental health section in the days following September 11 would be considered crisis intervention, these interactions occurred in the context of a warlike situation experienced by very few psychologists throughout the history of the profession. Informed consent in this circumstance was implicit. That is, the individual chose to reveal information specific to the disaster after learning Dr. Fissent was a psychologist. Although the firefighter knew nothing of the limits of consent, Dr. Fissent's action not to seek formal consent seemed appropriate for the extraordinary circumstance.

There was no documentation of this "therapeutic" contact. Dr. Fissent did not know anything about the firefighter except that he had been traumatized and wanted to talk about it for a few minutes. The ethical standards regarding documentation require psychologists to create records of their work to "facilitate provision of services later by them or by other professionals" (APA, 2002, p. 1067). Dr. Fissent might have asked the firefighter his name, asked him if it would have been alright to have someone follow up with him, and then taken his name to the mental health professional at the staging area, creating some documentation for the need to follow up. However, he knew that the firefighter would have ample opportunity to pursue mental health services in the future if desired, and he also felt that such a request during their interaction would have seemed inappropriate. Thus, again because of the unique context in which this crisis interaction occurred, Dr. Fissent did not believe that the usual requirement for documentation was indicated. Therefore, for each of the half dozen or so similar interactions that occurred that afternoon, evening, and night, no documentation was generated.

Case Disposition

With the exception of a few close friends and colleagues, Dr. Fissent reported to no one his presence at Ground Zero from the morning of September 11 to the morning of September 12.

Additional Commentary

It is potentially problematic whenever a psychologist makes a judgment that a section of the APA Ethics Code does not apply in a particular situation. One cannot generally defend ethical violations with the argument that a given case was unique, and the Ethics Code did not apply. Many ethical and clinical factors must be considered very quickly and often in the presence of strong emotions during crises. The Ethics Code addresses this unique set of events only to some extent. For example, the Ethics Code clearly allows individuals to practice beyond their scope (i.e., "psychologists may provide such services to ensure that services are not denied. The services are discontinued as soon as the emergency has ended or appropriate services are available" [APA, 2002, p. 1064]). Dr. Fissent clearly wanted to help and chose to do so in a way he considered to be appropriate given his background and his difficulty reaching authority figures. However, he did not appreciate the role his own emotions were playing in his decision making. Psychologists are not immune to the impact of sweeping traumatic events, and their reactions can affect their own sense of therapeutic effectiveness (Batten & Orsillo, 2002). Because of his drive to help, Dr. Fissent did not consider the potential risk he posed to coordinated disaster response efforts by operating independently. Although he was repeatedly thanked by firefighters with whom he spoke, Dr. Fissent's actions, no matter how well intentioned, were ethically questionable. Dr. Fissent was not a member of the disaster response team even though he possessed background that could prove useful. Although he checked in at the staging area, this was not the place of decision making and coordination for the ongoing disaster response. By independently going into the crisis area, Dr. Fissent risked hindering relief efforts as a result of not understanding the disaster protocols being implemented. If other psychologists had responded as Dr. Fissent did, a chaotic situation could have been made even worse.

Although one can be sympathetic to Dr. Fissent's actions, psychologists need to work within systems set up to respond to emergencies so that they do not hinder coordinated relief efforts. Psychology services have been successfully integrated into disaster response teams in multiple states, such as through the Disaster Response Network of the North Carolina Psychological Foundation and the National Rural Behavioral Health Center in Florida. In addition, psychologists can use technology for widespread dissemination of coping resources. For example, the sheer magnitude of the September 11 attacks dramatically increased demand for mental health information provided on the National Center for Posttraumatic Stress Disorder (PTSD) Web site (Ruzek, 2002). Similarly, there are resources for psychologists working in the trauma area. Several authors offer commentary on therapeutic issues and strategies that may be helpful for psychologists to be aware of when working on response teams or with clients who have experienced large-scale trauma (Call & Pfefferbaum, 1999; DeWolfe, 2000; La Greca, Silverman, Vernberg, & Roberts, 2002; Myers, 1989; Myers, 1994; Ruzek, 2002; Young, 2002). By responding appropriately, psychologists address crucial mental health concerns postdisaster, both immediately afterward and over the long term. However, this does not negate the unique nature of crisis intervention, especially in unanticipated and sudden disasters with wide-ranging contexts, and requires yet additional ethical clarification and elaboration (e.g., when emergency response teams can not be reached, consent, and follow-up).

CASE 1.2
PROVIDER CONFLICTS IN MANAGING
MILD TRAUMATIC BRAIN INJURY

Dr. Freida Brown had been a consultant to the Emergency Department of Community Hospital in Plains, North Dakota, just shy of two years. She had returned to the area as a "repatriated" native three years after receiving her doctorate in clinical psychology. Dr. Brown had done a two-year combined health psychology and neuropsychology postdoctoral fellowship in a primary care setting funded by a community training scholarship. This scholarship had been created by the county commission, which had correctly anticipated a shortage of rural health care providers. As a result of her community's generosity, Dr. Brown agreed to work in the community health system for five years. She was fulfilling this agreement by attaching herself to the largest general health practice in town and consulting to other smaller local health care facilities.

Dr. Lance Lowry had worked as a critical care physician at Community Hospital for almost 27 years. Over the decades, Dr. Lowry had managed to reduce his practice to three eight-hour ER shifts per week. The rest of the time he fished and hunted the pristine countryside, maintaining a comfortable, but modest lifestyle. Dr. Lowry had carefully crafted a reputation for being a minimalist in using health care resources. He rarely admitted patients; if they could walk and knew their own names, patients were discharged home with monitoring instructions from his nurse. The medical center appreciated his cost-conscious nature, and most of his patients valued their health care self-sufficiency. Dr. Lowry's critical care colleagues, however, held a less positive view of his practice style, even though there was no evidence that Dr. Lowry's approach ever contributed to subsequent patient morbidity.

Drs. Brown and Lowry had their first meeting in the evaluation suite of the ER, addressing the needs of Hope Knudsen, an 18-year-old snowboarder. Ms. Knudsen had attempted the county's first inverted 540-degree rotation move on the newly constructed X-Treme ski run just east of town. Hope had managed to complete the inversion portion of the trick before an unusually strong northern gust of wind blew her off course, slamming her upside down into the branches of a pine tree. She was lodged there until her friends arrived to assist her to the ground. She began to regain consciousness about 25 minutes after her collision.

Emergency Medical Services (EMS) quickly transported the confused young woman to the Community Hospital ER. Dr. Nora Knox, the critical care attending physician, consulted Dr. Brown for a cognitive evaluation. Dr. Knox, who was ending her shift, then handed the case, per protocol, to the incoming physician. That physician was none other than Dr. Lance Lowry.

Dr. Brown was in the middle of her screening when Dr. Lowry entered the room. He briefly glanced at the psychologist and introduced himself to the patient. Hope swiveled away from Dr. Brown toward the new voice speaking to her. Momentarily confused, she giggled at the beaver cap Dr. Lowry sported in the winter. "Hey man, that thing's still alive!" Dr. Brown interjected, "We're in the midst of a cognitive screening, doctor. Once it's completed, I'd like to discuss the results with you." Dr. Lowry ignored the statement, instead turning toward his newly assigned patient, "Young lady, please tell me your name." Hope hesitated for a moment and then complied. Before she could respond further, Dr. Lowry pointed across the room and said, "Please get up and take a few steps toward that sink." Hope followed instructions, although unsteadily, and with a look of pain on her bruised face. Dr. Lowry smiled, "I think we can send you home to your parents." As Dr. Lowry turned to leave, Hope said, "Hey, what about my friggin' headache? Feels like my head's gonna explode!" Dr. Lowry responded as he made his way to the door, "I've looked at the CT scan Dr. Knox ordered, and it was negative. Your head may hurt for a few days, but you'll have a prescription for pain. If things get worse, come back to the hospital and we'll do more extensive testing."

"Dr. Lowry, this woman's family is unavailable. Hope's friends told the social worker that she has been staying at home alone while her parents are out of town." Dr. Brown's voice had taken on a somewhat critical tone. Dr. Lowry stopped, removed his hand from the doorknob, and turned, "Oh, hello; I'm Hope's attending physician, and I've just released her. Don't worry, we'll let the social worker find someone to look after her." Again, he turned toward the door.

"I'm Dr. Brown, the psychologist Dr. Knox consulted to evaluate Ms. Knudsen's cognitive status. My findings indicate a possible mild traumatic brain injury (Berrol, 1992). I'd like to complete my examination before this patient leaves." The frustration was evident in Dr. Brown's demeanor.

"Take all the time you need. It will take the staff a while to complete the patient's discharge paperwork." With that, Dr. Lowry briefly smiled and exited the room. Dr. Brown was left with an even more puzzled Hope Knudsen leaning heavily on the examination table.

Relevant Ethical Principles and Standards

Principle A: Beneficence and Nonmaleficence

There are at least two levels of potential concern in this case: first, whether Dr. Brown believes Dr. Lowry acted inappropriately, and second, whether the discharge plan is warranted. Potential concerns based on the psychological evaluation include the ongoing headache, absence of home monitoring, and emerging evidence of mild traumatic brain injury (TBI). Does immediate discharge home place Ms. Knudsen at significant risk of harm despite negative CT scan results?

Principle B: Fidelity and Responsibility

Dr. Brown is faced with patient management and advocacy responsibilities not anticipated by the initial consultation. These represent a modification of her role as evaluative consultant (e.g., discharge planning, safety). She believes she has an ethical responsibility to educate Dr. Lowry about potential complications of TBI and resulting safety concerns.

Principle E: Respect for People's Rights and Dignity

Whether the patient has consented to the discharge plan is in question. Dr. Brown's assessment of Ms. Knudsen's decisional capacity should bear on how active a role she plays in her treatment plan. Dr. Brown also may find herself weighing the need to become a patient advocate to help safeguard the patient's welfare.

Standard 2.01, Boundaries of Competence

Lacking admitting or attending privileges, Dr. Brown cannot directly determine the patient's discharge plan. However, her assessment data can figure prominently in case disposition if the treatment team is open to her input. Dr. Brown possesses expertise to make judgments about the patient's safety secondary to the cognitive effects of injury. She must clearly state findings that bear on the discharge decision even if Dr. Lowry subsequently disregards this information.

Standard 2.04, Bases for Scientific and Professional Judgments

Dr. Brown can present a credible challenge to the evolving discharge plan based on her awareness of the literature regarding closed head injury sequelae. She knows, for example, that initial CT scan results can be normal in patients with mild TBI and that sequelae commonly unfold over time (Berrol, 1992).

Standard 3.04, Avoiding Harm

If Dr. Brown's interpretation of her assessment results suggest the discharge plan is unsafe, she must consider challenging the discharge order, potentially going to Dr. Lowry's supervisor. This person is not likely to be on site at the time.

Standard 3.07, Third-Party Requests for Services

This case is complicated by the fact that one physician requested consultation and another physician received the results. Dr. Brown may need to clarify her already established role with the new provider to prevent subsequent miscommunication and to help tailor presentation of recommendations to the new provider.

Standard 3.09, Cooperation With Other Professionals

Dr. Brown needs to question whether supporting the physician's discharge order effectively serves the patient.

Standard 3.10, Informed Consent

If Dr. Brown believes it is important to assess Hope's decisional capacity given the suspected TBI, she could potentially complete the mental status exam without initial consent. However, she should still strive to obtain assent.

Standard 4.05, Disclosures

Assuming she has appropriate capacity, Ms. Knudsen should be asked for authorization to discuss Dr. Brown's findings with the health care team to effect appropriate treatment and discharge planning. If Ms. Knudsen's confusion prevents such authorization, Dr. Brown may release information to assist the patient in obtaining appropriate services and to prevent potential harm from an unsafe discharge.

Standard 6.01, Documentation of Professional and Scientific Work and Maintenance of Records

Dr. Brown's assessment results and recommendations need to be specifically documented in Ms. Knudsen's medical record, particularly given the conflict regarding discharge readiness.

Standard 9.01(a), Bases for Assessment

Dr. Brown must be able to support any safety and health concerns as a result of her assessment that would influence her decision to accept or not accept the discharge plan.

Standard 9.02(a), Use of Assessments

If adaptation of a mental status examination is required based on Ms. Knudsen's presentation, clear documentation of this modification should be provided. This is particularly important given the mental status exam results are a significant factor in Dr. Brown's forming an opinion different from the physician's.

Institutional and Legal Concepts That May Apply

Dr. Brown must be cognizant of the legal scope of practice vis-à-vis her medical staff privileges. If they are restrictive (no admitting or discharge privileges, no prescription privileges, no attending privileges), then she must work within the designated role of psychologist consultant. However, her concerns for the safety of her patient may allow her to function in an advocacy role that remains in the purview of her consultant status.

Although the discharge is a judgment call, Dr. Lowry may be in jeopardy regarding his obligation to provide due care. If a formal medical staff review of his actions were initiated, the review board would compare his performance against established practice standards for delivery of care.

Relevant Context and Key Stakeholders

Dr. Lowry has approached this case in his usual practice style. He has reviewed the imaging data, read the medical chart, and evaluated the patient to his satisfaction. This manner of practice has allowed Dr. Lowry to perform his duties in Community Hospital without sanction for years. In fact, his method of clinical practice has earned him praise from bottom-line-oriented hospital management. There is no suggestion that he has treated Hope Knudsen in any way that departed from his usual style. Although Dr. Brown may disagree with Dr. Lowry's approach to the case, she remains an invited consultant, thereby constrained in her direct influence on the course of treatment to making recommendations. However, she was consulted by Dr. Knox, the physician of record, and a possible resource.

Dr. Brown has specialized knowledge of brain injury given her postdoctoral training emphases; that knowledge directly bears on Ms. Knudsen's case. She has clear concerns regarding discharge plans because she believes Ms. Knudsen has a traumatic brain injury and the 72-hour window of observation for subdural hemorrhage has not closed. She is obligated to act on that information to reduce the risk of adverse outcome. If Ms. Knudsen were to return home without supervision, complications could arise that would place her at risk for future harm.

The following parties were considered in resolving the conflict between providers.

Patient (Hope Knudsen). Hope Knudsen shows signs of mild TBI. Although her decision-making capacity is impaired, she appears to be able to participate in personally relevant decisions. She reports having a headache and expresses indirect concern about being discharged with this pain. Her family is absent, but Hope should have a supervised setting for several days to ensure no additional symptoms associated with brain injury develop.

Psychologist (Dr. Freida Brown). Based on her assessment and clinical judgment, Dr. Brown's professional opinion is that Ms. Knudsen has sustained a mild TBI. She has been consulted by Dr. Nora Knox but has to deal with Dr. Lance Lowry to whom the case has been transferred at shift change. She finds herself in the additional role of advocate for the patient in order to both respect the patient's right to be involved in decisions and to minimize risk of possible harm if Hope is discharged without adequate supervision. Her concerns appear to be falling on uninterested ears.

Covering Physician (Dr. Lance Lowry). Dr. Lowry has approached the Knudsen case as he typically does when covering the ER. His practice style has earned him kudos from the cost-conscious facility but veiled criticism from physician colleagues. Nonetheless, he has never been sanctioned for how he practices. Dr. Lowry ruled out major problems based on review of a CT scan and lab data and a brief clinical exam; he appears to have minimized concerns expressed by a consultant on the case. He nevertheless agreed to have a social worker find someone to supervise the patient.

Admitting Physician (Dr. Nora Knox). Dr. Nora Knox was on duty when Ms. Knudsen arrived at the ER. She planned to use medical and psychological consultation data to diagnose and treat Ms. Knudsen. Although it might have been reasonable to expect the case to be managed according to Dr. Knox's plan, the scenario changed when the case was handed to Dr. Lowry.

ER Staff. The case manager and nurse charged with crafting Ms. Knudsen's discharge plan gave tacit support to the idea of a short observational admission. Their position was justified by their views of due care, an obligation under which they too operate. However, they had to carefully balance their working relationships with the varied authority figures involved.

Proxy. Even though absent during the ER admission, the family is emotionally invested in their adult daughter's well-being. It may be reasonable to contact them to both inform and receive guidance regarding an acceptable discharge plan if the patient has no other person on file as a surrogate. Most states recognize a family member (usually the spouse, children, or parent) as the first authority to make decisions on behalf of an incapacitated individual or during an emergency. However, neither of these situations is clearly evident.

Facility. Community Hospital is responsible for the quality of care that occurs on its premises. The process of considering how to provide quality care at a reasonable cost reflects the principle of justice and is a daily challenge in the health care system. The balance struck between cost and quality has direct implications for service decisions by providers. Dr. Lowry is inclined to provide low-cost care, consistent with his practice style and his perception of the organization's cost-conscious approach to care.

Social Worker. Although not yet involved, the social worker has responsibility for arranging appropriate supervision. Her ability to do so will determine the level of risk associated with the discharge placement from the psychologist's point of view.

Case Resolution

Information Gathering

Prior to Hope Knudsen's discharge from Community Hospital, Dr. Brown carefully reviewed the patient's chart. She noted the pertinent information and then discussed the case with the ER case manager and the nurse charged with preparing the patient for discharge. Although they were reluctant to challenge Dr. Lowry's orders, they agreed that the patient might have needs that had not been met during the ER visit. They were willing to support Dr. Brown's idea of a short admission for observation. Dr. Brown indicated she would discuss this option with Dr. Lowry.

Consultation With Dr. Lowry

Dr. Brown approached Dr. Lowry and recommended a short observational stay, allowing for 72-hour follow-up radiologic studies and a discharge plan to home with adequately informed family present. Dr. Lowry politely but firmly rejected that recommendation citing the negative results of his clinical exam, not to mention the initial CT scan and lab results. He allowed that subdural hemorrhaging does appear postacutely in a minority of patients, but he was willing to rely on his clinical judgment in support of discharge. Dr. Lowry added that if complications arose after discharge, the patient could be reevaluated by another physician and admitted for treatment. When reminded that Ms. Knudsen had no family at home, the physician replied that the ER social workers were wonders at locating resources. Dr. Lowry expressed confidence that the patient would ultimately be well supervised. The conversation ended when he abruptly turned and headed to the nurses' station.

Consultation With Dr. Knox

Dr. Brown contacted Dr. Knox by phone and explained her concerns about the patient's presentation and discharge plan. The first question asked by Dr. Knox was, "Did Lance do his typical cursory exam and plan immediate discharge, as long as the patient wasn't bleeding out on the exam table?" Dr. Brown cautiously responded, "While I can't comment on the medical evaluation, he did recommend discharge." She paused, "I feel this patient is at risk to develop complications, and her parents are unavailable to monitor her. My recommendation is a short, observational stay. I documented that recommendation in the patient's chart." Dr. Knox agreed and announced her intention to contact the ER. As the ER admitting physician, she authorized the patient's transfer to an inpatient floor for observation.

Contact With Surrogate Caregiver

Dr. Brown followed up with the ER case manager, suggesting that he approach Ms. Knudsen's friends waiting in the ER in an attempt to obtain parental contact information. The case manager smiled and said that he had already done so and was hoping for a return call from a message placed in the parents' hotel.

Case Disposition

Dr. Brown observed Dr. Lowry and the charge nurse in conversation. The phone receiver was handed back and forth several times before the conversation ended, and Dr. Lowry headed in Freida Brown's direction. He walked right past her, then stopped, turned, and spoke, "Well, seems Dr. Knox has decided to admit our young patient for observation. It appears that you two think alike." With a smile, "Oh well, she's taken the case over now, so I'm free to meet other unfortunate souls who wander into our ER." That said, Dr. Lance Lowry wandered off.

Hope Knudsen stayed the 72 hours without incident. Her severe headache was brought under control with medication within 48 hours. Her unsteady gait and confusion also abated. A cognitive screening performed just prior to discharge by Dr. Brown demonstrated significant improvement. Hope's parents arrived at the hospital the next evening, having cut their vacation short after notification. They were grateful for their daughter's care and welcomed the information packet given to them regarding the expected recovery course of mild TBI and resources for follow-up care.

Additional Commentary

The most serious dilemma of this case is whether the psychologist has a clinical disagreement with another health care provider (in this case the physician with discharge privileges) or whether the psychologist is actually concerned that the provider has been negligent in his care of the patient. The fact that the psychologist found additional advocates for her position becomes secondary if she believes the physician is negligent. However, negligence requires that the provider has a direct relationship with the patient and the patient is harmed as a direct result of the lack of due care (i.e., breach of duty; Beauchamp & Childress, 2001). In this case, the provider's actions do not seem to rise to the level of negligence because Dr. Lowry evaluated the patient, acted on negative CT scan results, and agreed to a plan in which the social worker would arrange supervision, indicating he did take into account the psychologist's safety concerns. Therefore, although the psychologist believes the physician's approach is too loose, she does not have a strong case to pursue a complaint regarding care. It was, nevertheless, appropriate for the psychologist to mitigate the circumstances that might create a potential safety risk, which she did through her advocacy efforts.

On the other hand, the psychologist did not handle at least two situations well. First, it was almost immediately apparent that Dr. Lowry and Dr. Brown were at odds regarding discharge, which was played out in front of the patient. Although decisions are made quickly in an ER setting, the providers should have attempted to resolve the differing opinions between themselves and not in front of a confused patient. Second, the psychologist requested that the patient's friends be approached for parental information, which is a clear violation of the ethical principle of respect for people's rights and the standard of informed consent. Although it is very tempting to ask those immediately available for useful information, there was no indication in this case that the psychologist asked the patient for contact information or had identified the patient's correct surrogate. All we know is that the parents were out of town. It would require the patient's consent to solicit information from outside sources. If a competent patient refused to provide such consent, the psychologist would generally be obligated to respect this decision despite an increased risk of complications.

CASE 1.3
PROFESSIONAL BOUNDARIES AND
THE UNWANTED PSYCHOLOGIST

Dr. Leon Guenther took pride in the health psychology service he had pioneered at Midstates Regional Hospital in central Missouri. Three years earlier, Dr. Guenther had secured his chance to practice in Midstates when his close friend Dr. Manuel Moto, an internist, was elected chief of medical staff. Doors that had been closed to Dr. Guenther in the past reluctantly creaked open to allow him to start a limited outpatient clinic practice and hospital consultation service. However, the latter service was grossly underutilized from lack of acceptance of psychology's contributions to acute medical treatment. Dr. Moto's parting official action as chief of staff was to leverage Dr. Guenther's consultation service onto the critical care unit after Dr. Moto had seen the benefit of health psychology's interventions with several of his patients and families. Dr. Guenther had labored almost 18 months to establish a toehold in the critical care unit.

Late Thursday night, Dr. Guenther rushed to the hospital, having received his first page from the Midstates intensive care unit (ICU). He was confronted by a newly admitted 32-year-old man with a chronic spinal cord injury (SCI–T6 paraplegia secondary to a mountain bike injury three years earlier). The patient, Ron Beckman, had been admitted through the ER with symptoms of acute abdominal pain, nausea, hematuria, acute kidney failure, mild delirium, and lethargy.

By the time Dr. Guenther arrived in the ICU, Mr. Beckman and his family were quite distressed. Because staff constantly reminded them of the number of times Ron had required treatment for urinary tract infections (UTIs), the family felt the medical staff was accusing them of ineffectively managing Mr. Beckman's home bladder catheterization program. The family also resented that a "head shrinker" had been consulted but were mollified when Dr. Guenther explained the purpose of his visit. The ICU nursing staff greeted Dr. Guenther with skepticism and called Dr. Lisa Wetherstone, the attending physician, to verify the consultation request. Once the consultation was verified, a nurse handed Dr. Guenther the patient's chart and said, "As long as you are on the unit, maybe you could do something about that patient's temper."

The chart review revealed that the patient had been a "frequent flyer" (regular admissions to the hospital ER) since his injury, usually with UTIs and gradually worsening renal function. Mr. Beckman's medical condition was severe enough that he was unable to work or live independently. Interestingly, Mr. Beckman could cite chapter and verse regarding proper sterile self-catheterization technique. He had all the necessary equipment at home and had demonstrated good technique in the ICU after his delirium had abated. He nevertheless had returned to the ER at a frequency that indicated technique problems rather than resistant organisms. During the clinical evaluation with the patient and family, Dr. Guenther discovered the likely cause of the problem.

Dr. Guenther had completed a postdoctoral fellowship that included a rotation at an accredited rehabilitation center boasting a regional spinal cord injury center. He was aware that a sizeable number of patients sustain an intercurrent brain injury at the time of the spinal cord insult. Indeed, the family described Ron as a "changed man" after his spinal cord injury. He exhibited irritability, episodic temper dyscontrol, and distractibility, symptoms that resulted in ongoing family supervision, much to Ron's chagrin. Dr. Guenther's clinical examination identified a probable attention and concentration deficit and a personality disorder likely related to a TBI. He believed a more comprehensive neuropsychological evaluation after discharge would support these conclusions.

Returning to the nurses' station, Dr. Guenther made specific recommendations based on his interpretation of Ron Beckman's clinical presentation and history. His recommendations focused on behavioral approaches for Ron to improve bladder self-management. Dr. Guenther included instructions for the nursing staff to assist in deescalating Ron's temper when frustrated. He ended with a cautionary statement that the patient would likely continue to have recurring UTIs until his neurobehavioral condition was thoroughly assessed and an intervention program begun. When Dr. Guenther finished, several nurses gathered around to review the written report.

Dr. Guenther sat down with Ron and his family in the hospital room to discuss his findings. It was during this conversation that he discovered the size of the Beckman family. There were 11 people (5 adults and 6 children) living in the family's small two-bedroom house. No one had much privacy, and the routine noise level in the house fell just short of chaos. Ron was constantly distracted during his attempts at self-catheterization.

The family denied having been told about the possibility of a brain injury accompanying the spinal cord injury. Even though Ron's emotional dyscontrol was not at all like his preinjury personality, the family simply thought Ron was angry, as anyone in similar circumstances would be. The family expressed relief, concern, and guilt about Ron's situation. Had they known about the brain injury, they could have sought professional help for Ron. Dr. Guenther provided emotional support and then shared practical accommodations and compensatory strategies for the patient and family to use at home to help Ron be successful with his bladder management. Finally, Dr. Guenther promised to assist them in securing state and local agency support for outpatient assessment, treatment, and vocational rehabilitation.

Just as the conversation was coming to an end, a red-faced urology resident entered the room. The resident was accompanied by the ICU's head nurse. The resident said, in a harsh voice, "I wasn't aware that psychologists had a license to practice medicine." In response to Dr. Guenther's surprised look, the resident added, "*Anything* having to do with urological concepts, practices, and procedures is the purview of medicine. *Only* physicians can accurately discuss such information with patients." The nurse stood sullenly by, eyeing Leon Guenther as if he were an interloper.

Relevant Ethical Principles and Standards

Principle A: Beneficence and Nonmaleficence

By identifying the links between the spinal cord injury, brain injury, and UTI, Dr. Guenther contributes to a treatment plan that prevents future patient harm (e.g., reducing health risks and costs associated with repeated UTIs and the impact of TBI sequelae). Because both the patient and his family are affected by the problem, Dr. Guenther needs to consider the involvement of supportive players in the intervention to promote optimal patient welfare and effective family support and coping.

Principle B: Fidelity and Responsibility

Dr. Guenther attempts to define his relationship with the Beckman's through knowledge regarding TBI and modifications to their current approach and environment under which self-catheterization occurs. The provision of this information and recommended intervention strategies should help the patient and family adaptively alter troublesome behavior. Dr. Guenther also discharges his responsibility to the attending physician, the hospital staff, and the patient in his role as a consultant by providing them with information that could enhance the effectiveness of the medical care rendered to the patient.

Principle D: Justice

Mr. Beckman presents with a clear pattern of UTIs associated with his spinal cord injury and uses potentially avoidable high-cost ER services. By contributing to the prevention of both UTIs and use of the ER for treatment, Dr. Guenther indirectly saves health care resources.

Principle E: Respect for People's Rights and Dignity

Although Mr. Beckman has arrived with associated family, Dr. Guenther must be careful not to make assumptions about the family's role. It remains important for him to clarify if and how Mr. Beckman would like the family to be involved, given that he is an autonomous adult.

Standard 2.01, Boundaries of Competence

Because of his rehabilitation training and experience, Dr. Guenther is suited to render a professional opinion regarding potential behavioral causes of the patient's frequent UTIs. His recommendations regarding behavioral aspects of bladder management fall within the practice boundaries of a qualified psychology consultant.

Standard 2.04, Bases for Scientific and Professional Judgments

Opinions offered in the consultation report are based on published scientific literature regarding SCI–TBI comorbidities (Stutts et al., 1991). The opinions are further bolstered by Dr. Guenther's experience with dual-diagnosis patients encountered during his traineeship.

Standard 3.04, Avoiding Harm

Dr. Guenther has the expertise and has appropriately responded to a request for consultation services. At this point, if he were to condone the resident's and nurse's actions, he would be allowing the possibility of future harm to both the patient and family caused by the emotional, physical, and financial costs of the recurring UTI pattern.

Standard 3.07, Third-Party Requests for Services

The psychologist has a contractual relationship with the hospital for consultation services. Uninformed third parties do not have the authority to override these relationships. However, Dr. Guenther needs to clarify his role given that the individuals raising the concerns are providers affected by the type of relationship established.

Standard 3.09, Cooperation With Other Professionals

The resident and head nurse do not appear interested in cooperating with the psychologist to improve patient care. They have taken a strong position regarding role definition for the psychologist. Dr. Guenther should strive to seek a reasonable solution to the resident's and nurse's initial reaction, but he has no obligation to concur with actions he deems counterproductive to the patient's care.

Standard 4.01, Maintaining Confidentiality

From the moment Mr. Beckman entered the ICU, his family has been present. It is Dr. Guenther's ethical responsibility to ensure that the patient understands the limits of confidentiality and to identify clearly what will and will not be shared with his family based on Mr. Beckman's preferences.

Standard 6.01, Documentation of Professional and Scientific Work and Maintenance of Records

Dr. Guenther reviewed the medical record prior to seeing Mr. Beckman. Then, he documented his findings in the patient's medical record to provide consultative guidance in treatment. In this documentation, Dr. Guenther needed to take care to avoid language suggesting the exclusivity of the behavioral contributions to the recurring UTIs. Similar to the physician, Dr. Guenther only has one part of the diagnostic puzzle (e.g., behavioral but not physical contributions). Even if the behavioral or cognitive factors in this case ultimately turn out to be the only contributing factors to the recurring difficulty, using exclusive language would be suggestive of practicing outside the boundaries of one's competence (i.e., because such language implies that other hypotheses, such as medical contributors, have been ruled out).

Standard 9.03, Informed Consent in Assessments

Mr. Beckman's consent is solicited prior to the evaluation, a process that also serves to secure his cooperation with the consultation despite temper control problems. However, Dr. Guenther fails to obtain consent regarding family involvement and instead assumes involvement by their de facto presence during the exam.

Institutional and Legal Concepts That May Apply

The Medical Staff Bylaws of Midstates Regional Hospital define the psychologist's scope of practice as part of the criteria necessary for attaining consulting privileges. Dr. Guenther's addressing behavioral influences on the medical condition of Mr. Beckman is within the psychologist's domain of documented expertise as established during the credentialing process. The fact that Dr. Guenther is recognized as a health psychologist in his consulting privileges allows him to render professional opinions regarding cognitive, behavioral, and emotional factors contributing to less than optimal health.

Relevant Context and Key Stakeholders

Dr. Guenther has been practicing at Midstates Regional Hospital for three years. There has been ongoing underlying resistance to his consultative role by specific staff, although this resistance is no longer widespread. However, because his expansion to the ICU has been more recent, practice barriers have not yet been addressed. The resident and head nurse are suspicious of psychological practice and are very protective of their unit. Nevertheless, Dr. Guenther received a request for consultation from an attending physician, who was called into surgery before Dr. Guenther arrived. The patient has a clear history of recurring UTIs associated with his spinal cord injury, but no one until Dr. Guenther has raised the issue of TBI. Mr. Beckman's family is exasperated, both by the recurring UTIs and staff accusations that they are not appropriately managing Ron's care. The potential for a very dysfunctional outcome based on the dynamics among the patient, family, and hospital staff is quite high and is now further complicated by the rejection of Dr. Guenther's recommendations by the resident and nurse.

The patient, family, medical team, and hospital were all considered in determining a resolution to the conflict.

Patient (Ron Beckman). Mr. Beckman seems to have good knowledge of needed care and yet has recurring UTIs. He manages his and his family's distress by accessing emergency care services. He seems invested in improving his health and consented to and cooperated with the psychological consultation. He is upset by staff who believe he is not taking care of himself.

Family (Ron's parents). The family lives in a crowded home. Despite cramped living conditions, they are very supportive of each other and serve as Ron's primary caregivers. They noticed a change in Ron's personality after his SCI, but have not inquired about it with a professional. They are resentful of staff who accuse them of not helping Ron. The family is receptive to information provided by the psychologist. The Beckman's were party to the confrontation by the urology resident physician and head nurse.

Psychologist (Dr. Leon Guenther). Dr. Guenther has exercised his consultative responsibility by securing patient consent, performing a bedside evaluation, giving recommendations to the medical staff, and giving feedback to the patient and family. He expects some suspiciousness from the medical staff, given they have no previous experience with psychology consultants. However, he believes the confrontation by the resident physician and head nurse exceeded the apparent benign mistrust or suspiciousness displayed by the staff nurses.

Attending Physician (Dr. Lisa Wetherstone). The attending physician requested the psychology consult. She believes Dr. Guenther's opinion in the case could be of benefit because previous medical interventions were unsuccessful in changing the increasingly dangerous pattern of renal damage caused by repeated UTIs. The attending physician reconfirms the consultation when queried by the ICU staff after Dr. Guenther's arrival.

Resident Physician and Head Nurse. These individuals have accused the psychologist of practicing outside professional boundaries of competence. They imply that the patient's health will be compromised by the psychologist, who is not trained to treat someone with a UTI. If this accusation has merit, it could result in serious sanctions against the psychologist.

Medical Staff Office and Hospital. The medical staff office grants practice privileges to health professionals serving in the hospital. An unsettled accusation by the medical resident and head nurse could possibly lead to a formal medical staff review. If exculpated, the medical staff office might reprimand the complainants for unfounded, potentially damaging accusations. However, if Dr. Guenther is found to be practicing beyond the scope of his privileges, sanctions against him might include institutional privilege revocation or restriction. Importantly, the process also might produce legally discoverable information, opening the door for later civil court action.

Case Resolution

Confront the Resident and Head Nurse

After excusing himself to the patient and family, Dr. Guenther promptly asked the resident and nurse to accompany him into a nearby consultation room. Once the door had been closed, he immediately expressed his dismay,

"I am profoundly saddened by your unprofessional display in front of the patient and his family." He went on, "If any hospital staff had questions about my consultations, they were welcome to raise their concerns. However, I demand respect due a fellow professional."

This change of momentum nonplussed the young physician and nurse but did not prevent them from restating their accusation that the psychologist was "practicing medicine." Dr. Guenther asked them for an explanation by way of an example. The resident produced a photocopy of the consultation note from the patient's chart and showed Dr. Guenther a highlighted line in the recommendation section where bladder management was mentioned. Stabbing at the paper, the resident stated, "Such matters are the sole purview of medicine, not psychology."

The nurse then spoke up for the first time and said, "Psychologists should only address emotional issues and leave medical treatment to qualified health care professionals."

Rather than respond promptly to the accusations, Dr. Guenther turned and began pacing slowly around the room. After a short time, he stopped, hands folded behind his back, and asked, "What do you two plan on doing about your complaint?"

This question again took the pair aback. They looked at one another, each waiting for the other to answer. Finally, the physician said, "I expect you to admit that you have overstepped your privileges and apologize for your actions."

Dr. Guenther looked puzzled and retorted, "Such an action would imply that I've done something wrong, an implication that I strongly dispute." Again, he asked the question of his accusers, staring intently at each of them, "What *formal* action do you plan to take?"

They replied in tandem, "We'll consult with our supervisors." With that comment, and a worried look between them, the resident and nurse promptly left Dr. Guenther in the room alone.

The psychologist then returned to the patient's room, finished discussing his recommendations, and departed the unit. He did not comment to the staff beyond a polite adieu.

Contact Attending Physician

Dr. Guenther called the consulting physician upon returning to his office in the hospital's outpatient clinic. First, he reported his findings and answered questions regarding behavioral management and follow-up options. He then brought up the negative interaction he had experienced with the resident and head nurse. As the conversation progressed into details of the exchange, Dr. Wetherstone began to shed some contextual light on the situation. She had known of the resident's attitudes toward mental health professionals through overheard conversations in the nurses' station. She was unaware of any reason the head nurse, whom she had known for several years, would have participated in such a dramatic confrontation. She volunteered to speak to the head nurse and express support for psychology consultation services, especially given the helpful perspective contributed in the Beckman case. She also said that she would talk to the resident and the head of urology, if needed. Dr. Guenther thanked her for her assistance and ended the conversation.

Contact Dr. Manuel Moto

The next call Dr. Guenther made was to Dr. Manuel Moto. The call was best characterized as a strategy session geared at avoiding such confrontations in the future. Anger was evident in his friend's voice as Dr. Guenther provided detailed answers to Dr. Moto's onslaught of questions. When Dr. Guenther mentioned the attending physician's offer to follow up with both the head nurse and the head of urology, Dr. Moto's affect deescalated. The political winds in the hospital blew in unpredictable directions at times. Both men agreed to let the situation develop of its own accord and only respond reactively to any challenges raised.

Case Disposition

The situation was never brought to the chief of medical staff's office for review. The attending physician's intervention provided the necessary corrective direction for both the head nurse and the urology resident through his department head. Several of the nurses implemented the temper management strategies recommended by the psychologist, and Mr. Beckman's temper outbursts resolved. These positive results enhanced the staff's confidence in psychology. Dr. Guenther then offered to conduct a behavioral management in-service for the ICU staff, an offer that was received positively by staff and reluctantly approved by the head nurse.

Once the family saw that the staff was following through with Dr. Guenther's recommendations, their distress notably decreased. In addition, the psychologist's review of the evaluation results with the patient and family served as an explanation of the patient's behavior. It also introduced the patient and family to other assessment options, interventions, and community resources. In subsequent weeks post discharge, Mr. Beckman retired his "frequent flyer" moniker. He and his family had successfully reduced distractions during sterile self-catheterization.

After case resolution, the psychologist could not help but wonder about such strong reactions to the consultation. Dr. Guenther later learned that the ICU head nurse had had negative interactions with psychologists during her divorce, the aftermath of which included her losing custody of her two children to her ex-husband. Thus, she harbored a generalized ill will against the profession. The night of the consultation, she had challenged the attending physician when she heard the consultation order had been written. The physician stated her rationale for the consult, hoping for an alternative, behavioral strategy for Mr. Beckman's recurrent UTI problems. Failing in that gambit, the nurse contacted the on-call urology resident, whom she knew was biased against mental health professionals. She had rather dramatically described Dr. Guenther's interaction with the patient as meddling in medical matters. She did not have to provide much substantive data for the resident physician to "fill in the blanks." They both decided to confront the psychologist and actively discourage him from performing such consultations in the future.

Additional Commentary

It is often the case that psychology consultation services on acute care units develop over time and typically with some pockets of resistance and some pockets of support as relationships develop (Gatchel & Oordt, 2003). Critical to success are efficient, succinct responses to consultation questions, particularly when laying out recommendations, and following up with providers after initial recommendations are made. This approach, combined with positive patient results, can speak volumes regarding the value of psychology consultants as they make inroads into previously uncovered hospital units. Psychologists need to be careful, like all professionals, to practice within their boundaries of competence and to be able to defend recommendations offered. When facing resistance, it may not be helpful, as Dr. Guenther did, to challenge resisting professionals regarding what they will do with their complaint. More facilitative can be attempting to understand the nature of concerns, and consistent with the standard of third-party request for services, use the specific consultation question at hand to educate those less supportive regarding psychology's contributions. In addition, the psychologist may have needed to briefly and directly address the inappropriate interaction occurring in front of the patient rather than ignoring it. Finally, he failed to obtain consent for family participation and was ethically obligated to do so even though the family was a clear presence in this case.

2

ACUTE CARE

Hospital-based psychologists usually provide services through consultation and liaison services or positions assigned to specific departments, such as family practice. Service is commonly provided when other health care providers, most typically physicians working on acute treatment units, request assistance for their patients or patients' loved ones who are attempting to manage the psychological, cognitive, and behavioral manifestations of disease or disability. Patients tend to be very sick and can be quite diverse in their diagnostic presentations, both across and within patients. It is part of the routine for psychologists working in acute health care settings to familiarize themselves with varied acute and chronic illnesses, diagnostic procedures and treatments, and anticipated patient recovery or progression to serve their patients effectively.

Providing services on acute hospital floors necessarily implies a collaborative model of health care through consultation with referring professionals and other stakeholders in the patient's care (Belar & Deardorff, 1995; Rozensky et al., 1997). Psychologists typically take advantage of the multiple information sources present in acute care to gain the picture needed to engage in sound decision making. These sources may range from chart review, patient and family interviews, and limited consultation with physicians and nurses responsible for managing the patient's medical care to complex negotiations for time with the patient and contacts with a broad array of disciplines. To obtain the breadth of data needed to make complex decisions, psychologists may consult with such diverse personnel as medical specialists (e.g., oncologists and radiologists), nurse practitioners, social workers, and hospital chaplains. Psychologists also may need the assistance of institutional ethics committees when ethical dilemmas that place institutional policy at odds with ethical practice arise or when dilemmas present two or more equally compelling challenges for effective practice.

Psychologists are challenged by the very nature of the acute health care setting to uphold their ethical obligations to their patients, ranging from protecting patient privacy to conducting succinct yet useful and valid evaluations. Working with multiple sources creates interesting questions regarding what to disclose and document, given the short time in which the psychologist may be involved in a case. Confidentiality is difficult to uphold simply because of the design of semiprivate rooms. Control regarding the implementation of specific assessment and intervention plans may be limited because of procedural interruptions. Patients may be too sick to complete assessment instruments or other evaluations in one sitting, if at all, and patient discharges may come unexpectedly. It is not an uncommon phenomenon for the psychologist to receive a request for consultation in the morning and to find that by the afternoon the patient is no longer on the floor, having been discharged prior to the psychologist's being able to evaluate the patient's cognitive, behavioral, or psychosocial health. In addition, because of shorter hospital stays coupled with the patient's presentation and a hospital milieu in which the patient may be whisked off for a medical procedure at any time, psychological evaluations may be short and focused on specific areas raised by the consultation request rather than comprehensive in nature. The overall name of the game in acute care is flexibility and efficiency (Gatchel & Oordt, 2003). Quick, professionally appropriate response to both the patient and the referral source, although not as quick as required in emergency care, is critical to success.

CASE 2.1
MANAGING DOCUMENTATION IN THE MEDICAL RECORD: THE IMPACT OF THE HEALTH INSURANCE PORTABILITY AND ACCOUNTABILITY ACT GUIDELINES

Bonnie Goode, a 34-year-old, twice-divorced woman, sustained a compound fracture of her right femur in a fall down an escalator while shopping. Although shopping for nothing in particular, she made it a habit to go to the mall each Monday to spend a portion of her alimony checks. In addition, if she had problems with the salespeople, she had easier access to store management.

Bonnie was admitted to the local hospital closest to the mall. Despite her pain and her instructions to emergency medical service (EMS) personnel to get her to the hospital *now*, she was quite angry that she was not taken to the somewhat more prestigious University Hospital across town. One EMS worker was quite impressed by Ms. Goode's fluent use of profanity and her creativity in combining curses when she addressed ambulance crew. He thought what she really wanted was a heavy dose of pain medication, which he promptly administered with the help of his partner.

Following surgical repair of her femur, including open reduction and internal fixation (ORIF), Bonnie was given a bed in the intensive care unit, where she continued to receive substantial doses of pain medication that left her sleeping much of the time. During the following two days, her arousal improved as her medications were reduced. Unfortunately, there was a corresponding increase in anger and frustration, culminating in what the morning nurse, Marilyn Teeter, termed *rage* in her progress note. In her bouts of anger, Bonnie would yell about not only her pain but also about how she now felt like a freak with the metal in her leg.

Bonnie's nurse on the third shift, Pauline Binder, could not understand the necessity of the colorful adjectives used by some of the nurses on earlier shifts to describe Bonnie's behavior. To Pauline, Bonnie was the epitome of the perfect patient. She was polite, appreciative, complimentary, and generous. It was Bonnie's father who was the problem. Malcolm Goode was an attorney, as he liked to inform everyone, and a member of the city council. Apparently, when not drinking, he was quite the litigator. He assured those who would listen that he planned to sue the mall and anyone else who mistreated his daughter.

Ms. Binder was glad that some of the doctors and aides agreed with her assessment of Bonnie, despite the awful things that other staff members had said. In fact, Pauline was becoming particularly disappointed and upset with Marilyn Teeter's assessment of Bonnie and believed it was Marilyn's insensitivity that led Bonnie to scream numerous times that she would kill herself if she did not get a new morning nurse.

Dr. Reilly Watson was called to evaluate Bonnie's suicide potential and to address her angry and unpleasant behavior. Having recently completed an excellent postdoctoral fellowship in psychodynamic therapy in an outpatient psychiatric setting, Dr. Watson felt particularly confident in assessing suicidal ideation. Nevertheless, his hospital-based work was being closely monitored by the supervising psychologist, Dr. Roberto Franco.

To obtain Ms. Goode's consent for the evaluation, Dr. Watson thoroughly described the purpose of the evaluation and potential implications and use of his findings. He then reviewed the medical records in greater detail, interviewed staff and Ms. Goode, and administered both questionnaire and projective psychological tests. His findings were clear: Bonnie did not want to die. Consistent with Borderline Personality Disorder, she used threats, and he suspected that she might use gestures of self-injury to manipulate people into doing what she wanted. Unfortunately, if she did not get her way, such gestures could result in inadvertent death.

Dr. Watson believed that Bonnie had developed this pattern of behavior when she was a child as the only means of getting positive attention from her father, who beat her during alcoholic binges at home. It was also Dr. Watson's opinion that Bonnie's behavior may have contributed significantly to her two divorces and that this type of behavior would likely continue to interfere with the establishment of stable relationships in the future. She would likely remain an essentially unhappy, unfulfilled, and unstable person.

Dr. Watson diligently documented all of this information in his report. He was about to hit the enter key to make his report part of Bonnie Goode's electronic medical record when Dr. Franco stepped up to the computer. As Dr. Franco read the report a look of concern crossed his face. He suggested that they make modifications to the report before entering it into her medical record.

Relevant Ethical Principles and Standards

Principle A: Beneficence and Nonmaleficence

In deciding what to document, the psychologist should determine the extent to which the patient's psychopathology is affecting current treatment and the information considered essential to help staff effectively treat Bonnie and protect her welfare. The psychologist needs to consider the interaction between the team dynamics and the patient's presentation in determining how to address the concerns raised. He also should address staff biases if these increase the likelihood of harm, such as failure to provide appropriate treatment to Bonnie. Both Drs. Watson and Franco need to report findings that facilitate the development and acceptance of an appropriate treatment plan.

Principle B: Fidelity and Responsibility

Dr. Watson established a relationship of trust with Bonnie during the psychological evaluation. By reporting his findings as originally written, he could violate that trust. He must carefully evaluate how to present necessary information to the referring physician and nursing staff while still maintaining Bonnie's trust in psychology.

Principle E: Respect for People's Rights and Dignity

Dr. Franco is keenly aware of Bonnie's and her father's privacy rights and that a violation of their privacy in the context of the psychological report could challenge respect for their dignity. Dr. Franco is somewhat obsessive about including in reports only information that is pertinent to the patient's immediate care. In addition, he needs to consider potential actions psychology might take with the staff to facilitate respect for the patient.

Standard 2.03, *Maintaining Competence*

Dr. Watson is competent to assess mood, personality, and behavior, but he practiced within a very different model during his training than is operating in the acute hospital setting. He needs to establish and maintain appropriate supervision with Dr. Franco until competent to practice independently in this new setting. He also needs to ensure that he familiarizes himself with documentation procedures in this setting.

Standard 2.05, *Delegation of Work to Others*

As his supervisor, Dr. Franco needs to ensure the level of autonomy given to Dr. Watson is appropriate for his training and expertise.

Standard 3.04, *Avoiding Harm*

Avoiding harm encompasses all aspects of a psychologist's role with patients, and therefore, includes both direct and indirect interactions, such as documentation. Although neither psychologist wants to document findings or impressions that will result in more distress for Bonnie or further alienate certain staff from her, Dr. Franco is sensitive to the statements in the report that may do just that. If Bonnie were to access her medical record (a right supported by the Health Insurance Portability and Accountability Act [HIPAA] and her state's law) and read a detailed description of her personality and her prognosis, she might be devastated. Similarly, the reporting of her father as an alcoholic and former child abuser (unsubstantiated) could ruin his standing in the community if hospital personnel with access to the electronic medical record were to share that information with others. In addition, Malcolm Goode has initiated personal injury litigation against the mall, and thus, Bonnie's medical records would be discoverable by involved parties. Dr. Watson must rely on Dr. Franco's assistance in deciding what information included in his report may be harmful versus helpful in this setting.

Standard 3.07, *Third-Party Requests for Services*

Third-party requests are inherent in psychology service provision through consultation. It is critical for the psychologist to review his or her relationship with all appropriate parties. In addition, Dr. Franco is sensitive to the limits of confidentiality in acute medical settings and in the context of litigation. Although he wants the referring physician to get the information needed to maximize Bonnie's care, he does not want potentially unnecessary, hurtful, or embarrassing information about Bonnie or her father to be available to unintended persons. Therefore, the language used and the documentation chosen should be done in the context of assuming unintended persons may have access to the electronic record.

Standard 3.09, Cooperation With Other Professionals

Dr. Watson realizes that, although he is a licensed psychologist, he needs Dr. Franco's input on report writing for acute medical units. He also realizes that there is a conflict among nursing staff that could detrimentally affect patient outcome. He must therefore establish a relationship with both nurses to serve Bonnie effectively.

Standard 3.10, Informed Consent

At the beginning of the evaluation, Dr. Watson needs to inform Bonnie fully about the purpose and nature of the evaluation, the nature of the results and how they would be handled, any possible risks, and the potential threats to privacy and confidentiality. The information in his report should not exceed the boundaries described to Bonnie. Given that Dr. Watson uses an electronic record to document his patient interactions, it is appropriate for him to document his solicitation of and patient's granting of informed consent via this record as well.

Standard 4.01, Maintaining Confidentiality

Psychologists must be particularly sensitive to the issue of electronic storage of information, which potentially offers quick access and delivery to unintended parties. Dr. Watson generally understands the importance of confidentiality but needs input from Dr. Franco to help recognize the extent and limits of confidentiality in the current context.

Standard 4.02, Discussing the Limits of Confidentiality

Dr. Watson has an obligation during the consent process to inform the patient that the psychological data, as part of the medical record, will be stored electronically by the hospital and not solely by the psychologist.

Standard 4.04, Minimizing Intrusions on Privacy

Dr. Watson has gathered significant data regarding Bonnie's background and familial history. Although all of this information has been helpful to the psychologist in formulating a diagnosis, he must now determine which information is directly relevant to the requested consultation. Only germane material should be included in his written and oral communications.

Standard 9.10, Explaining Assessment Results

Dr. Watson should take reasonable steps to ensure that evaluation results are provided to the patient. However, he needs to consider what to share in the context of risk of harm to the patient given her psychological status.

Institutional and Legal Concepts That May Apply

The Health Insurance Portability and Accountability Act of 1996 (retrieved November 2003, from http://www.hhs.gov/ocr/hipaa) is a federal law to improve patients' access to their medical records and to improve privacy related to health information in any form that is personally identifiable. In the hospital setting, the patient or a representative is provided with a Privacy Notice at the time of admission; therefore, individual clinicians may be removed from this process. Although Drs. Watson and Franco are aware that health care providers using an electronic format to transmit or store health information must comply with HIPAA requirements, state law preempts this privacy rule. Therefore, more stringent access could exist than is allowable by the privacy rule alone (Gostin, 2001). On the other hand, ethical standards do not take precedence over HIPAA. If Dr. Franco or Dr. Watson believes that specific ethical standards, such as avoiding harm, are in conflict with Bonnie's right of access, they need to try to resolve this conflict. Ultimately, however, the law would need to be followed.

Because Dr. Watson is providing a psychological evaluation and not psychotherapy, HIPAA would allow Bonnie access to the report if not prohibited by state law. The privacy rule under HIPAA grants patients access to protected health care information but not to psychotherapy notes if they are stored separately from the medical record unless permitted by law, as in Vermont (Holloway, 2003). Under HIPAA there is also an exception to the patient access provision in forensic contexts. It is questionable, however, whether this exception applies in this case. The purpose of Dr. Watson's evaluation is to contribute to treatment planning and not for use in litigation, even though litigation may result. If it is anticipated that litigation will include the psychological evaluation, then Bonnie's access could be prevented, depending on state law regarding record access (Connell & Koocher, 2003).

Relevant Context and Key Stakeholders

Bonnie Goode's injury, although a serious fracture, will not result in an extended hospital stay. The original treatment plan was to monitor her for 48 hours, establish a pain management protocol, provide instruction on performing activities of daily living given her restricted range of motion and mobility, and discharge her with home-based physical therapy. However, the psychological issues have complicated that plan and engaged two nursing staff members in a dysfunctional dynamic.

If these issues are not resolved, Bonnie Goode's reported suicidal comments could become suicidal ideation through impulsive reaction to her hospital situation. This is complicated by the fact that Bonnie's father is perceived as a threatening presence on the unit (although he plans to return to work as soon as Bonnie is discharged). Bonnie's affect vacillates between being irritable and angry and being sweet and rather dysphoric. Dr. Watson is consulted because of the behavioral manifestation of what he subsequently diagnoses as Borderline Personality Disorder. Dr. Watson is inexperienced on an inpatient general medical floor, although he has extensive psychiatric training and experience. As Dr. Watson's supervisor, Dr. Franco realizes (based on the review of Dr. Watson's report) that he needs to work closely with Dr. Watson to determine the next steps in the treatment plan and the essential information to include in the electronic report.

The following critical parties were considered in weighing what to document.

Patient (Bonnie Goode). Bonnie has a strong sense of entitlement, modeled by her father. She is quick to anger and directs that anger toward others. She is quite upset about her injury and is worried that it may have terrible functional and cosmetic effects. Her father, her primary source of support in the hospital, must return to work in the coming days. She feels alone and frightened of going through the recovery process by herself. Bonnie lacks insight into the effect her behavior has on others; she perceives others as being rejecting, thus increasing her anger.

Psychologist (Dr. Reilly Watson). Dr. Watson is quickly learning how to manage sensitive patient information in acute medical settings. He also is learning how to balance staff needs for psychological patient information with the need to respect that patient's right to privacy. The psychologist must address how the patient can decrease this tendency to alienate others. Although Dr. Watson is struggling to establish his own professional identity and is somewhat defensive when approached by Dr. Franco, he quickly realizes that he needs the perspective of someone experienced in this setting. He becomes both open to and appreciative of Dr. Franco's guidance.

Bonnie's Father (Malcolm Goode). Bonnie's father is genuinely upset and concerned about Bonnie's injury, but he is coping by accusing others of maltreatment and threatening litigation. His style of interaction is isolating staff. He is not a man open to hearing others' opinions of his behavior and has no tolerance for what he considers Dr. Watson's "mumbo jumbo." He attempts to resolve problems with money and litigation and expects to be served.

Psychology Supervisor (Dr. Roberto Franco). Dr. Franco has seen many family members and patients with personality disorder in acute medical settings and has developed a reporting style that he believes accurately conveys the patient information necessary for optimal care without compromising the patient's privacy, dignity, or coping. He is obligated to share his experiences and reporting style with Dr. Watson, whom he supervises. Dr. Franco believes that Dr. Watson has not considered key medical and psychological contributors to the patient's presentation. He believes he can successfully address situational factors to enhance the patient's participation in her medical care.

Medical and Nursing Staff (Including Marilyn Teeter, Pauline Binder, and the Referring Physician). The hospital staff value and respect psychological services, particularly when patients are in crisis. They further appreciate having psychologists take the lead with interventions with difficult family members. Although there are no illusions that anyone is going to be cured or show significant personality changes as a result of brief psychological intervention, the staff hopes the psychologist can help the patient improve her behavior so they can be free to focus on Bonnie's medical care. They have not considered the possibility that they have gotten caught in the web of patient psychopathology.

Case Resolution

Perform Psychological Evaluation

Understanding Ms. Goode began with the psychological evaluation process. This necessarily involved solicitation of informed consent and assessment of Bonnie's personality and behavior as well as team consultation regarding their observations of Bonnie's distress. On the basis of Ms. Goode's manipulative behavior and outbursts as well as familial history and team reports of inconsistent and erratic behavior, Dr. Watson's results were consistent with the diagnoses of Borderline Personality Disorder and Adjustment Disorder with Depressed Mood. He made the decision not to share the results with Bonnie under a misguided application of the ethical standards of avoiding harm and use of assessment results. He considered the findings to be relevant only for the staff treating Bonnie, and he believed that telling Bonnie about his impressions would likely be quite upsetting to her, which he wanted to avoid because of its toll on Bonnie and the team who was the endpoint for Bonnie's anger.

Consult With the Supervising Psychologist

Dr. Watson was going to submit his results without consultation with Dr. Franco. This is inconsistent with ethical practice given Dr. Watson's inexperience in the acute medical setting. Dr. Watson should have reviewed his findings, plans, and report with Dr. Franco prior to interacting with staff and submitting an electronic report. When Dr. Franco stopped Dr. Young, he found the report problematic, particularly the documentation of abuse that was not critical to current treatment planning given that the patient did not live with or have regular contact with her father. Dr. Franco also discovered through supervision that Dr. Watson had not considered factors outside of the personality disorder and fracture that were potentially contributing to Bonnie's presentation. For example, he had not considered the potential effects of anesthesia or the psychological impact of perceived body distortion from the ORIF. He therefore had Dr. Watson follow up with the patient and physician on these concerns. Dr. Franco acknowledged the inexperienced psychologist's concerns regarding the patient's coping and offered to join Dr.

Watson in discussing the findings. In addition, he counseled Dr. Watson on the importance of sharing the results with Bonnie, consistent with ethical practice.

Report Results to Appropriate Personnel and in the Chart

Appropriately reporting the results involved contact with Bonnie, the team, and Bonnie's father as well as chart documentation. Dr. Watson provided verbal feedback to Bonnie about the results of the psychological evaluation. He described the findings in terms of her anger and dysphoria as well as her style of interacting with others. She was open to the feedback and agreed that the findings represented her emotional state and behavior but that she did not mean to act that way. What she had not considered before was how others felt when she lashed out at them. She was overly apologetic.

The same general information was provided to the hospital staff, who were educated about how they had been pulled into the patient's psychopathology. Dr. Franco and Dr. Watson discussed staff reactions that had inadvertently resulted in an exacerbation of the patient's symptoms. They focused on the staff's achieving a broader understanding of the impact of psychopathology on the patient's presentation. This discussion affected the staff's self-monitoring when with Bonnie and their choice of language when describing the patient, thereby directly and indirectly increasing respect for the patient. The psychologists met their ethical obligation to not knowingly condone the inappropriate activity of others.

With patient consent, Dr. Watson also provided direct feedback to Mr. Goode regarding how he could help Bonnie, including balancing advocating for his daughter with being understanding of the staff. He provided specific examples regarding how to modify his behavior to better serve his daughter. Importantly, Dr. Watson arranged for Mr. Goode to observe a successful application of this approach during a staff interaction with his daughter. This information also served to lay the foundation for continuation of mental health services on an outpatient basis.

Dr. Watson collaborated with Dr. Franco in editing the written report, including tactful yet clear descriptions of Bonnie Goode's personality disorder, and addressed what information should not become part of her permanent medical record (e.g., the report included comments regarding family stress contributing to problems coping with acute injury and distress expressed in an angry and displaced manner, especially toward staff but excluded unsubstantiated abuse). The final product was considered sufficient to assist in her treatment, yet acceptable should Bonnie, her father, or others who know them (e.g., attorneys or judges) later read it.

Review Outpatient Treatment Recommendations

Dr. Watson met with Bonnie before discharge to briefly reassess her mood and to emphasize his recommendation for outpatient psychotherapy.

Dr. Watson explained that to help her avoid alienating the therapists coming into her home she could benefit from education about the impact of her behavior on others. She could also benefit from supportive psychotherapy to address her coping difficulties and body image concerns (which were anticipated to be short term given the acute nature of the injury).

Set Up Discharge Plan

Dr. Watson consulted with the home therapy agency to coordinate continuation of mental health services. The agency contracted with a social worker experienced in working with patients coming from the hospital and respected in the community. Dr. Watson provided this option to Bonnie as well as the possibility of pursuing a psychotherapist independently.

Case Disposition

As a result of Dr. Watson's consultation, the hospital staff tried to apply their understanding of Ms. Goode's negative behavior in their interactions with her. However, they believed the discrepancy in how they perceived Bonnie was only of Bonnie's doing. Those who absorbed the brunt of her attacks kept interactions to a minimum and were very task focused when with her. Those who benefited from her charm continued to give her extra time and attention.

Approximately 72 hours after admission, Bonnie returned home with an aide. She was apparently verbally abusive to the aide during the first week. She was frustrated with the home care agency not being able to begin services for about two weeks, something to do with insurance authorization. Once she began physical therapy and counseling with the social worker, her mood and behavior improved somewhat, although she remained quite demanding. Malcolm Goode continued the litigation against the store and the mall, but he brought no formal complaints against any medical providers.

Additional Commentary

As a result of HIPAA, health care facilities and providers across the country must reevaluate and revise how they store medically sensitive material and how they inform patients about their rights to privacy regarding personally identifiable health information. In addition, the American Psychological Association (APA) has developed materials to facilitate psychologists' compliance with HIPAA (APA Practice Directorate, 2003, http://www.apapractice.org). In this case, although Dr. Watson attempted to gain consent from Bonnie to conduct an assessment, the nature of the consent obtained was insufficient. He did not anticipate potential limits of confidentiality related to litigation, which he should have given the earlier lawsuit threats made by Mr. Goode. He also did not explain what aspects of the psychological evaluation (which included sensitive information) would be stored by the hospital and how these would be protected. Therefore, both he and his supervisor had compromised their ethical obligation to their patient. Although potentially damaging to the relationship given Bonnie's psychopathology, it would still behoove the psychologist to explain these limits even after completion of the assessment. If the patient then refused to allow documentation based on true informed consent, the psychologist would have been obligated to record only a general summary documenting the reason no further documentation was provided unless true suicidal ideation had been identified. The potential for refusal is significant given that the majority of people feel they have lost control over their personal information (Gostin, 2001). The psychologist would also be in a very vulnerable position regarding billing.

CASE 2.2
TRUTH TELLING: THE DISCLOSURE OF
EMOTIONALLY DIFFICULT INFORMATION

The pathology report whirred out of the Midville Regional Cancer Unit's printer. It was 6:30 a.m. and the change-of-shift meeting in the nurses' lounge was underway. Nurse Robin Nielsen, the charge nurse covering for her staff, retrieved the report. She quickly scanned the label, which read Manita "Mandy" Lopez. Reviewing the case from memory, Nurse Nielsen reluctantly skipped to the interpretation at the bottom of the report and closed her eyes, shoulders slumping under the emotional weight. Her fingers let the sheet of paper float lazily to the floor. Mandy was going to die. Mandy's primary carcinoma had grown over the past two weeks, and bone scans had identified several additional metastases scattered throughout her body. The 42-year-old was a mother of two young children and married to the local state's attorney, an ascending political star. She also was a veteran pediatric nurse at Midville Hospital and well known to most of the staff. The cancer unit's physicians and staff had given Mandy all they had over the past 18 months. They had called on reputed consultants, used the latest treatment technology, and helped her enroll in new clinical trials. In every possible way they had supported her; she just couldn't be taken away from them.

Dr. Elizabeth Jenkins, the health psychologist, walked onto the unit at the moment the pathology report hit the floor. She saw Nurse Nielsen standing alone in the nurses' station, eyes closed, tears flowing. Quietly approaching, Dr. Jenkins gently rested her hand on Nurse Nielsen's shoulder and asked if there was anything she could do to help. Nurse Nielsen abruptly turned, pulling away from Dr. Jenkins's touch. After recognizing the newcomer, anger and embarrassment briefly flared in her eyes, "Yeah Dr. Jenkins, you can tell Mandy that she's gonna die. I . . . I just can't do it." Robin Nielsen's head dropped, and she sat heavily on a nearby chair, retrieving the report, freely crying. Dr. Jenkins pulled up a chair next to Nurse Nielsen. She steadied her own emotions and replied in as calm a voice as she could muster, "Robin, what can I do?"

The moment had passed. Nurse Nielsen looked up through tear-soaked, reddened eyes and said, "I'm sorry Beth. I shouldn't have snapped at you . . . but I just got the path report back on Mandy. The results are grim. I know Dr. Portnoy will try to avoid saying anything negative. He doesn't want Mandy to lose hope." Staring off into a private place, she said, voice trembling, "I . . . I simply can't do this one. Mandy's too close to me . . . to all of us. She's like family. Please help us with this." Turning toward Dr. Jenkins, the look in Robin Nielsen's eyes bordered on desperation.

Dr. Jenkins, 26-years old, was newly hired out of her health psychology postdoctoral training program at the National Cancer Institute in Washington, DC. She had never been confronted by this challenge in her clinical training. Her postdoctoral fellowship had focused on developing behavioral approaches to boost medical treatment adherence in outpatients. Although she knew some patients died during the treatment protocol, she had never had direct responsibility for those patients and so had never dealt with the impact of a patient's death on loved ones. Dr. Jenkins had not even experienced death in her personal life, as both her family and circle of friends were healthy. Her position on the cancer unit in the small urban medical center had just been created. There were no other psychologists working in the facility. Dr. Jenkins felt like the Lone Ranger with a capital L.

Relevant Ethical Principles and Standards

Principle A: Beneficence and Nonmaleficence

Dr. Jenkins is challenged by the prospect of truth telling, a responsibility that superficially appears to risk significant distress to the patient and her family, who to this point have been protected from the realistic and difficult issue of death as a near term outcome. Dr. Jenkins must consider the timing and depth of truth telling to maximize the patient's welfare and prevent additional pain or needless time spent on unanticipated issues. In addition, how Dr. Jenkins manages this case has repercussions for developing relationships with team members she hopes to work with long term for the benefit of future patients.

Principle B: Fidelity and Responsibility

Dr. Jenkins must be cognizant of the importance of clarifying her role in this situation: Is she being a supportive colleague, thereby focusing on providing support to the team, or is she a team member providing care to patients on the cancer unit? She must be clear regarding what is required for patient access and whether there are conflicts of interest inherent in this case that must be identified up front. If she determines her role is to evaluate and treat the patient, then she needs to determine whether truth telling is the appropriate immediate course of action. She must ensure her value system of supporting disclosure does not excessively influence her perception of Mandy's needs.

Principle C: Integrity

Dr. Jenkins must determine whether providing support to Nurse Nielsen creates the perception of an unclear or unwise commitment given that Dr. Jenkins is also being asked to consult on the case itself. To prevent a detrimental relationship from developing with either the team or patient, she needs to clarify the boundaries under which she will operate, particularly given that she can be affected by the process of coping by other team members.

Principle D: Respect for People's Rights and Dignity

The consideration of truth telling embodies the principle of the patient's right to self-determination. The team has apparently overstepped its boundaries in trying to protect Mandy's welfare by negating her right to health information. The psychologist must be careful not to be pulled into this dynamic on the basis of her own emotional reactions to working with someone with a terminal illness or eagerness to join the team.

Standard 2.01, Boundaries of Competence

Gaining some perspective on death and dying should be helpful to Dr. Jenkins as she begins working with Mandy. In addition, given that Dr. Jenkins has not worked with families who have experienced the loss of a loved one to terminal illness, she will need to address her own limits in understanding. This could potentially be accomplished through consultation with another appropriate professional or through continuing education using critical literature. Because there is no other psychologist at the hospital, Dr. Jenkins needs to explore other avenues for consultation. In addition, if she chooses to present health information to Mandy, she should anticipate medical questions outside her boundaries of competence and determine an appropriate course of action to address these. For example, Dr. Jenkins would be wise to discuss the patient's situation in detail with Dr. Portnoy prior to meeting with the patient and family. In addition, although the physician has avoided the potentially distressing interaction of sharing difficult news, the psychologist must consider a plan that will secure the physician's commitment to deal directly with questions or issues that only a physician can address.

Standard 3.06, Conflict of Interest

Dr. Jenkins has an inherent conflict of interest in trying to address the staff's emotional needs when part of that same team and when simultaneously consulting on a patient served by that team. These conflicts must be proactively resolved.

Standard 3.09, Cooperation With Other Professionals

Truth telling regarding terminal illness does not simply imply sharing diagnostic information. Rather, it encompasses a host of factors, ranging from disease progression to expectations regarding family and patient coping. To engage in truth telling effectively and sufficiently, Dr. Jenkins will need to solicit the cooperation of other key professionals on the team and other experienced psychologists to best serve her patient. Dr. Jenkins also needs to be aware of the murky territory into which she treads if she chooses to communicate information traditionally handled by another discipline. Even if invited to do so, reactions to this role shift that require direct response can occur.

Standard 4.04, Minimizing Intrusions on Privacy

The risk of intrusion on privacy is quite high given the nature of the established relationship between the staff and the patient. Dr. Jenkins needs to take particular care to share information only with appropriate personnel.

Standard 6.01, Documentation of Professional and Scientific Work and Maintenance of Records

Dr. Jenkins has to consider how to document her interactions with the patient and family in the patient's chart, recognizing that well-meaning staff not directly associated with the case may be tempted to review how Mandy is doing. The psychologist also needs to weigh how to present information regarding staff roles given the importance of their support and access to psychological reports.

Standard 10.01, Informed Consent to Therapy

The provision of supportive therapy after presentation of the health status information requires that Dr. Jenkins secure Mandy's consent to treatment. The focus on the dying process needs explication to clarify treatment goals.

Standard 10.09, Interruption of Therapy

Depending on the aggressiveness of the cancer, therapy with Mandy and her family may be interrupted by needed treatment, resulting side effects, or deteriorating health. Both she and her family need to understand the implications of these types of events on treatment progression and likely outcome. In addition, a straightforward conversation regarding family treatment in the event of Mandy's death should occur prior to commencement of therapy.

Standard 10.10, Terminating Therapy

Dr. Jenkins may need to evaluate treatment in the face of unmet goals if the patient and family desire to put their remaining energy and time into private moments. Dr. Jenkins also needs to attend to the patient's and family's goals as somewhat separate issues given their needs and intervention endpoints will likely differ.

Institutional and Legal Concepts That May Apply

Given the gravity of Mandy's diagnosis, Dr. Jenkins needs to be aware of any advanced directives Mandy possesses. For example, if Mandy specified in her advanced directives or in her interview with Dr. Jenkins that she did not want to know when the end was upon her, Dr. Jenkins would rightly need to respect the patient's choice. Respect for autonomy encompasses the concept of the right *not to know* just as it supports the right *to know*. In addition, Dr. Jenkins needs to clearly demarcate the limits of her expertise to avoid potential liability created by provision of inappropriate information. Dr. Jenkins also needs to be aware of any legal determinants in her state covering what must be included in informed consent to treatment.

Relevant Context and Key Stakeholders

Mandy Lopez's admission to Midville Cancer Unit marks a significant decline in her physical status. Mandy has been in constant pain, requiring a moderately aggressive course of narcotic analgesics. Her cognitive awareness has been variable, depending on her level of sedation. There has been no indication of brain involvement in her work-up. With the latest downturn in her health, Mandy and her husband formally created advanced directives preventing artificial nutrition, hydration, and use of resuscitation.

Mandy has been upbeat during her 18-month fight against cancer. She frequently visited the cancer unit nurses when she was in the building for outpatient treatments. Mandy, her husband, and her children have become enmeshed in the families of the nursing staff, as most of them have contributed in one way or another to supporting the Lopez family during Mandy's course of treatment. Mandy's husband frequently stays with her in her hospital room overnight, and her children visit every weekend, passing the time by playing games with the aides.

Importantly, no staff member has allowed the subject of negative prognosis to enter formal or social conversations. When the children have expressed their fears about their mother's health, they have been told that Mandy would "beat this problem." The staff and family are clearly uncomfortable about the direction the disease has taken. Although the tacit taboo placed on this topic during the admission is evident, the decision to pursue a palliative course of treatment needs to be addressed. Traditionally, the unit has followed a pattern in which the nursing staff shares bad news with patients. This pattern breaks down in this case because of the relationship between the staff and patient. It is unclear what Dr. Portnoy's role could be in disclosing the prognosis because he too has been actively involved in ensuring that Mandy has all treatment options at her disposal. Sharing prognostic information would require someone breaking the taboo and who better than an "outsider" to take on that uncomfortable task.

There are several key parties to consider in determining an ethical response.

Patient (Mandy Lopez). Mandy has been diagnosed with terminal cancer. Given her experience as a nurse, she is very familiar with cancer diagnoses and progression. She has many supportive friends on the cancer unit where she is now being treated. She also has good social support from her spouse, who could be called on to help her cope if the truth is shared regarding her prognosis. She has advanced directives allowing for palliative care but not invasive procedures such as CPR and tube placements for artificial nutrition and hydration. She has discussed in general terms her cancer progression with her children but not the possible outcome of death should her health deteriorate further.

Staff. Every health care professional in Midville Cancer Unit has focused on helping Mandy through her illness. The energy expended in treating Mandy has been motivated by the desire to ameliorate, if not cure, her cancer. Several staff have used third-order denial (denial of outcome; Van Servellen, 1997) to cope with Mandy's diagnosis and declining health. Nursing staff in particular have been emotionally devastated by the news that Mandy's prognosis is terminal. The nurse practitioners have worked with Mandy for years and have been great sources of support. Because some of these individuals are now Mandy's providers, they have become entangled in the inability to maintain appropriate boundaries for delivering care. Not one of them wants to discuss Mandy's prognosis with her, even though it is typically part of their professional role to do so.

Psychologist (Dr. Elizabeth Jenkins). Dr. Jenkins is the new and only psychologist on the cancer unit. She brings an eagerness to serve the team and wants to make a good first impression, which she realizes can have a lasting effect on the acceptance of psychology's services. Mandy Lopez's treatment is complicated by the sheer number of staff with whom she has worked. Dr. Jenkins knows that she must handle the staff issues very carefully, particularly when discussing appropriate professional boundaries and in documenting any information acquired from the patient and her family. Dr. Jenkins lacks the necessary background to manage the case independently, but there is no other psychologist employed at the hospital to offer consultation. She suspects that Mandy is already aware of the gravity of her deteriorating health given her nursing background. In general, Dr. Jenkins adheres to the principle of truth telling when communicating with patients about changes in their health status. She believes presenting information in a straightforward manner usually allows the reality of the situation to be accurately appreciated by the patient and her family and supports the process of coping with this negative information.

Physician (Dr. Samuel Portnoy). Dr. Portnoy and the nurse practitioners have supported an unquestioned pattern in which nurses deliver bad news to patients. It is unclear whether Dr. Portnoy is willing to be involved in the delivery of the prognostic information, but he seems receptive to psychology's input. He has in all other respects been heavily involved in the case. He personally met with each treating specialist and contacted several prominent cancer researchers on Mandy's behalf.

Family. The family has been by Mandy's side since the illness began. They provide pivotal support. Mandy and her husband have engaged in end-of-life discussions as evidenced by the advanced directives. However, their children have been relatively protected from the possibility of their mother dying; their likely reaction to this news is uncertain.

Case Resolution

Clarify Role

As a team member, Dr. Jenkins realized that her primary responsibility was to the patients on the cancer unit. She therefore clarified the appropriate procedure for patient access, which was through physician consultation. She obtained a request for consultation from Dr. Portnoy through Robin Nielsen. It was Dr. Jenkins's first official consultation, as she was still being oriented to the program.

Gather Information, Particularly Regarding Staff–Patient Relationships

In preparation for her first meeting with Mandy Lopez, Dr. Jenkins familiarized herself with the patient and her situation. She reviewed the chart, paying particular attention to any documented wishes regarding information sharing and the progressive medication record, and discussed Mandy's course of treatment with the staff. Dr. Jenkins was especially interested in the staff's views of Mandy's cognitive and emotional status over the past 10 days, including level of consciousness, orientation, understanding and following commands, pain perception, lability, and observed interactions with family and visitors. Related to this formal record review, she questioned the staff about their relationship with Nurse Lopez prior to her illness, and how they perceived Mandy was responding to her course of treatment. A primary purpose of this latter line of questioning was to gain insight into the level of enmeshment between the staff and the patient. In addition, she discovered that very early on in her treatment, Mandy had indicated wanting to be informed about health changes.

Establish Contact With Dr. Portnoy

Dr. Jenkins knew her early contacts with Dr. Portnoy could greatly facilitate or hinder her ability to develop a consultation service. In addition, she believed he was an important ally in the process of truth telling even though he too was likely to have strong emotional reactions to Mandy's prognosis. Dr. Jenkins needed Dr. Portnoy to be available to answer medical questions outside her areas of competence.

After reintroducing herself to Dr. Portnoy, she sought his summary of the case to date, including his response to the recent pathology report. She hoped this approach would communicate respect for his perspective and lay the groundwork for the needed collaboration. The physician responded openly to Dr. Jenkins's request for a detailed verbal summary of Mandy's case. Dr. Jenkins discovered that the physician had decided to recommend palliative care. Dr. Jenkins mentioned the request from nursing for her to be the team representative to break the news of this momentous change to the patient and her family. Dr. Portnoy readily agreed with this strategy as he recognized he was heavily emotionally invested in Mandy's care. The psychologist was struck by Dr. Portnoy's empathic response when discussing Mandy's care. He volunteered to follow up with Mandy and her spouse to answer any specific medical questions. Thus, the groundwork was laid for Dr. Jenkins to meet with Mandy.

Consult With Professional Organization

Dr. Jenkins contacted her state psychological association to obtain a list of health psychologists in her area. Having received resource contacts, she called two psychologists for collegial assistance in dealing with dying issues, one of whom had consulted with hospice in the past. The psychologist whom Dr. Jenkins consulted volunteered to provide additional assistance as the case progressed.

Intervene With the Patient

Armed with specific case information and a plan to approach Mandy, Dr. Jenkins met with her new patient. Although initially difficult to rouse, Mandy maintained a friendly demeanor as Dr. Jenkins introduced herself and explained that she had been consulted by Dr. Portnoy and asked to join her treatment team.

Dr. Jenkins said calmly, quietly, "Ms. Lopez, I have some bad news for you." Dr. Jenkins dutifully shared the latest prognostic information in some detail.

Mandy looked away for a while, crying softly. Then she turned to Dr. Jenkins, reached out to hold her hand, and said, "I knew the team couldn't bear to tell me if the cancer took a turn for the worse. I had even asked my husband to let me know if he had received any selective information from the staff, but he hadn't." Looking out the window opposite the bed, "I tried to ignore the signs but . . . I just couldn't. I've been feeling so much weaker and more nauseated, and the pain, even the strongest analgesics haven't been working." Looking sympathetically at Dr. Jenkins, Mandy said, "I'm sorry that you had to be the one to tell me." Dr. Jenkins was deeply touched by Mandy's concern.

After sharing the poor prognosis, Dr. Jenkins offered psychotherapy and explained that appropriate team members would follow up with Mandy to provide specific information about her altered treatment plan and answer any questions she might have. She ended the session by asking Mandy how she would like her family involved in her care. As Dr. Jenkins prepared to leave the room, Mandy expressed relief that the news had been broached so that she could begin planning with her family for her death.

Intervene With the Patient and Family

Mandy established with Dr. Jenkins that she would like her spouse involved in all sessions and that information would be shared equally. All subsequent sessions occurred with Mandy's husband present. In the first joint session, Mandy told her husband about her prognosis. Mandy and her husband indicated they wanted to tell the children themselves but would appreciate strategies for doing so. Dr. Jenkins offered advice regarding how to use simple, straightforward language to concretely answer their children's questions about dying.

Therapy then focused on discussing Mandy's present status, behavioral pain management strategies, the effects of dying on the patient and family, coping with loss, and facilitating a sense of contentment by putting things in order. It also was agreed that after Mandy died the family would seek psychological support through the local chapter of the American Cancer Society rather than through the cancer unit at the hospital. Mandy's funeral would represent the end point of treatment with the family.

Communicate With the Staff

In both oral and written communication, Dr. Jenkins was careful to share information only with those staff directly assigned to Mandy's care and only information directly relevant to planning for palliative care and preparation for death. After consulting with Mandy regarding whom she did and did not want to have access to her health information, Dr. Jenkins established clear boundaries regarding staff not on the case who were concerned friends.

Case Disposition

Through the process of this case, Dr. Jenkins determined that information was not being shared with a patient who had the right to know, evaluated the emotional dynamics hindering the truth-telling process, and took steps to ensure that the patient's and family's need to know was met. Dr. Beth Jenkins's mentor in this case was Nurse Mandy Lopez. Walking down the hall towards the nurses' station after a therapy session with Mandy and her spouse, Dr. Jenkins was struck by how much Mandy had contributed to the truth-telling process. Mandy had turned the case from a burdensome responsibility into one with meaningful opportunity.

Dr. Jenkins followed up with Mandy and her family through her funeral three weeks later. They had almost daily contact until the funeral. Dr. Jenkins had become a communications' nexus for the case, ensuring that a balance of information was shared among the appropriate people. Although Mandy's death was a time of sadness, it also embodied the concept of death with dignity.

Additional Commentary

This case reflects some of the history of truth telling from the perspective of other health care professionals. Western medical literature in particular has evolved over time from supporting very limited information sharing to the commonly recognized practice today of sharing emotionally charged, negative news such as terminal illness to allow the patient and family time to address what is personally meaningful to them (Boyle, 1997a). Consensus guidelines for medical practitioners breaking bad news were presented in a 1995 summary of the literature (Girgis & Sanson-Fisher, 1995). This shift in sharing news has been influenced by court decisions guiding the informed consent process, in which it has been recognized that patients have a right to information relevant to selection or rejection of treatment (Annas, 1994). Similarly, Petersen et al. (2003) have discussed the importance of patients with cancer being able to implement their own decisional style (rather than having one imposed) to facilitate self-efficacy and minimize potential psychopathological reactions to cancer, such as anxiety and depression. Psychologists working in medical settings may nevertheless encounter physicians and patients with differing value systems, affecting who should be told what (Carrese & Rhodes, 1995; Thomsen, Wulff, Martin, & Singer, 1993). In addition, many physicians feel neither prepared to share difficult news nor deal with patients' emotional reactions to such news (Fallowfield, 1993; Frankel & Beckman, 2004; Girgis & Sanson-Fisher). Psychologists can play a critical role in both training others to share information effectively on the basis of a patient's values and needs and educating others regarding the impact of cognitive, behavioral, and emotional issues on coping, including during the very final stages of life. Ptacek and Eberhardt (1996) offer a summary of recommendations as well as caveats cited in the literature regarding breaking bad news. In this case, if the physician or nursing staff had not concurred with the psychologist's decision to share the prognosis with the patient, then the psychologist would have needed to do what was appropriate from a psychological point of view (i.e., determining reasons for reluctance to share news and potentially sharing information acquired from the physician regarding prognosis to facilitate positive coping). In this context, of course, the psychologist is obligated to attempt to seek resolution with the other providers through an educational process regarding what is helpful to the patient in her specific situation. In this case, the psychologist was keenly aware of the dynamics of the enmeshed relationships at play; however, she was able to implement appropriate actions by participating in the truth-telling process without directly challenging any specific individual.

CASE 2.3
MALINGERING AND THE MANAGEMENT OF CHRONIC PAIN

The voluminous medical record being reviewed by the psychologist, Dr. Norton Adler, was that of 33-year-old Tyvek Havel. Ty had been newly admitted to the inpatient Pain Control Center of the South City Medical System in New Orleans and was undergoing presurgical evaluation for lower back and neck pain. On balance, Mr. Havel's history was not that unusual for someone being seen at a large metropolitan pain center: a mixture of emotional and behavioral symptoms (including a history of alleged substance abuse and depression) combined with multiple injuries. However, Mr. Havel's current behavioral presentation was another matter. Dr. Adler entered Ty's hospital room to find him attired in sunglasses, a tattered Hawaiian shirt, surfer jammer shorts, and his neck in the death-grip of a dirty gray foam support collar. A young woman was also in the room and sat meekly in a chair in the corner. She identified herself simply as *Abandon* and was wrapped tightly in various articles of black mesh and leather clothing. After asking Ty's permission to perform the evaluation, Dr. Adler asked if the patient minded if his girlfriend was involved in the evaluation process. Ty agreed without argument. The broad smile he beamed at Dr. Adler highlighted a gold tooth with an inlaid skull and cross-bones.

During the course of the psychologist's evaluation, Ty volunteered to demonstrate his gait. He moaned his way out of bed, dramatically illustrating his unsteady stance, and then began to limp around the room. He banged his carved wooden walking stick on furniture, loudly demanding that the young woman move each offending obstacle out of the way before he tripped and "broke the only remaining intact bone" in his body. After dramatically yet gingerly sitting on the edge of the bed, Ty pointed with his stick to a chair across the room, indicating for his companion to take a seat, which she did without comment.

During his record review, Dr. Adler had noticed that one week earlier Ty had been injured (yet again) in a fender-bender accident while driving a company car. At the scene, he had been observed jumping out of his car, checking the vehicle for damage, and then abruptly falling to the ground writhing in pain and yelling for EMS. At the nearest ER, where he was transported, negative imaging results did nothing to deter Ty from declaring a disabling injury with excruciating low back pain. He *reluctantly* accepted an analgesic injection, reminding the resident physician that he had a drug abuse history. However, when the same physician balked at his request for oral morphine at discharge one hour later, Mr. Havel screamed about mistreatment of a newly injured patient and demanded to see the administrator. He was given the prescription and left quietly, but not before being observed placing a collect call to the regional Workers' Compensation office to report his injury. Ty then returned one week later complaining of worsening pain and was referred for a comprehensive pain evaluation.

Mr. Havel presented a bland psychosocial history devoid of any information that might explain his behavioral presentation. In fact, without the medical record, the psychologist would have learned little of Ty's history. By contrast, Mr. Havel's closing monologue was telling and went something like, "Okay, Doc, you can see that I'm severely injured as a result of that terrible car wreck while I was on the job, mind you. So let's skip the psychobabble and cut to the bone. It's as simple as this . . . I was already in constant pain, and it's tripled with this new injury. I want . . . no I need, back surgery. And because of this disability, I must be entitled to some type of settlement from the insurance company of the guy who hit me. Just say the word, and I'll submit to the knife with a smile on my face." He lay back in his bed with a gold-hued toothy grin, calmly awaiting Dr. Adler's response.

Norton Adler was in a bind. He knew that Mr. Havel was scheduled to see Dr. Rudy Kohl for the surgical evaluation. Dr. Adler had worked in the clinic for several years and knew that Dr. Kohl had the reputation of rarely refusing a surgical candidate. Dr. Kohl had been thoroughly trained as a surgeon and plied this skill with singular focus. He also was well-known as the physician least likely to accept the counsel of psychology. Yet, here was a patient who clearly had psychological factors mitigating any decision to move forward with surgery.

The psychologist begged off directly addressing the patient's comments regarding surgery other than to state that any decision would be made by a team of professionals. The only other physician on the case was the consulting anesthesiologist, Dr. Payne Fulbright. Dr. Adler needed time to think.

Relevant Ethical Principles and Standards

Principle A: Beneficence and Nonmaleficence

Although the patient has clearly indicated that there is secondary gain associated with his willingness to undergo surgery, Dr. Adler must take care not to discount the patient's concerns or make generalizations regarding the patient's needs that result in appropriate evaluation and treatment being missed.

Principle B: Fidelity and Responsibility

Dr. Adler clearly anticipates problems with the physician's recommendation on the basis of his experience, but the physician's position is not yet known. The psychologist must caution against making generalizations that negatively impact his ability to interact effectively with other health care providers. Even though the outcome may be fairly predictable, Dr. Adler must seek a reasonable solution to best serve Mr. Havel.

Principle D: Justice

Dr. Adler has a responsibility to support equitable and justifiable distribution of scarce public funding, and justifiable behavioral intervention is less expensive than surgical intervention. The use of health facilities unnecessarily increases overall health care costs, and the psychologist's intervention can potentially help break the patient's pattern of abusing health care resources either by addressing the malingering behavior, if present, or by increasing the facility's awareness of the behavioral pattern.

Principle E: Respect for People's Rights and Dignity

Mr. Havel is due complete information disclosure to give valid, fully informed consent regarding the surgery he prefers versus noninvasive alternatives. The psychologist must ensure that Mr. Havel comprehends these alternatives to be confident that consent is valid rather than simply reflecting the patient's predetermined response.

Standard 2.01, Boundaries of Competence

Dr. Adler is working with a pain management team, each member possessing expertise in a particular area. He clearly brings the specific expertise that allows an appreciation of the behavioral and emotional components of the patient's current presentation, and in particular, may identify the diagnosis of malingering. Dr. Adler has an obligation to share this expertise and can rightfully present this diagnosis as a primary causal agent of current symptoms. However, he must be careful not to negate the physician's surgical recommendation, as this is a medical determination.

Standard 2.04, Bases for Scientific and Professional Judgments

Dr. Adler possesses an awareness of relevant outcome literature regarding effective interventions in chronic pain. The fact that he is employed by a multispecialty facility attests to the fact that this literature is relevant to current practice standards. In addition, he has significant experience understanding potential psychosocial causal agents of pain expression. His recommendations take such information into account.

Standard 3.09, Cooperation With Other Professionals

To the extent possible, Mr. Havel's welfare is promoted if Dr. Adler and Dr. Kohl can design a treatment program that both support. This is particularly important when the patient's psychological presentation suggests some abuse of a medical system in which splitting across providers can contribute to inappropriate patient management. Dr. Adler must work with the rest of the team to avoid unintentionally reinforcing a maladaptive pattern of coping with pain.

Standard 3.10, Informed Consent

Dr. Adler has to present the patient with alternatives to his stated treatment of choice to obtain valid, fully informed consent. This information necessarily includes a description of the risks and benefits of each alternative in the context of Mr. Havel's life.

Standard 4.02, Discussing the Limits of Confidentiality

In addition to disclosure of the limits of confidentiality regarding personal and other's safety or harm, Dr. Adler should explain the interdisciplinary nature of the Pain Control Center, particularly how patient information is necessarily shared during the process of treatment planning.

Standard 4.05, Disclosures

The nature of the relationship between the Pain Control Center and the Department of Workers' Compensation has to be explained as it relates to sharing clinical treatment planning information.

Standard 6.01, Documentation of Professional and Scientific Work and Maintenance of Records

Dr. Adler has right of access to records as a member of the direct treatment team and should document only information necessary to ongoing evaluation and treatment. Evidence supporting behavioral interventions should be concretely documented. Diagnostic information, including supportive descriptive examples and behavioral history suggesting the patient exaggerates his symptoms, should be clearly noted as well. He should document material under the assumption that outside parties, such as Workers' Compensation and the insurance company covering the driver who ran into Mr. Havel, will request access to records.

Standard 9.01, Bases for Assessments

Any chronic pain assessment tools used by Dr. Adler should have adequate validity and reliability relevant to the patient population served by the Pain Control Center. If the population is not well represented, then Dr. Adler needs to be very cautious in the weight he gives these data. He must be able to defend the use of the instrument and his interpretations of data with other corroborating evidence, which should be available to him if he capitalizes on team interactions. He also must take into account the potential mitigating effects of acute pain from the recent accident.

Standard 9.10, Explaining Assessment Results

In explaining his findings, Dr. Adler should take into account whether sharing that the patient is exaggerating his symptoms is counterproductive or helpful to the treatment process. He may conclude, for example, that deception is necessary in treatment to most appropriately facilitate treatment benefits.

Institutional and Legal Concepts That May Apply

Given the questionable circumstances and negative imaging results surrounding the most recent injury, the question of malingering needs to be raised. There is a clear suggestion of secondary gain associated with augmenting the stream of public monies already received by the patient through the Workers' Compensation system. The challenge for Dr. Adler and the other professionals of the Pain Control Center is to minimize the risk of fraudulent claims of disability being inadvertently supported by unrelated clinical findings.

Relevant Context and Key Stakeholders

Tyvek Havel has a long history of accessing medical care for injuries lacking medical support. He recently experienced an accident that could precipitate unknown injuries, and he presents with back and neck pain, which he indicates existed previously and is now exacerbated. Dr. Adler, possessing many years of experience with chronic pain management, hypothesizes that Mr. Havel is malingering and may not be a surgical candidate. However, he has not yet clarified this hypothesis with Dr. Kohl, the physician of record, who almost always favors surgery over noninvasive procedures. Although Dr. Fulbright, the anesthesiologist, may be an ally of Dr. Adler's, Dr. Kohl might not appreciate the double-teaming, and the patient has clearly and unambiguously requested surgery.

The following individuals were considered in weighing key information.
Patient (Tyvek Havel). This patient presents several challenges to the health care system. Ty has clearly stated in his personal account that having surgery would increase his chances of securing his disability status. He plans to pay for surgery through public resources. However, Ty presents clinically with behaviors both dramatic and inconsistent with the conventional understanding of biomechanical effects of neuromuscular and orthopedic in-

jury. The only symptom that cannot be contested is his subjective pain report. Therefore, standard surgical treatment for his reported maladies may be inappropriate. Should surgery prevail as the primary course of action without further evaluation, Mr. Havel may be subjected to multiple consequences he has not adequately considered.

Psychologist (Dr. Norton Adler). The providers' appointment schedules at the Pain Control Center program have placed the psychologist first in the evaluative pipeline for Mr. Havel. Therefore, he bears some responsibility for triage through the Pain Control Center's available evaluative pathways. Dr. Adler's opinion that the patient has significant psychological factors influencing his clinical presentation is motivating him toward emphasizing the importance of behavioral factors in any proposed treatment plan. He has to exercise political astuteness to ensure that such a treatment plan emphasis occurs and that public funding is spent justifiably within the prevailing social context.

Surgeon (Dr. Rudy Kohl). Dr. Kohl is a highly skilled surgeon with a high rate of success, defined as patients reporting decreased pain, increased mobility, and minimal complications. The surgeon has a reputation for offering surgery as a first option to his patients and minimizing the importance of psychological factors in pain management.

Anesthesiologist (Dr. Payne Fulbright). Dr. Fulbright is the program's consulting anesthesiologist and is well versed in the behavioral nuances of acute versus chronic pain presentation. He usually is amenable to multimodal treatment intervention. Dr. Fulbright offers a possible moderating influence in the treatment planning process, allowing psychological factors to assume more weight in the final decision. Additionally, being a physician, he may be able to bolster the opinion of the psychologist in the decision-making process. However, he is also faced with determining a safe and effective medication or nerve block intervention for a patient with a likely substance abuse history.

Patient's Girlfriend (Abandon). Abandon is a potential ally for the psychologist and the evaluation team. The extent to which she can influence the patient, either directly or subtly, may assist Ty in making a constructive informed decision. Her rather submissive behavior during the psychological evaluation suggests that she may not be effective in persuading the patient to alter his initial wish for surgery. Clearly, Abandon's role in the case needs exploration.

Case Resolution

Secure a Consultation With Dr. Fulbright and Gain Dr. Kohl's Support

The psychologist felt obligated to involve Dr. Fulbright in the case to balance the decision-making process toward the goal of maximizing the patient's overall benefit. Dr. Adler was aware that the physician's influence over formulating the treatment plan was powerful, and he believed his collaboration with Dr. Fulbright would increase the valence of psychological factors affecting the planning process.

Dr. Adler obtained Mr. Havel's schedule for the Pain Control Center evaluation. He noticed that there was a 45-minute block of time before the patient was scheduled to see the surgeon. He made a hasty call to Payne Fulbright to ask a favor. Could the physician see a patient *stat*? Dr. Adler presented the case as that of a very challenging and needy gentleman who could benefit greatly from Dr. Fulbright's eclectic view of pain treatment. The challenge was too tempting for his colleague to ignore. Dr. Fulbright managed to spend half an hour with the patient. With prompting from Dr. Adler, he caught Dr. Kohl just before the surgeon saw Ty. Dr. Fulbright explained the unusual circumstances of the precipitating car incident and told Dr. Kohl that such patients (those with virulent psychopathology) were more likely to sue surgeons for "unremitting" postoperative pain.

That timely contact was enough to make the surgeon wary of honoring the patient's insistence on surgery. Before he left Ty's room, the surgeon told him that such decisions were made by the whole treatment team (a first for this surgeon). He assured the patient that he would bring his request for surgery before the team. Dr. Kohl then made his way to the radiology department to review Mr. Havel's MRI films personally.

Implement a Purposeful Plan to Blend Persuasion and Informed Consent

During Payne Fulbright's visit with the surgeon, the psychologist returned to Ty's room. He secured the patient's permission to share additional information with Ty's girlfriend in the room. Dr. Adler quickly outlined a number of possible lifestyle benefits for avoiding surgery. He knew that the surgeon would address potential negative surgical complications in his discussion. At first the patient balked at the suggestion of less invasive alternatives, but as the list went on, he listened more attentively. The potential benefits described included lifestyle preservation (avoiding postsurgical limitations like not driving), not having to endure postsurgical pain, avoiding possible painful surgical complications, avoiding postsurgery contingencies that the Workers' Compensation system might impose (e.g., monitored exercise regimen and postural or movement prohibitions that could last for months), and introducing the possibility that if the agency ever changed its disability qualification criteria, Mr. Havel might be dropped from the rolls or have benefits reduced despite the surgery. Dr. Adler did not try to convince Mr. Havel to change his mind nor did he directly address his girlfriend. He simply broadened the patient's perspective regarding possible unintended consequences attached to surgery. These were purposely described in a concrete, specific manner given the patient's tendency to manipulate his situation to his own financial advantage.

Secure Reinforcement From Workers' Compensation

Dr. Adler then placed a call to Tyvek's Workers' Compensation counselor (the funding source for the evaluation) from the nurses' station. He expressed his concerns regarding the patient's insistence on surgery after Dr. Kohl agreed that surgical intervention was not mandated. The counselor stated that she shared the same concerns and was not encouraging her client to pursue surgery.

Discuss the Treatment Recommendations With Mr. Havel

The team met with Mr. Havel to discuss the recommended treatment plan, which included gradually increasing mobility through exercises and behavioral pain management. An important challenge facing the psychologist was the patient's view that surgery was his "badge of disability," somehow increasing the likelihood that his bad back was worthy of disability payments. Subscribing to less invasive or behavioral interventions would require Ty's commitment and cooperation, not to mention a significant adaptive lifestyle modification. Dr. Adler hoped that his description of the expectations of the disability system becoming increasingly stringent regarding the individuals it financially supports struck a chord with Mr. Havel. In short, he might realize that the system could cramp his style.

Shortly after the meeting, Dr. Adler saw Abandon standing at the nurses' station. She requested to speak with him. Stating that he could not share more than she already knew, Dr. Adler agreed to talk with her in a private consultation room. The young woman volunteered social information about her boyfriend. Tyvek Havel emigrated from the former Czechoslovakia to the United States with his parents when he was eight years old. His father was a master machinist and had quickly found employment in a Los Angeles fabrication shop. Tyvek's mother, Georgia, was trained as a seamstress, and once Ty and his older brother, Goran, were safely ensconced in school, she was hired part time by a film studio wardrobe department. Within two years of entering the country, the Havel family had established themselves in a relatively comfortable social niche. Miran Havel, the family patriarch, doted on the boys. He viewed America as the land of opportunity, and debt was just another inconvenience. He never quite grasped the subtleties of interest payments. Nonetheless, the family was successful in contrast to their life abroad. All was well until Goran was killed in a bicycle accident at 13 years of age.

Miran Havel was never the same afterward. He worked sporadically, drifting through a series of jobs. Georgia was saddled with being the consistent breadwinner, and Ty was alternately ignored and doted on. Ty became withdrawn and opted out of many school activities. His grades dropped and the rest of his schooling, through high school, became a struggle that he barely survived. Ty experimented with and then wholeheartedly mired himself in the drug culture. By age 18, Ty had crafted an alternative lifestyle that involved working enough minimum wage jobs to pay for his modest habit. Living under the roof of his guilt-ridden parents, Ty additionally benefited from the largesse of some local pushers, who often employed him as a "sales consultant" for new initiates into their street chemistry fraternity.

The "good life" Tyvek Havel had cultivated was short-lived. A change in management of the drug ring he had depended on resulted in increased product prices, several painful beatings, and two brief incarcerations. Ty's intellectual acumen had gradually dulled with his chemical experimentation over the years. When Miran Havel finally learned of his son's illegal activities, he disowned him. The gradual change in cognitive capacity and the abrupt change in social support marked an economic downturn, during which time Ty had varied encounters with the health care system seeking treatment for social diseases and violent injuries. By age 24, Ty was destitute, in chronic pain from his multiple bone fractures, and begging for drugs from anyone who would listen. In retrospect, the morning he awakened to find himself in jail, recovering from withdrawal and sentenced to a drug rehabilitation facility, was a turning point in Ty's life. After graduation, he embarked with dispatch on a decade-long career development path aimed at becoming a professional "disabled" person. Along the way, Ty managed to qualify for temporary partial Workers' Compensation benefits. At the time of this incident, he had an open case pending a disability determination panel's decision regarding permanent partial disability status.

Abandon then told Dr. Adler that she had tried to get Ty to reconsider his choice after the *alternatives lecture*. Although Ty had not answered her directly, he agreed to think about all the treatment possibilities after talking with the surgeon. Dr. Adler thanked Abandon and returned to reviewing the medical record for any more helpful information that might affect the treatment plan.

Case Disposition

Mr. Havel heard the recommendation, politely thanked the team for the advice in an uncharacteristically somber manner, and left the facility with his girlfriend in tow. The team breathed a collective sigh of relief, and the immediate feedback to the Workers' Compensation counselor triggered a similar response. She reciprocated with a plan to fund the recommended treatment at the Pain Control Center. In the flurry of conversation after the meeting, the consensus of the team was that they had done the right thing, for the sake of the patient and society.

Two days later, Tyvek Havel underwent a lumbar decompression laminectomy in a nearby facility, paid for by "old friends" who had owed him a favor. The surgery was successfully completed, and Ty received word of his permanent partial disability award while recovering in the hospital.

Additional Commentary

Because malingering implies intentional misrepresentation of symptoms for an undeserved (health care) benefit, appropriate ethical responses to suspected malingering are often founded in the principles of utility and justice, that is, valid, equitable use and distribution of scarce health care resources. In cases in which the veracity of signs and symptoms is dubious, and there is evidence for secondary gain, the health care professional is justified in limiting or denying access to services that would be more appropriately used in another manner. Johnstone, Schopp, and Shigaki (2000) outline well-known indicators of malingering. These include a history of antisocial personality, recent substance abuse, a wide discrepancy between physical findings and functional impairment, reports of bizarre or unrelated symptoms, and obvious bias in favor of symptom endorsement. Other indicators include a natural healing course that is inconsistent with the facts of the case as well as reports of equal decline across all daily activities. Chiu and Lee (2002) also suggest there may be common patterns of faking on memory tasks across ethnic groups. Vanderploeg and Curtiss (2001) suggest the most common reasons neuropsychologists question an evaluation's validity are (a) inconsistencies in test performance and behavior outside of the testing session and (b) inconsistencies between actual and expected test performance coupled with poor performance on validity measures. Several authors offer specific assessment recommendations for malingering (Baker, Hanley, Jackson, Kimmance, & Slade, 1993; Colby, 2001; Cullum, Heaton, & Grant, 1991; Etcoff & Kampfer, 1996; Rogers, 1997).

In this case, several of the indicators Johnstone et al. (2000) highlighted lead to diagnostic consideration of malingering. The clinic staff collaborated to ensure that unneeded or unwarranted surgery was not prescribed for the patient. Indeed, the psychologist made a point of arranging for the patient to receive information regarding possible harmful consequences of surgery and adaptive alternative services in lieu of aggressive and costly treatment for his complaints. Despite this attempt at adaptive redirection, the patient found another avenue to achieve his personal goal and exercised his autonomous choice. Although the interdisciplinary clinic professionals can be confident that they handled this case in a just manner, the freedoms inherent in the health care system fostered informed choice despite a likelihood of negative personal and social consequences.

CASE 2.4
OVERRIDING TREATMENT REFUSALS DURING EARLY RECOVERY FROM CATASTROPHIC INJURY

The oxyacetylene explosion occurred without warning on a quiet Saturday morning in the Custom Fabrication Shop. A safety device on a valve that mixes the volatile gases in two nearly empty tanks failed, causing a leak. An errant spark ignited a broad jet of flame that flared for only a few seconds before running out of fuel. Unfortunately, Fergus MacGonagle was in the path of that incandescent jet. For those few seconds, the deadly flame bathed his upper body as he sat working at the programming console for his CNC milling machine. Fergus had the presence of mind to dive for the floor, rolling to extinguish his burning clothes. Then he struggled to stand and desperately staggered to a phone, successfully dialing 911. Slumping in a nearby office chair, Fergus was momentarily stunned as he looked down at his charred clothes and mottled flesh underneath. He then succumbed to shock and lost consciousness.

Dr. Satya Vajra, a 31-year-old assistant professor in the Clinical Psychology Department, had just finished a rather disturbing long-distance phone call from her father when the request for consultation arrived from the burn unit. The University Medical Center had established a psychology consultation and liaison service several years earlier, and the burn unit was one of the first programs to request psychology's assistance. In addition to providing direct care, Dr. Vajra served as a supervising psychologist to graduate students and interns. Dr. Vajra knew from past experience that a call from the sixth floor meant that a patient had regained consciousness. The patient had survived the initial medical crisis, having been maintained in a medication-induced coma to allow unobstructed fluid volume stabilization, initial plastic and orthopedic surgeries, and the harvesting of epidermis allografts. The patient was now awake and believed in need of psychological services.

Just prior to the psychology consultation, a neuropsychology intern attached to the neurology service had been asked to conduct a mental status examination with Mr. MacGonagle. The intern found the patient's behavior challenging, but he believed Mr. MacGonagle had cooperated well enough with the evaluation to warrant a valid interpretation of the assessment data obtained. The intern's conclusion was that the patient was capable of making health care decisions on his own behalf. That piece of information is what triggered the burn team to call Dr. Vajra for a treatment consult.

When she arrived on the unit, suitably gowned, masked and gloved, Dr. Vajra encountered a severely disfigured Fergus MacGonagle. Tragically, all but two digits on his hands had required amputation. He had marked facial alterations, except around his eyes. Safety goggles had protected Fergus, leaving a mask-shaped ring of healthy tissue around his orbits. Despite the liberal patient-controlled analgesia (PCA) pump program, Fergus cried out in distress. Although still on significant doses of narcotics, Fergus was beginning to realize that he had lost 2 months' time and his upper body had been gruesomely ravaged. His persona had been transplanted into a horribly gnarled shell that he neither recognized nor wanted to inhabit.

Dr. Vajra introduced herself to her new patient, adopting an upbeat style, "Good afternoon, Mr. MacGonagle. I'm Dr. Vajra, your psychologist while you're here on our burn unit." Her pronounced English accent gave an air of probity to the introduction. She smiled and waited.

Rolling his eyes toward her, Fergus managed to croak, "Get the hell out of my face and go back to where you came from, lady. Unless you can take away this godawful pain, I don't want nothin' to do with you." That said, he closed his eyes and turned his head away, breath whistling wetly around his tracheostomy tube.

"Mr. MacGonagle, the burn team has requested that I see you. They feel that you need psychological support. They're experts in the field, and I trust their judgment." Dr. Vajra smiled sympathetically, trying to help her patient understand that establishing a working relationship was an inevitability. Then, adopting a more serious tone and expression, she added, "I've been serving patients with burn injuries for several years now. You can be confident that I am quite familiar with the pain and discomfort you are experiencing. I am well versed in hypnosis and other techniques that can help lessen your pain." Smiling again, Dr. Vajra went on, "We will make it through this experience together."

Fergus turned his head slightly, opened one eye and studied the psychologist for a moment. Then he said, "Hypnosis! You're not trying any voodoo on me. You tell that team of ghouls that they're wasting valuable medical resources on a man who doesn't want 'em. There are people in our country who don't get health care simply because they can't afford it. Cut me off and give them my share. I don't want any more treatment!" At that moment the pain gripped Mr. MacGonagle. His lips opened in a gurgling yell that turned into a hacking cough, blowing the cap off his tracheostomy tube. Mr. MacGonagle shut his eyes again, and passively refused to interact further with Dr. Vajra.

Relevant Ethical Principles and Standards

Principle A: Beneficence and Nonmaleficence

Both the burn team and the psychologist serving as consultant are focused on supporting Mr. MacGonagle's recovery and preparing him for the lengthy rehabilitation process. He likely is going to survive the burn injury, so treatment is not considered futile. If services are withdrawn, per the patient request, the consequences would likely be life-threatening wound and respiratory infections, unchecked and debilitating scar formation, and significant pain, all preventable with continued treatment. Because the team possesses knowledge regarding long-term recovery that the patient may not yet be in a position to assimilate, the team overrides the patient's autonomy to protect his health. On the other hand, they must consider that emotional harm might be a consequence of providing treatment against the patient's wishes.

Principle B: Fidelity and Responsibility

The psychologist's duty to her patient is to provide the requested psychological services within a professional relationship built on trust. Unfortunately, Dr. Vajra's introductory comments tended to minimize the patient's concerns and implied she understood the patient's situation before a relationship with the patient had been developed. Therefore, she immediately challenged her capability to build trust by placing distance between the patient and herself.

Principle D: Justice

The patient has suggested his expensive and scarce health care resources should be allocated to other individuals who need basic care to use limited health care funds more efficiently. On the other hand, lack of acute treatment for Mr. MacGonagle may contribute to costlier subsequent intervention for medical complications or psychological crisis. Therefore, Dr. Vajra must use her psychological knowledge and expertise to attempt to predict the likelihood of a future patient crisis if she does not proactively offer psychology services.

Principle E: Respect for People's Rights and Dignity

Although the patient initially requested treatment by calling 911, he has the right to refuse health care at any reasonable time, assuming that such a refusal is fully informed. The psychologist needs to carefully consider whether Mr. MacGonagle has provided true informed consent to refuse therapy given his distressed emotional status.

Standard 2.03, Maintaining Competence

Dr. Vajra's actions and experience must support her competence to work with individuals on the burn unit. Consistent with this standard, Dr. Vajra has been involved in several national burn conferences and presented a collaborative paper with the medical chief of the service the year before. In addition, she attends monthly clinical and research educational rounds sponsored by the burn program. Finally, she continues to gather field experience through managing several consultations from the burn team each month.

Standard 2.06, Personal Problems and Conflicts

Dr. Vajra has to take care that the contentious relationship with her family, particularly her father, does not intrude upon her professional duties.

Standard 3.04, Avoiding Harm

By providing services the patient appears to be refusing, Dr. Vajra could contribute to the patient's overall emotional distress. She also must consider that lack of early intervention may have long-term consequences not immediately apparent to the patient. Therefore, in weighing whether to forgo or provide psychological treatment, Dr. Vajra must attempt to determine which decision will result in the avoidance of the most emotional harm.

Standard 3.09, Cooperation With Other Professionals

Dr. Vajra has to maintain a collaborative relationship with the health care professionals on the burn team. Her behavioral data gathering and intervention carryover depend on the cooperation of the burn team professionals who will bear responsibility for implementing part of her treatment recommendations.

Standard 3.10, Informed Consent

The patient has to consent to psychology services. Although at first this appears to be a hindrance to intervention, the psychologist and the burn team may well work to soften the patient's negative view of psychological services through encouragement and provision of information regarding treatment effectiveness. If Dr. Vajra believes the patient's mental status is waxing and waning, which is not uncommon in acute medical patients, she should implement serial assessments of that capacity (Holzer, Gansler, Moczynski, & Folstein, 1997).

Standard 3.12, Interruption of Psychological Services

Dr. Vajra should anticipate the likely disruption of psychological services as a result of the patient's need for continuing medical services. It is likely the patient will be transferred between the burn and surgical units for skin grafting, reconstruction, and restoration of function. She should consider making arrangements to provide service across hospital settings to ensure continuity of patient care.

Standard 4.02, Discussing the Limits of Confidentiality

Dr. Vajra has to inform Mr. MacGonagle that confidentiality might be broken and protective measures taken if she perceives that he or someone else might come to harm. Discussing the limits of confidentiality with someone who has sustained a traumatic injury is critical. The patient may experience unpredictable challenges in the course of recovery over which he perceives little control, increasing his risk of emotional crisis.

Standard 9.01, Bases for Assessments

Dr. Vajra bears the responsibility for ensuring that any test instruments used on the burn unit are validated and found reliable for that specific special population as evidenced in research literature.

Standard 9.03, Informed Consent in Assessments

Mr. MacGonagle must give his consent before any assessment instruments may be used. An exception is defensible if Dr. Vajra suspects that Mr.

MacGonagle's emotional presentation interferes with his capacity to given an informed opinion about his burn treatment. She can proceed with an evaluation for the purposes of clarifying his emotional status impacting on that capacity.

Standard 10.01, Informed Consent to Therapy

In soliciting patient consent to therapy, the psychologist should provide a treatment rationale and expectations for outcomes couched in terms of measurable, objective goals. If the patient does not consent and is judged to have the capacity to make this decision, the psychologist has a heavy burden to defend a decision to override this decision and attempt additional contact.

Institutional and Legal Concepts That May Apply

Mr. MacGonagle originally requested emergency medical services (EMS), and treatment was initiated. However, he later expressed the desire to withdraw treatment. Although the patient's wish to terminate treatment is inconsistent with his initiation of the 911 call, a decision made during an emergency does not necessarily reflect the patient's wishes after the emergency has subsided. The team is obligated to reevaluate consent and their course of action.

Given this case does not occur in a state legally condoning physician-assisted suicide, measures to hasten Mr. MacGonagle's death were not directly addressed despite his requests to let him die. The patient does not have a terminal condition, and his ongoing treatment cannot be construed as futile given that his risk of injury-related death had significantly decreased by the time of transfer to the burn unit. Therefore, the burn team has weighed the benefits and burdens of withdrawing treatment and is unwilling to terminate preventive and curative treatment based on the patient's wish to do so upon regaining consciousness.

Relevant Context and Key Stakeholders

Patient's History

Fergus MacGonagle is a quiet, intense man of 47 years. Throughout his life he has prided himself on being the best at whatever he undertakes. His coworkers acknowledge that he was the wizard of the fabrication shop. The rookies and some experienced machinists went to him for how-to advice. He had "the knack." Fergus could visualize, calibrate, and then turn any billet of metal into a customer-pleasing part after being given only the vaguest of specifications. He took great pride in the satisfied customer reactions he observed. The owner of the shop was wise to let Fergus be the front man when complex orders came their way. Fergus has been employed in this shop for 14 years after failing in an attempt to operate a solo business. Exacting work habits in that solo effort did not allow him the productivity necessary to pay his bills. Fergus finally threw in the towel after realizing that arguing with himself was a rather boring exercise.

Fergus's wife Maida finds him to be a demanding partner. His perfectionistic character results in frequent bouts of irritability when others do not meet his standards. Yet, Maida can reliably rein him in when he oversteps his bounds. Fergus never intends to impose his will on others; it just escapes and runs amok now and then.

The MacGonagle's only son Iain moved out of the house when he was 16 years of age, citing his father's intolerance as the reason. He moved in with his girlfriend's parents, a living arrangement that continued until the couple wed three years later. Iain is now 26 years old, and he and his wife have a son. Only recently has there been a thawing out, a rapproachment, in the relationship between Fergus and Iain. This occurred at Maida's insistence when Iain introduced his 2-year-old son Willem to his grandfather.

Fergus is a man with very conservative views of the world. His nationalistic beliefs border on radical isolationism at times. He resents immigrants' receiving government assistance that is fast being cut back for everyone because of budgetary shortfalls. No one has the courage to remind Fergus that his Scottish lineage would have placed him in the same category several generations earlier.

Fergus also supports the activities of Dr. Jack Kevorkian, having read everything in print about the man and his exploits regarding assisted suicide. Fergus often has discussed his thoughts on the matter with his coworkers and family, stating emphatically that if he had a debilitating illness, he would be first on Kevorkian's list. A man just should not have to live without pride in his ability to work around a problem, and being unable to use his hands is one problem no one has succeeded in beating, even with fancy electronic prostheses.

Psychologist's History

Satya Vajra, age 31, was educated at Oxford, and spent most of her adult life living in London. She received clinical experience with catastrophic illness during her professional training in the British National Health Service. Dr. Vajra moved to the United States four years earlier as part of an extended health care exchange program. Two years remain on the training grant. Dr. Vajra's family belongs to the Brahmin caste and is quite wealthy. Her father is an importer, her mother a pediatrician. The family maintains a comfortable lifestyle in England. Dr. Vajra is unmarried, a break with her cultural tradition and a source of puzzlement and disappointment to her family. She has tirelessly devoted her life to helping her patients and teaching budding psychologists. By all accounts, she is a highly successful professional.

Dr. Vajra recently learned, through a cousin, that her father has been diagnosed with a terminal illness. Her father asked that she not be informed. She does not understand her father's behavior and has been especially distressed by the fact that her mother has not confided in her. Additionally, Dr. Vajra feels that she lacks a substantial social–emotional support system in the United States. She tried allying with the local Indian cultural center, but discovered it is family oriented and does not offer her a personally supportive connection.

The day following her initial contact with Fergus MacGonagle, Dr. Vajra found herself becoming frustrated and angry during a supervision session with her current graduate students, Adam Lerner and Francesca Vasari. They were discussing the MacGonagle case and speculating on intervention strategies. Exploring her own feelings, Dr. Vajra could not help but feel that the patient had rejected her on ethnic grounds. He had not given her the opportunity to demonstrate her professional expertise. She began to wonder if she could adopt an objective professional stance with respect to her relationship with him because of her own emotional reactions. These reactions were further complicated by the difficult situation with her family.

When weighing the relevant information in this case toward resolution, the following people were considered.

Patient (Fergus MacGonagle). The patient has refused treatment from the burn team except for dressing changes and mobility exercises. Control is very important to Mr. MacGonagle. He has a history of clearly expressing his ideas about assisted suicide should he find himself in a position of not being able to use his hands, a situation he associates with an unacceptable quality of life. However, he initiated rescue services from the health care system after sustaining severe burns. Mr. MacGonagle has a strained, but supportive relationship with his wife. Recently Fergus's relationships with his formerly estranged son, daughter-in-law, and grandson have improved, and they might be allies in treatment planning.

Family (Wife Maida, Son Iain and His Wife, Grandson Willem). Despite a demanding relationship, the patient's spouse is supportive and encouraging. She also has been supportive of their son during the 10-year period of estrangement. However, it is not likely that anyone in the family can effectively impact the patient's strongly held opinion regarding assisted suicide. No one questioned the patient's stance on this issue prior to his injury. The family has been unified around the curative and preventive treatments provided by the burn unit during the patient's two-month medication-induced coma. They have been distressed by Fergus's insistence on withdrawing treatment since he emerged from the medication-induced coma.

Psychologist (Dr. Satya Vajra). The psychologist experiences conflict regarding her role vis-à-vis the patient. He has rejected her initial overture for intervention. She attributes this, in part, to his long-held attitudes toward foreigners and possibly gender issues. Although Dr. Vajra is aware of the importance of respecting this patient's values, she also is aware that some patients sustaining burns initially reject services and then later thank the team for ignoring this rejection. She possesses the experience to work through most patient resistance. Nevertheless, Dr. Vajra needs to weigh the potential impact of her own family issues and values on her professional decision making. Because of her personal problems with her family, Dr. Vajra is beginning to feel that she may not be able to maintain an objective stance with regard to patient evaluation and treatment.

Burn Team. The interdisciplinary team is distressed that the patient, now able to make capacitated decisions regarding his care, refuses their ministrations. The team hopes that Dr. Vajra will be able to convince the patient to continue needed burn treatment. However, the team is unified in their opinion that they are obligated to provide both curative and preventive care to Mr. MacGonagle whether he desires it or not. He does not have a terminal illness, and they cannot, in good conscience, contribute to his demise through negligence.

Consultants (Dr. Merlyn Oates, Supervising Faculty; and Dr. Ford Monroe, Postdoctoral Trainee). Entering the case near the end of the patient's burn unit admission are Dr. Oates and Dr. Monroe, both attached to the chronic pain treatment program at the University Medical Center. Merlyn Oates is a collaborator by nature. He has a reputation as a psychologist who assists fellow faculty when they encounter problems that require a team approach. He often is the first choice among his peers when faced with a challenge. Ford Monroe, on the other hand, is a rather headstrong individual raised in a culturally mixed family that lives in a small community in northern Maine. He is rather difficult to fathom interpersonally as he is a very private person. Dr. Monroe's father had been a chief mechanic earlier in his life for a British Formula One racing team, a potential link to Fergus's vocation. Once the family returned from the United Kingdom, Dr. Monroe worked his way through school. He has struggled throughout his life to attain his professional goals on his own terms. Fortunately, he has learned the value of empathic regard when working with patients exhibiting resistance to treatment.

Case Resolution

Evaluate the Impact of Family Stress on Professional Effectiveness

Dr. Vajra had concerns that her family stress would affect her focus on this case. However, she was a determined individual and was not accustomed to transferring cases to colleagues. After careful consideration and deliberation with a colleague, she determined that she could manage her family stress and continue to work with the patient. The consultation helped her recognize she was not simply being obstinate in retaining Mr. MacGonagle as a patient; she felt she could maintain appropriate boundaries.

Solicit Informed Consent

Dr. Vajra attempted to acquire consent across several sessions to facilitate the development of rapport that might lead to the patient's consent for more formal assessment and intervention. These attempts failed.

Seek a Means to Align With the Patient

Because Dr. Vajra's initial attempts to offer psychological services failed, she tried to identify a means to align with Mr. MacGonagle. She knew that she and Mr. MacGonagle were similar in that Fergus was feeling alienated from his life because of his self-defined quality-of-life stipulation. She experienced social family alienation because of her choice to pursue professional goals over her cultural traditions. If she could present those similarities to the patient and achieve some mutual identification, she might be able to get through to him. As part of this process, she also evaluated the inconsistencies in the patient's behaviors and expressions (i.e., he allows some wound treatments but rejects others), which might help her set up a more effective alignment strategy. This attempt was also rejected. In this situation, the psychologist might also involve the team in attempting to reinforce positive interactions. However, Fergus did not consistently act positively toward anyone on the team.

Evaluate Whether the Patient's Value System Is Inconsistent With the Provider's Ability to Provide Care

Dr. Vajra had mounting evidence that the patient's value system contributed to his rejection of psychological services. Initially she had a nagging suspicion that her gender and ethnicity influenced his rejection of her attempts to provide care. This information was corroborated by family report, Fergus's own demeaning comments, and his tacit acceptance of a personality-testing evaluation that he then sabotaged, making her question the validity of any data gathered. Dr. Vajra then considered the possibility of working indirectly with Fergus through her graduate students. This strategy would allow her to supervise any intervention without provoking the patient's negative cultural or gender bias. Thus, the patient could receive benefit from her knowledge while she showed respect for his values. However, Mr. MacGonagle proceeded to harass both of the students once he discovered that the "foreign shrink" was their supervisor. This gave further credence to Dr. Vajra's ultimate decision to ask a colleague to take over care of this patient.

Involve the Family

Prior to transferring the case, Dr. Vajra arranged to meet with Fergus's family, who happened to be gathered in the burn unit lounge. Families commonly are supportive players in the care of individuals with traumatic injuries, and Fergus had given permission upon admission to allow the team to talk with his family (another inconsistency in his presentation). During the meeting, Dr. Vajra encouraged the family to visit Fergus regularly so that he could connect with something meaningful outside the hospital context. The family expressed concern that Fergus insisted on withdrawing treatment. They loved Fergus and took heart in the burn team's decision to continue treatment.

With Dr. Vajra's encouragement, the family agreed to visit Fergus again. This time she asked that Willem accompany them. She had gotten the sense that Fergus's attitude toward his son had softened through his feelings for his only grandchild. She cautioned the family to allow this to be a social visit with no mention of their concerns about his treatment refusal.

When the family returned, they entered the room with Iain in the lead, holding his son. Dr. Vajra stood in the doorway, out of direct eyesight, and observed her patient's reactions. The tears she saw on Fergus's face were the only signs of emotion not related to anger that she had observed since meeting the man. Iain held his son out to his grandfather, and Fergus managed an awkward hug. Willem appeared delighted with the visit. He was interested in all the machinery. He did not seem put off by his grandfather's appearance, approaching his grandfather after only a few moments of reticence during his initial visit several days earlier.

Fergus spoke to his grandson, ignoring the rest of the family, "Hello, my little man. You're looking chipper today." Iain broke in saying that Willem had just cut another tooth. Fergus responded, "Boy you're gonna have a nice set of choppers when this tooth cutting is over." The mood of the family appeared to brighten as a result of this interaction. Maida laid a hand on her husband's bandaged arm, and he tolerated that gesture without protest. He appeared lost in the joyful moment of Willem's visit. The family talked about things going on in their lives outside the hospital, and Fergus made occasional comments regarding their family news.

When the burn team nurse entered the room for a wound dressing change, the visit effectively ended. The family members bid Fergus goodbye and promised to bring Willem to visit the next day. As they filed out of the room past Dr. Vajra, Fergus said, "This don't change a thing." To his wife's questioning look, he stated, pointing with his bandaged, deformed hand toward the nurse arranging her bandaging supplies, "She's doing this to me under protest. I want all of them to leave me alone . . . let nature run its course . . . let me die." What started as a potential emotional breakthrough ended like every other interaction with Fergus MacGonagle.

Consult Colleague for Transfer of Care

Dr. Vajra opted to consult Dr. Merlyn Oates regarding transferring the case. Dr. Oates was the director of the University Medical Center's pain program and usually covered Dr. Vajra's service when she was away. After explaining the challenging case and her reservations about continuing, including personal issues influencing her judgment, Dr. Oates agreed to take over. At that juncture, Dr. Oates offered personal support to his colleague, suggesting that she discuss her issues with one of the clinical faculty therapists. She agreed, feeling an emotional weight had been removed. Later that day, Dr. Vajra let Mr. MacGonagle know that she would no longer be providing care. He stated again that he did not need any shrinks.

Dr. Oates had immediately thought of Dr. Ford Monroe when Dr. Vajra mentioned her patient's occupation. This lifestyle–history connection might be just the strategic leverage needed to secure an emotional foothold with Mr. MacGonagle. Never a person to turn down a challenge, Dr. Monroe agreed to take the case immediately after Dr. Oates described the situation later that week. He especially liked the strategic approach to intervention suggested by Dr. Oates.

Case Disposition

Before Dr. Monroe could introduce himself to Mr. MacGonagle, the burn team had decided to transfer Fergus to the University Medical Center's inpatient rehabilitation center. His wounds had healed to the point that Fergus's care could be provided by the rehabilitation nurses who had trained on the burn unit. Additionally, he had regained the ability to ambulate several feet (with hands-on assistance) to the restroom. This was a privilege he requested frequently, another curious inconsistency in Mr. MacGonagle's treatment-resistant presentation.

During a discussion about going to rehabilitation with the burn unit's medical director, Fergus was presented with the opportunity to perform more of his self-care and to walk greater distances in rehabilitation than he had been allowed on the burn unit. To the surprise of the surgeon, he agreed to the rehabilitation transfer. His previous treatment refusals were pointedly not addressed during this conversation. Learning of the impending transfer to the inpatient rehabilitation unit, Dr. Oates, in consultation with Dr. Monroe, opted to transfer supervision to the rehabilitation psychologist manning the rehabilitation unit. Dr. Oates made the call, presented a summary of Mr. MacGonagle's situation in the form of a clinical heads-up to the rehabilitation psychologist, and secured her agreement to allow Dr. Monroe to continue following the patient.

Additional Commentary

In this case, the psychologist must decide two key issues: whether to treat this patient against his wishes and whether to recuse herself from the case. In Western culture, one's respect for autonomy is strongly embraced. In this case, however, the providers must make a decision whether to override the patient's wishes in the interest of protecting the patient's welfare. The decision of teams to override the autonomy of individuals with traumatic injuries very early in the recovery process is fairly common. One rationale supporting this position, as expressed in this case, is that given the patient's emotional and physical stress, the patient cannot truly assimilate the long-term implications of lack of treatment, and thus informed consent is not acquired. The famous case of Dax offers a dialogue over many years between Dax Cowart and his physician. The physician treated Dax for severe burns for months against Dax's very loud protests (Cowart & Burt, 1998).

In deciding whether to recuse herself, Dr. Vajra had to evaluate how her own ethnicity and gender shaped her assessment of and reactions to Mr. MacGonagle. She also had to acquire knowledge regarding Mr. MacGonagle's value system. Through this process of assessing her multicultural competence, it became clear to Dr. Vajra that she should transfer the patient's psychological care. Hansen, Pepitone-Arreola-Rockwell, and Greene, 2000, offer a detailed discussion of 12 specific multicultural competencies and whether psychologists know when they are competent to treat individuals with differing values from their own. In addition, the APA (2003) offers guidelines for addressing multiculturalism and discusses the importance of cultural awareness and sensitivity in clinical practice.

Despite engaging in this competency self-assessment, Dr. Vajra's introductory comments seriously compromised her ability to establish rapport regardless of whether the patient held strong values regarding Dr. Vajri herself. She placed herself in an even more difficult position than she was already facing by increasing the emotional distance between her and the patient through the subtleties of her language. For example, stating that Mr. MacGonagle needed a psychologist exacerbated the patient's already defensive position. Therefore, Dr. Vajra did not get the chance to offer potentially effective pain management techniques applicable to early burn wound care and other painful procedures. (See, for example, a summary of hypnosis and clinical pain by Patterson & Jensen, 2003.) Respect for the patient is clearly displayed only if the psychologist matches the context, which Dr. Vajri failed to do in her introduction to the patient.

3

INPATIENT REHABILITATION

Acute medical rehabilitation typically serves individuals who have residual deficits from acute trauma or chronic illness. The hallmark of rehabilitation is a team-based model of care. Unlike many other settings in which psychologists serve as consultants or work fairly independently, rehabilitation psychologists usually are core members of a multi- or interdisciplinary team. Rather than offering independent assessment and treatment, psychologists' choices are continuously influenced by and integrated with those of other disciplines. Psychologists work closely with such diverse professionals as physicians, nurses, case managers, occupational and physical therapists, speech–language pathologists, and rehabilitation counselors. Additional disciplines may include dietitians, audiologists, recreation therapists, and medical consultants. Adaptation to the team milieu is a critical skill for all psychologists working in inpatient rehabilitation to acquire. (Blair & Gorman, 2003, offer commentary on the importance of this skill to neuropsychologists for survival in this setting.)

Psychologists working in rehabilitation provide neuropsychological and psychological evaluations and participate in individual and group treatment independently and as cotherapists with other disciplines. It is not uncommon for psychologists to see patients in other disciplines' treatment areas such as the physical therapy gym or the speech–language pathologist's office.

Because the primary goal of rehabilitation is to maximize the patient's independence and progress toward successful lifestyle adaptation after injury or illness occurs, psychologists may visit schools, homes, or work settings or participate in community reentry interventions as part of the team's discharge planning. Finally, psychologists may have to advocate for patient services or testify in court months or even years after termination of patient care related to litigation attempting to establish the permanence of disability.

Individuals with residual deficits from catastrophic conditions must face the implications of these functional challenges, which can evolve rapidly. Families who have successfully coped with crises attendant to acute medical care must attempt to plan for an uncertain future with loved ones. Families routinely participate in treatment sessions with the patient and can serve as the linchpin for successful transition from the structure of inpatient rehabilitation to the home environment. Therefore, psychologists work with families as much as patients.

The intersection of intrapersonal, familial, team, and social forces provides unique ethical challenges. In this milieu and with the types of patients served, these challenges may range from balancing the patient's right to be involved in care decisions when cognitively compromised to making decisions regarding pharmacological and behavioral restrictions to handling team conflicts in which role boundaries are questioned. Strict standards of confidentiality simply do not work when families must be involved early in the process to maximize recovery. One of the most common ethical dilemmas raised in this setting is balancing respect for the patient's right to self-determination and privacy with the need for family involvement to protect and promote the patient's interests and welfare. This is of particular importance when the patient does not have the ability to recognize the consequences of treatment decisions or may be overwhelmed by the rehabilitation process itself early in the treatment course. Psychologists must thread the needle carefully in a setting in which ethical challenges abound and coordination of care with several other disciplines, each with their own code of ethics, is a prerequisite for effective practice. (For a contemporary presentation of the contributions of psychologists in rehabilitation, see Frank & Elliott, 2000a).

CASE 3.1
OPPORTUNITIES AND CHALLENGES IN USING NONSTANDARDIZED TESTING

Seventy-year-old Emma Pollack sustained a left middle cerebral artery infarct at her home in Junction City, Tennessee, population 700. Bud Pollack, Emma's spouse of 45 years, drove Emma all the way to Metropolitan Hospital for Special Neurological Services (MNS). The "Metropolis," as Emma called it, was a two-hour drive. By the time they arrived, Mrs. Pollack had developed a dense right hemiparesis and a severe expressive language deficit. Her receptive language appeared intact. The language problems were extremely frustrating for Emma, who was the center of the social universe in Junction City. She knew everything that was going on in town, and different people stopped by her place all day long just to sit and chat. Mrs. Pollack was even more distressed by her inability to use her right, dominant hand, given that she loved to bake. Everyone in Junction City knew of Emma's famous double-chocolate caramel nut cookies. No matter how many people tried to make them (Emma was generous with sharing her "secret" recipe), their cookies were never quite as good as Emma's.

On the third day of her hospitalization, Emma felt stronger and Bud thought it might lift her spirits to get her out of her room. Unfortunately, Mrs. Pollack fell while attempting to transfer herself from her bed to her wheelchair. She did not break any bones and the rest of her medical work up was negative, but the mishap did nothing to lift Emma's spirits. Fortunately, the remainder of her stay was uneventful, and eight days after admission to Metropolis, Mrs. Pollack was transferred to the acute rehabilitation unit.

Upon admission, Emma was referred to Dr. Will Cole for a psychological evaluation. Dr. Cole introduced himself to Mr. and Mrs. Pollack, conducted a clinical interview, primarily through yes or no questions and use of a picture board, and then left, stating he did not want to tire Emma any further on her first day, especially given that she had been having trouble sleeping. He stated he would return the next day to complete a more comprehensive assessment. From the results of the initial interview, Dr. Cole believed Mrs. Pollack was experiencing adjustment-related dysphoria as well as short-term memory deficits; however, he wanted to assess further and quantify Mrs. Pollack's difficulties.

In the subsequent session, Dr. Cole administered his usual screening battery, flexibly modifying test selection and administration to accommodate Mrs. Pollack's linguistic and motoric impairments, as he had done numerous times with other patients. Because of Mrs. Pollack's expressive language problems, he selected performance-based measures when possible. For tests that normally required a verbal response, he instead offered a multiple-choice format. A head nod sufficed for simple yes or no questions. To assess emotional status, he administered a brief inventory of items characteristic of different emotional states. Although typically self-administered, Dr. Cole very slowly read both the questions and choices to her. For motor-based and timed tasks measuring visuospatial construction ability and visual memory (e.g., simple and complex designs), Dr. Cole asked Mrs. Pollack to use her left (nondominant) hand. She complied but expressed concern about her inability to draw with her left hand.

Mrs. Pollack's scores on the verbally based measures of this modified battery were relatively strong, falling within normal limits for her age group. In contrast, her scores on the performance-based measures generally fell in the impaired range. Dr. Cole noted that the obtained pattern of results was inconsistent with what would be expected given Mrs. Pollack's left hemisphere stroke. He stated so in his report, hypothesizing that she had sustained a diffuse axonal injury when she fell on her third day of hospitalization. The results of the mood questionnaire fell within normal limits compared to a female psychiatric population; Dr. Cole reported that Mrs. Pollack was coping well given the changes she had recently experienced.

Relevant Ethical Principles and Standards

Principle A: Beneficence and Nonmaleficence

Competence in test use, particularly test adaptation, is a prerequisite for ethical practice in acute rehabilitation (Caplan & Shechter, 1995). Although tests and norms adapted for medical populations are sometimes found in materials initially commercially distributed, it is more common to find test modifications in subsequent journal articles or texts on assessment. Dr. Cole is responsible for selecting appropriate tests, which will require adaptation given the effects of Mrs. Pollack's stroke, and for selecting appropriate norms for comparison of Mrs. Pollack's results. The psychologist must guard against naïve interpretation of test data based on his own lack of knowledge with specific populations. For domains in which standardized modifications or norms are not yet available, Dr. Cole should consider modifications to standard administration as needed to best reflect Mrs. Pollack's status. However, interpretations should be tempered accordingly. A lack of familiarity with or failure to use relevant modifications or norms may result in inappropriate and potentially harmful interpretations and recommendations. Cognitive test results can carry great authority regarding rehabilitation treatment planning, affecting decisions such as restriction of privileges and choice of medications. Inappropriate treatment or unnecessary patient monitoring may occur as a consequence of inappropriate testing and interpretation.

Principle B: Fidelity and Responsibility

It is likely that the hospital administrators would consider Dr. Cole's diagnosis and suspected etiology troubling. It behooves Dr. Cole to evaluate the availability of corroborating data. On a rehabilitation unit, reporting findings as fact without first seeking the perspectives of other team members with overlapping areas of expertise might be considered irresponsible. Dr. Cole has a responsibility to reconcile findings that do not concur with those of other rehabilitation professionals to attempt to determine a reasonable explanation for differences that could affect treatment decisions.

Principle E: Respect for People's Rights and Dignity

The results of the cognitive evaluation have significant implications for further treatment as well as the level of independence the patient may be afforded on the rehabilitation unit. Dr. Cole must ensure that he is using appropriate data to prevent overinterpretation of poor test performance needlessly resulting in restriction of patient autonomy.

Standard 2.03, Maintaining Competence

Staying abreast of emerging research regarding the validity and reliability of modifications to tests used with medical populations will allow Dr. Cole to select appropriate assessment tools for Mrs. Pollack as well as other persons with disabilities. He also would benefit from consulting colleagues regarding adaptation of test instruments.

Standard 2.04, Bases for Scientific and Professional Judgments

In addition to comparing Mrs. Pollack's pattern of results with appropriate norms, Dr. Cole must compare Mrs. Pollack's performance over time in the rehabilitation setting, given that it is expected her performance will change as she continues to recover from her stroke.

Standard 2.05, Delegation of Work to Others

Dr. Cole has access to a psychometrist who administers standard neuropsychological batteries. However, because the need for unanticipated modifications can arise during test administration for patients with evolving medical issues, Dr. Cole is extremely cautious in considering using a psychometrist for this type of evaluation.

Standard 3.09, Cooperation With Other Professionals

Other health care providers will use the results of the evaluation in their own treatment planning. Dr. Cole can and should assist them in appropriately interpreting the information available.

Standard 3.10, Informed Consent

Given that the patient's receptive language is intact, Dr. Cole can achieve appropriate consent through modification of normal consent procedures to match Mrs. Pollack's strengths.

Standard 4.06, Consultations

The rehabilitation team possesses significant information regarding cognitive and emotional function based on their own treatment sessions with the patient. These data should not be overlooked by Dr. Cole in drawing conclusions regarding test performance.

Standard 6.01, Documentation of Professional and Scientific Work and Maintenance of Records

Departures from standardized administration should be described in the written report.

Standard 9.01(a), Bases for Assessments

When possible, Dr. Cole must base his opinions on appropriate techniques and information and not solely on his own determination of how measures should be modified or on his subjective "internal norms" for how patients perform on such measures.

Standard 9.06, Interpreting Assessment Results

Dr. Cole must describe any limitations in the confidence he has in his findings or interpretation, particularly given testing modifications and situational variables can easily affect the presentation of patients in rehabilitation (e.g., energy level, noise and distractions, and medication changes).

Institutional and Legal Concepts That May Apply

By suggesting that Mrs. Pollack's cognitive deficits are due in part to a traumatic brain injury sustained while in the hospital, Dr. Cole opens his institution up to the possibility of a personal injury claim. Although psychologists may find themselves in situations in which appropriate documentation of their results places a hospital at risk, Dr. Cole's documentation is troubling given the limited information on which he offers the TBI hypothesis. The hospital also may be vulnerable to sanctions from accrediting organizations or the state board of health.

Relevant Context and Key Stakeholders

Emma Pollack has sustained a severe stroke, and her spouse has expressed concern about her mood. She may be experiencing cognitive and emotional difficulties that need to be addressed as part of her rehabilitation program. Dr. Cole is unable to administer commonly used neuropsychological measures in the standardized manner. He therefore modifies his test battery as well as the administration and scoring of the tests within his battery. Cautious interpretation of the test data is indicated. Reporting of questionable findings is made without consultation with colleagues.

The following parties were considered in weighing key information.

Patient (Emma Pollack). Mrs. Pollack's linguistic and motoric deficits preclude assessment of cognition and mood through standardized administration of common psychological measures. However, she is anxious to cooperate with any assessment procedures that will help her get better so that she can return to her social circle. She has consented to having her spouse involved in all aspects of her care. She has demonstrated some dysphoria and frustration over her situation as well as difficulty sleeping since entering the Metropolis.

Psychologist (Dr. Will Cole). Dr. Cole attempts to assess Mrs. Pollack's cognitive and emotional status as accurately as possible, taking into account her expressive language deficits. He demonstrates sensitivity to the fact that many standardized measures were not developed with patients with aphasia and hemiparesis in mind, and he has attempted to modify his procedures and interpretation accordingly. However, he has not researched the types of modifications that would be appropriate and has not effectively taken into account any emotional overlay to the cognitive difficulties. If his conclusions prove inaccurate, he will have needlessly contributed to inappropriate treatment decisions based on these conclusions.

Patient's Spouse (Bud Pollack). Mr. Pollack provides key support to his wife. They have had a long, happy marriage, and he knows Emma better than anyone else. He is worried Emma may be depressed because she believes she will not be able to successfully return to her prominent social circle. Mr. Pollack is available to provide critical social information if Dr. Cole requests it.

Rehabilitation Team. Team members, particularly the occupational and physical therapists, have observed a gradual but steady progression in Mrs. Pollack's strength and visual-spatial skills. In addition, the rehabilitation nurse and occupational therapist have noted that Emma has some movement in her right arm but it is not functional yet. Emma's affect and frustration appear to be worsening.

Hospital Administration. If the patient's fall results in injury, as Dr. Cole's report suggests, the hospital could be held liable, as discussed in the legal concepts section of this case. However, regardless of the accuracy of Dr. Cole's report, the hospital is interested in evaluating the circumstances under which the fall occurred. This assessment will help determine whether preventative steps (e.g., additional caregiver training, changing room layout, or monitoring) could be put into place to decrease the risk of falls among future patients.

Case Resolution

Review Patient's Chart

Dr. Cole thoroughly familiarized himself with the patient's identified deficits based on the physician's history and physical. He used this review to select his tests and adapt them accordingly. However, he appeared to minimize the negative medical data subsequent to Emma's fall.

Talk With Patient and Family

With Emma's permission, Dr. Cole involved Mr. Pollack in all sessions in which information was gathered or interpreted to maximize data collection. He ascertained that Emma has no psychiatric history (no previous depressive episodes) and that her social activities include visiting with friends and cooking. He did not inquire about responses to any previous health changes or the patient's general coping skills when faced with stressful events.

Modify Test Materials and Procedures

Dr. Cole limited his test battery on the basis of Mrs. Pollack's fatigue level. He attempted to modify the tests to match her response strengths according to what he thought would work (e.g., slowing instruction rate and use of nondominant hand).

Interpret Data

Dr. Cole used standardization norms for the cognitive tests and well-cited psychiatric norms for the emotional state questionnaire to interpret Mrs. Pollack's scores. He did not take into account the consistency or inconsistency of the patient's presentation with other providers, and he appeared to overemphasize test data at the expense of clinical observation regarding the patient's emotional presentation.

Integrate Test Results Back Into Treatment Planning

Dr. Cole recommended in the chart that occupational therapy and speech–language pathology address the visual–spatial and expressive language concerns, which they were already doing. He did not recommend psychological services, as Dr. Cole reported Mrs. Pollack was coping well emotionally given her recent stroke. This conclusion was based on the use of inappropriate norms and insufficient familial information regarding Emma's general coping.

Case Disposition

Mrs. Pollack made significant gains while on the rehabilitation unit. At discharge, her speech was slow but understandable and her right hemiparesis had improved to the point of her being able to grasp a spoon with adaptive equipment. She required both speech and occupational therapy services as an outpatient. Despite her medical progress, she continued to be extremely frustrated by the slow pace of recovery and seemed to have difficulty with mood swings, which were partly related to her social circle falling apart. She ultimately sought outpatient psychotherapy to help manage the impact of the lasting effects of the stroke on her social life.

Although Dr. Cole had attempted to meet Mrs. Pollack's needs, he was insufficiently trained to do so. His lack of familiarity with relevant studies led to inappropriate modifications from which misleading data were obtained. He did not attempt to resolve inconsistencies in the patient's presentation or consider other providers' data, which was shortsighted and inappropriate. He did not consider the impact of timed tasks on performance and used inappropriate norms for emotional status. Although he did adapt his testing length to accommodate the patient's fatigue level, he did not consider the impact of potential sleep deprivation on the test results (Stepanski, Rybarczyk, Lopez, & Stevens, 2002). Therefore, he drew inaccurate conclusions regarding Mrs. Pollack's cognitive and affective functioning. He represented his discipline poorly among team members, failed to provide appropriate service to his patient, and put his institution at risk for legal action, even though the statement that Mrs. Pollack's cognitive difficulties were because of the fall sustained in the hospital went unnoticed.

Dr. Cole had no psychology colleagues present in his setting and did not believe he had the time to pursue continuing education beyond that required by his state license. As a result, he continued to practice in the same manner until one of his assessments came to the attention of a board-certified rehabilitation psychologist, Dr. Irma Riviera. Dr. Riviera practiced in an outpatient setting and had received a referral on one of Dr. Cole's former patients. When she received the record, she was a bit surprised, to say the least, by the neuropsychological report. Consistent with Ethical Standard 1.04, Informal Resolution of Ethical Violations, Dr. Riviera contacted Dr. Cole. She explained her concerns and stated that she would have to report the ethics violation if Dr. Cole did not take steps to gain the necessary training to perform competently. Ideally, this might include regular professional peer contact and continuing education focused on the needs of the patients in Dr. Cole's work setting. Dr. Cole decided to retire instead.

Additional Commentary

Nonstandardized assessment is commonplace in the inpatient rehabilitation setting. Modifications usually are required because of the sensory, cognitive, and physical limitations prevalent in patients seen in rehabilitation. In addition, there are a multitude of mitigating factors associated with recovery, such as overall fatigue level, reactions to medications, success in managing pain, and inconsistency in responding, that necessitate adaptations to the test process (Wilde, Bush, & Zeifert, 2002). These modifications can range from simplifying test instructions to testing across multiple sessions. Unfortunately, data for test interpretation remain somewhat limited for specific diagnostic groups. What data are available should be part of the knowledge base for anyone working with individuals with disabilities. Because of his lack of familiarity with test adaptations, Dr. Cole drew inaccurate conclusions preventing early psychological intervention. Both Caplan and Shechter (1995) and Crewe and Dijkers (1995) offer detailed discussions of the use of nonstandardized testing in rehabilitation. The American Psychological Association (APA) Division 22 journal, *Rehabilitation Psychology*, also is a place where test modifications are commonly reported for patients with disabilities (see, e.g., Nelson, Dial, & Joyce, 2002.)

Ultimately, the purpose of neuropsychological assessment in rehabilitation is to help facilitate treatment that results in optimizing the patient's level of independence. Neuropsychological tests were not originally designed as tests to predict everyday function to the level of specificity needed by rehabilitation psychologists. Therefore, there is always a slight leap of faith regarding the interpretations made. Sbordone (2001) offers a brief but pointed discussion surrounding the issues of using neuropsychological tests to predict everyday function for individuals with brain injury, and Ruchinskas and Curyto (2003) provide an analysis of common cognitive screening tools used in geriactric rehabilitation.

In this case, Dr. Cole selected tests he believed lent themselves to the necessary adaptations required by Mrs. Pollack. However, his leap of faith was simply too large. Sound ethical practice is supported not just by an awareness of and good faith attempt to meet the patient's needs but also by ensuring the contemporary knowledge base available in the profession is brought to bear in the attempt to protect the patient's safety and promote his or her welfare. Conway and Crosson (2000) discuss some of the clinical areas in which psychologists should receive training to practice competently in the area of neurorehabilitation. Only with appropriate training and sensitivity to contemporary challenges can the psychologist effectively serve the patient and profession.

CASE 3.2
THE OVERWHELMED PSYCHOLOGIST'S RESPONSIBILITY TOWARD VERY SICK PATIENTS

Dr. Earl Byrd, the medical director of the Physical Medicine and Rehabilitation (PM&R) department in Pleasantville Regional Hospital (rural setting in southwestern Texas), was a favorite of top administrators in the Pro-Health Care System. He was quickly climbing toward a vice presidency. Dr. Byrd's success was attributed to his business acumen and its resultant aggressive rehabilitation philosophy. Aggressive did not mean that he provided patients with more therapy or state-of-the-art therapy. Aggressive rehabilitation, to Dr. Byrd, meant admitting as many patients as soon as possible, requiring therapists to treat three to four patients an hour, using group instead of individual therapy when possible, treating 7 days a week, and discharging patients after 15 days, before rehabilitation benefits were exhausted. PM&R was the most financially successful program in the Pro-Health Care System. Earl Byrd was a hero to the hospital president; his therapy staff hated him.

Because of the high medical compromise of the patients admitted to rehabilitation, few were able to engage adequately enough in the therapy provided to benefit from the program, and more than a few had died in recent months. Staff morale was an oxymoron. Staff turnover was high despite excellent pay and benefits. Dr. Peter Wilmott, the rehabilitation psychologist, admittedly took the high-paying job to put a dent in his student loans. The only time not spent with patients was spent in meetings trying to determine how the team could get their patients' functional independence evaluation numbers up.

It was within this context that Dr. Wilmott was consulted to perform a psychological evaluation on 89-year-old Hyman North. Mr. North had been admitted to the hospital three weeks earlier because of a general decline in overall functioning. His daughter, Velda, with whom he lived, reported that his ability to get around and do things in the home had been declining for the last two months. She had not seen any of her father's usual medication bottles out on the kitchen counter for several days. Then one evening after getting home from the two jobs she worked, Velda discovered several half-empty vodka bottles and cigarette cartons hidden in a closet. The next morning, she took her father to his primary care physician who, on finding significantly elevated blood pressure and some open wounds on his feet, admitted Mr. North to his service at the local hospital.

An initial inpatient examination revealed uncontrolled diabetes, decreased renal and liver functions, hypertension, and hypercholesterolemia. After three days in the hospital, Mr. North developed pneumonia and sepsis. His blood, sputum, and wounds tested positive for methycillin-resistant staph aureus (MRSA). Mr. North was placed on oxygen, contact isolation, and heavy-duty antibiotics. He remained in bed for most of his three-week stay with the first week being touch and go for survival. Because of his compromised health, Mr. North's level of arousal was poor, and he responded to staff questions only on rare occasions and in a confused manner.

Finally, after being stabilized with no fever for two days, Mr. North was transferred to the rehabilitation unit with a diagnosis of "debility." Observing his patient's complex treatment regimen and ongoing confusion and lethargy, Dr. Philip Maris, the attending physiatrist, ordered a psychology consult in addition to implementing a standard strengthening therapy program. Dr. Wilmott received the order for psychological consultation early on Friday afternoon, and he was already behind schedule to meet his productivity quota for the day. After reading the order, he thought that this very sick elderly patient was less in need of rehabilitative and psychological services than he was in need of appropriate medical care on an acute unit. That is, Dr. Wilmott thought his time would be better spent with other patients than with another inappropriate rehabilitation admission, reasoning that Mr. North might "crash" and be transferred off the rehabilitation service before Dr.

Wilmott could complete his evaluation. Consequently, he intended to put the consult off until early the next week.

Relevant Ethical Principles and Standards

Principle A: Beneficence and Nonmaleficence

When a patient is admitted to a service to which a psychologist is affiliated, that psychologist has a responsibility to provide appropriate and timely care to prevent harm and facilitate recovery. Dr. Wilmott is responsible for evaluating patients who are referred to him for signs of psychological difficulty. Failure to do so based on preconceived ideas about appropriateness or inappropriateness of the patient's presence in rehabilitation would be to neglect his responsibility. Dr. Wilmott also needs to consider whether the timing of the evaluation contributes to benefiting or harming the patient.

Principle B: Fidelity and Responsibility

Dr. Maris expects Mr. North to receive appropriate interdisciplinary care, including psychological services. Dr. Wilmott has developed an atmosphere of trust with his physiatrics colleagues on the provision of quality and timely evaluations and treatment. He must maintain that trusting relationship to be effective as a provider on that health care team. He also must ensure that he is making a sound decision not to evaluate based on the patient's needs and not his own desire to be done for the day.

Principle D: Justice

Dr. Wilmott is aware that Mr. North deserves a psychological evaluation regardless of whether he is a good rehabilitation candidate. However, in an environment in which services cannot be equally distributed among all who need them, the psychologist must consider what constitutes a fair distribution of his services. If Mr. North is too ill to participate adequately in the evaluation, resources have then been inappropriately allocated.

Standard 1.03, Conflicts Between Ethics and Organizational Demands

If Dr. Wilmott believes the pace at which he is required to work results in inadequate quality of services, he is ethically obligated to discuss this problem with Dr. Byrd in an attempt to reach a compromise regarding caseload or service provision. Dr. Wilmott hopes that Dr. Byrd will be willing to discuss some type of resolution or compromise. However, even if Dr. Wilmott believes his efforts with Dr. Byrd will be futile, he still has an obligation to try to achieve a resolution.

Standard 3.04, Avoiding Harm

It is appropriate for Dr. Wilmott to consider the timing of an evaluation with a patient who is severely deconditioned and lethargic. Evaluating

Mr. North too early could result in a paucity or misinterpretation of data, negatively affecting the types and range of treatment offered. In addition, documenting the results of an inappropriate evaluation could negatively influence future provider's judgments regarding similar symptoms with different etiologies.

Standard 3.09, Cooperation With Other Professionals

The referral question regarding "confusion and lethargy" in this case is descriptive but imprecise. Therefore, as part of his evaluation, Dr. Wilmott should clarify the nature of the referral with Dr. Maris before seeing the patient. He could use this conversation as an opportunity to ask questions about the patient's medical status and to clarify concerns regarding psychological symptoms.

Standard 3.10, Informed Consent

If Dr. Wilmott decides to proceed with the evaluation of a patient whose alertness is in question, informed consent needs to be sought from the patient's documented surrogate or legally recognized proxy. Generic hospital consent forms sometimes cover this consent, but it remains Dr. Wilmott's responsibility to ensure this consent exists.

Standard 9.01, Bases for Assessments

Dr. Wilmott upholds this standard if he determines that an examination is not warranted because of the patient's level of alertness. He also upholds this standard if he believes he will not be able to acquire enough evaluative information through a brief exam to address the referral question. If he chooses to administer an exam, such as the Mini-Mental State Exam, then he must clearly articulate its limits under the circumstances.

Institutional and Legal Concepts That May Apply

Dr. Wilmott believes that some of the billing practices performed on the unit are fraudulent. On occasion, therapists feel pressured to bill for services not fully provided because of the patient's inability to engage in or tolerate an acute level of rehabilitation. The psychologist further believes that such billing practices are not only condoned but also subtly encouraged by program administration. However, he has no direct knowledge that such practices have occurred. He has overheard vague, unsubstantiated complaints from staff and some physicians regarding this issue. Dr. Wilmott feels the pressure himself but has steadfastly avoided inaccurate billing or documentation. If he had engaged in either fraudulent or inaccurate billing, he would be in violation of the APA (2002) Ethics Code and would also be subject to criminal investigation and any resulting penalties.

Relevant Context and Key Stakeholders

The Pro-Health Care System supports a practice environment in which there is significant pressure for providers to see and bill for a high volume of patients. Although Dr. Wilmott is aware that colleagues in other rehabilitation centers also are under pressure, he believes that Dr. Byrd's requirements are extreme and risk compromising care for individuals needing more time and intensive services. The high rate of staff turnover supports his beliefs. Although Dr. Wilmott knows that all patients admitted to the rehabilitation program deserve the highest possible quality of psychological services, he must distribute his time to provide the most effective services to the greatest number of patients in need.

The following parties were considered in attempting to resolve the caseload issue.

Patient (Hyman North). Mr. North does not appear medically stable or appropriate for rehabilitation at this time. Since being admitted to the rehabilitation unit, he has become more ill and lethargic. He deserves the highest quality service available to address his needs. However, he is in a vulnerable position because of his health status and should not be given unnecessary service (that he is not in a position to refuse), consistent with the principles of beneficence, fidelity, and justice.

Psychologist (Dr. Peter Wilmott). Dr. Wilmott is caught between his desire to provide quality services to appropriate patients and the administrative demands of his department. Despite being well trained and initially highly motivated, Dr. Wilmott sees that his frustration, disappointment, and feelings of helplessness are leading toward job burnout. This is evidenced by decreased empathy for the patients that Dr. Maris and others continue to admit to the rehabilitation unit inappropriately. Dr. Wilmott has a sinking feeling that he ultimately will have to make a determination about whether he should make the most of his present position or seek employment elsewhere. He also is aware of the potential legal implications of the billing practices of the institution.

Unit Physiatrist (Dr. Philip Maris). Dr. Maris is excellent at keeping the unit full, thus currying favor with Dr. Byrd. However, he does want patients to get maximal benefit from rehabilitation. He knows he is admitting more acutely ill patients, but he is responding to direct pressure from the acute care unit discharging these patients. If he refuses to admit the sicker patients, they will go to an extended-care facility where needed rehabilitation services are not consistently available. He respects the role of psychology and has high regard for Dr. Wilmott, who is approachable and effective at considering differing professional points of view.

PM&R Medical Director (Dr. Earl Byrd). Dr. Byrd has seen physiatrists, psychologists, and members of every other discipline come and go. The average length of stay for staff members in his department is proportionate to the length of stay for patients; that is, both are short, and he really does not care. Given the isolated geographic location of the hospital, there is little competition, so he is not dependent on the department's reputation to keep the beds full. He ensures that appropriate "product lines" are in place and that documentation is sufficient to satisfy accrediting bodies. He keeps the whole hospital in the green financially. He is seen by many, including himself, as the cutting edge of for-profit health care.

Case Resolution

Psychological Evaluation and Consultation

The psychologist has to ensure that all of his patients are treated fairly. Therefore, Dr. Wilmott is obligated to initiate at least an abbreviated assessment to assist him in making a just decision regarding how to prioritize his time rather than operating on assumptions without data. In addition, this prioritization of time might include consideration of the family's as well as the patient's needs. Thus, Dr. Wilmott began reviewing Mr. North's medical record at the nurses' station and was considering doing a brief mental status exam and obtaining family support information. Dr. Maris was also there reviewing charts. After examining the patient's chart for a few minutes, Dr. Wilmott asked Dr. Maris about Mr. North's ability to respond to basic questions. Dr. Maris confirmed Dr. Wilmott's impression that the patient was generally quite lethargic and responded sparsely even when more alert, although some improvement had been noted in the last few hours. Dr. Wilmott and Dr. Maris concurred that the patient could benefit from additional bed rest and medical treatment prior to Dr. Wilmott's psychological evaluation. Dr. Maris modified the request for consultation accordingly. He also indicated that the patient's daughter would be visiting her father on Monday.

Meeting With Organizational Management

Although Dr. Wilmott did not want to ruffle any feathers, he had an ethical responsibility to try to resolve the discrepancy among quality service, caseloads, and billing demands with Dr. Byrd. Dr. Wilmott made an appointment to meet with Dr. Byrd early the following week. The past relationship between the two men had been pleasant and professional. At the meeting, Dr. Wilmott began to outline his concerns.

"Earl, I've come to the point that I can't provide quality care and effectively serve the number of patients cycling through our facility. Therefore, I've got a proposal for you to consider. It promises to allow us to deal more effectively with our patient population." He paused a moment, waiting for some kind of reaction. Dr. Byrd sat silently behind his mahogany desk, hands laced behind his head. Dr. Wilmott continued, "I propose that we hire a part-time psychologist."

The irises of Dr. Byrd's blue eyes abruptly constricted, he said, "Go on."

"Well, by my calculations, this new part-timer could bill enough time to cover her or his salary and benefits. More important, the extra time afforded me would be spent providing better coverage to the whole unit. Quality of care is my motivation here."

Smiling with momentum established, Dr. Wilmott continued to sweeten the pot, "And that's not all. Some of my freed-up time could be devoted to securing grant funding for the projects we've discussed in the past."

Earl Byrd cleared his throat. "Son, I sincerely appreciate your ideas and forward-thinking style."

Then, Dr. Byrd switched gears, smiling gratuitously, "Tell me about that lovely wife of yours. How are things at home?" Grinning even wider, "And those kids! Bet they're growing up like weeds."

Taken off stride, Peter Wilmott answered, "Uh . . . well . . . they're all fine, just fine."

Before the psychologist could regain his cognitive equilibrium, Dr. Byrd interjected, "Let this title sink in some, Dr. Peter Wilmott . . . Director of Psychological Services. How does that sound? Sweet, eh? Maybe, well deserved?"

Dr. Wilmott responded, unsure of the new direction the conversation had taken, "Well, Earl, that's an unexpected turn of events. As you know, there are only two of us in psychology at present. Dr. Flanders has been doing fine on the other unit."

Swiveling to the side in his office chair, Dr. Byrd stood up. Stretching his 6-foot 3-inch frame to its full height, he extended a hand to the psychologist. "Just think what an $8,000 raise means to those kids. A quality college education just became a reality. Congratulations."

Peter Wilmott accepted the very firm handshake, and said, "I'm flattered by your offer, sir, but . . ."

Dr. Byrd maintained control. "Flattery nothing. My boy, you deserve this promotion." Smiling, he paused just a moment, then added, "However . . . our budget prevents us from hiring any new psychologists at this time. Your new title of Director of Psychological Services gives *you* the authority to enforce *your* responsibility for providing quality of psychological care to our patients and families. Be creative son! That's the nature of this business."

Case Disposition

After taking a few days to consider Dr. Byrd's proposal and do some intense soul searching, Dr. Wilmott accepted the new position. He was pleasantly surprised to find that he felt rejuvenated and had a renewed level of motivation and commitment. He turned his attention toward developing a triage system. This system included use of a clinical screening questionnaire, which focused on select symptoms representing the more commonly seen diagnoses with computer administration either by himself or self-administered by the patient. He believed this system would satisfy the multiple demands created by Dr. Byrd's admission practice to the rehabilitation unit.

Additional Commentary

As reimbursement restriction practices continue to take hold in acute rehabilitation, psychologists who were once fairly free to treat patients as often as deemed necessary have had to critically reevaluate how to deliver services. Rural health care facilities, in particular, face the possibility of closing their doors if not aggressively managed given the substantial losses they have sustained under the Balanced Budget Act (Stensland, Moscovice, & Christianson, 2002). When hospitals, particularly those serving underrepresented populations, shut down, no one is really well served. Families are forced to drive hours to see a loved one in rehabilitation and no longer able to participate at the level needed to ensure safe discharge. Telehealth may offer some hope for providers and families in this regard (Glueckauf, Pickett, Ketterson, Loomis, & Nickelson, 2003; VandenBos & Williams, 2000), but it presents its own ethical and practical challenges, such as how to protect patient privacy and manage the treatment environment.

It is not inherently unjust to admit patients and not provide the full complement of services available. Decisions are made every day in rehabilitation (as well as other settings) regarding prioritization of services based on staffing levels and patterns and patients' perceived needs. Provider actions become unjust when policies are implemented inconsistently and when services not offered are promised or services are offered that are inappropriate. Most important psychologists need to ensure they do not inadvertently perpetuate fraudulent practice through their inaction when unjust policies or processes are unveiled. Differing expectations regarding performance between supervisors and their team members can create conflict that clearly needs to be resolved (Kline, 2001).

In this case, the psychologist must question his own motivation regarding the timeliness of his response to the consultation request for Mr. North. There is some suggestion that he made a decision to delay before gathering enough information on which to base such a decision. Although he did interact with Dr. Maris to clarify the intent of the referral (and secured a delay), the issue of personal lifestyle preferences versus professional responsibility remains murky and could be cause for concern regarding the timing of clinical judgments.

Finally, the conversation between the psychologist and administrator did not address concerns regarding suspected billing fraud. Burying this risky issue beneath talk of job satisfaction, program development, and financial rewards places the institution and involved providers at considerable legal risk. Although the psychologist might not be held directly accountable for the billing practices of his institution given scrupulous management of his own paperwork and documentation, he is still obligated to attempt to rectify this perceived problem.

CASE 3.3
USING PLACEBOS AND DECEPTION IN TREATMENT

Ginger Hawthorne was a 33-year-old homemaker named after the character on Gilligan's Island. The show had brought countless laughs to her parents who otherwise struggled to make ends meet on their small cattle ranch in eastern Wyoming. Unfortunately, Ginger's adult life had been anything but paradise.

Ginger's early life started out fine. She finished high school, met the man of her dreams, and had three wonderful children. Recently, however, her husband Rollo lost his part-time construction job when the economy turned sour, and he began drinking heavily. The financial loss came at a particularly bad time. Ginger's mother Beatrice had just moved in with them because of her own failing health, and Ginger's 15-year-old son, Archie, had entered an inpatient drug rehabilitation program for cocaine abuse.

One evening while leaving the drug rehabilitation center, Ginger slipped on wet stairs, fracturing her fourth thoracic vertebra and sustaining multiple bruises. She underwent surgical repair of the vertebra, including removal of bone fragments impinging on her spinal cord. The surgery was deemed successful, and Mrs. Hawthorne was transferred to an acute medical rehabilitation unit.

The transfer order indicated that Ginger was deconditioned and had not regained movement in her legs when expected. After thoroughly reviewing the patient's scans and conducting a neuromuscular examination, which showed inconsistent lower extremity resistance and normal reflexes, Dr. Greg Yee, the attending physiatrist, suspected Mrs. Hawthorne was faking her paralysis. He contacted Dr. Roberta Eidelman, the rehabilitation psychologist who would be evaluating Ginger as part of the initial team assessment, to give her the heads up that "we might have a malingerer."

Dr. Eidelman had been working as a rehabilitation psychologist for nine years. She was known as a great team player and a tough but fair supervisor. Patricia O'Malley, a postdoctoral fellow, was partway through her rotation with Dr. Eidelman. Dr. Eidelman thought Ms. O'Malley would be the perfect intern to give this case to because Ms. O'Malley needed to stretch her developing skills and gain better insight into her professional strengths and weaknesses. Dr. Eidelman explained Dr. Yee's suspicions and told Ms. O'Malley to read up on malingering and conversion disorder. In addition, she advised Ms. O'Malley to make no assumptions about the diagnosis because the results of the psychological assessment could suggest neither diagnosis was accurate.

After two days, Ms. O'Malley asked to meet with Dr. Eidelman. She had thoroughly reviewed the *DSM* criteria and had completed the reading Dr. Eidelman had given her on the two diagnoses. She had interviewed team members, including nurses, occupational therapists, and physical therapists, and had completed her initial assessment. The evidence was mounting that Ginger was feigning a spinal cord injury. The physical therapist had noted some inconsistent resistance during passive exercises. The occupational therapist and rehabilitation nurse had both noticed that Mrs. Hawthorne showed slight movement in her legs when trying to transfer during self-care tasks like bathing and toileting. However, Nurse Donovan firmly believed that inpatient rehabilitation was just the break from family stress Ginger needed, and she advocated for Ginger to stay on the inpatient unit.

Ms. O'Malley's initial assessment clearly supported a conversion disorder rather than malingering. She based her conclusion on the findings that Mrs. Hawthorne was not suing the drug center for damages, did not discuss any obvious secondary gain, and seemed genuinely concerned about how to get the family back on track. She also seemed to lack adequate coping resources. Ms. O'Malley agreed with the nursing staff's assessment that inpatient rehabilitation could be of benefit and wanted to begin therapy immediately. Dr. Eidelman agreed to let Ms. O'Malley initiate psychotherapy (to develop stronger rapport) until the initial team conference was held, at which point the team would determine whether to keep Mrs. Hawthorne on the unit. If Mrs. Hawthorne stayed, Dr. Eidelman would reevaluate Patty's treatment plan.

The fairly heated discussion in team conference focused on whether it was a waste of rehabilitation resources to keep a patient who was not really sick. At this point, Dr. Eidelman joined the debate, stating unequivocally that this patient did have a disease. She argued that the rehabilitation team was better equipped than a psychiatric facility to handle Mrs. Hawthorne's treatment because the team's intimate knowledge of spinal cord injury and consistent approach to treatment were key to Mrs. Hawthorne's recovery. After much discussion, the team agreed to a 10-day trial of rehabilitation. If Mrs. Hawthorne had not shown significant progress by the end of that time, she would be discharged.

Most team members had no idea how to proceed and clearly indicated that the psychology staff would have to take the lead. Ms. O'Malley sat there looking a little dazed. Then she turned to Dr. Eidelman and said, "Now what do I do?" Dr. Eidelman calmly turned to Ms. O'Malley and stated, "You and the team are going to design a placebo program and convince Mrs. Hawthorne she will walk again in 10 days.

Relevant Ethical Principles and Standards

Principle A: Beneficence and Nonmaleficence

Dr. Eidelman's advocacy for treatment supports the principle of benefi-cence. As she and Ms. O'Malley develop a treatment plan, they will need to consider how to coordinate Mrs. Hawthorne's care across all team members to maximize benefit to the patient. Given the patient's primary presenting concern, the psychologists have a responsibility to protect the patient from team biases regarding psychiatric illness that influence treatment decisions. Because it appears that Mrs. Hawthorne has developed a conversion disorder to protect herself from the stressful familial circumstances that have exceeded her capacity to cope, Ms. O'Malley and the rest of the team must be careful not to rush treatment or prematurely challenge Mr. Hawthorne's beliefs about her illness or they could shatter her delicate emotional state. The team must also consider the consequences of Mrs. Hawthorne's discovering the decep-tion. If the team is successful, they likely will have contributed to health care cost savings in the future.

Principle B: Fidelity and Responsibility

If Mrs. Hawthorne were to discover that the rehabilitation team does not believe she has a spinal injury, the trust between the psychologist and patient could be destroyed. Therefore, the psychologist has to be vigilant to ensure the team's message to the patient is consistent and that no one "spills the beans." Dr. Eidelman also must discharge her duties as an intern supervi-sor in an appropriate manner.

Principle D: Justice

The rehabilitation team must consider the possibility that they are de-priving someone else of rehabilitative care while Mrs. Hawthorne occupies an inpatient bed for a psychiatric diagnosis. On the other hand, depriving Mrs. Hawthorne of the benefit and expertise of the rehabilitation team is worthy of consideration in attempting to develop an appropriate health care plan given the focus of patient concern is spinal cord injury. The team has clearly weighed these issues and decided the just action is a time-limited stay. The team needs to appreciate that they may be placing themselves at financial risk, given an insurance company might challenge a medical reha-bilitation stay based on the diagnosis.

Principle E: Respect for People's Rights and Dignity

The treatment team needs to weigh the benefit of selecting a placebo treatment and the deception they employ for its implementation against the rights of the patient to be fully informed about her care. They clearly need to have an ethically cogent argument that they are acting in the best interest of the patient and this interest outweighs their obligation of comprehensive disclosure.

Standard 2.04, Bases for Scientific and Professional Judgments

The use of a placebo in psychological practice is not a new concept. However, its use in rehabilitation has not received widespread attention. Dr. Eidelman's actions are consistent with this standard if she can make the case that the general practice literature supports the therapeutic value of a placebo and these findings are applicable to the rehabilitation setting in which the conversion disorder presents itself.

Standard 2.05, Delegation of Work to Others

Dr. Eidelman has delegated direct assessment and intervention with Mrs. Hawthorne to her intern. Although she may not believe Ms. O'Malley has the competency to handle this case independently, she upholds this standard only if she believes Ms. O'Malley will manage Mrs. Hawthorne's psychological care appropriately under supervision.

Standard 3.04, Avoiding Harm

Dr. Eidelman may place herself at ethical risk regarding harm to Mrs. Hawthorne in at least two respects. First, if Mrs. Hawthorne discovers the deception, she may choose not to seek psychological or other health services in the future because of the loss of trust in the provider–patient relationship. Second, if Dr. Eidelman and the team choose not to treat Mrs. Hawthorne and refer her to a psychiatric facility, Mrs. Hawthorne may infer that the team does not want to help her or does not believe her, creating the same outcome, lack of trust, treatment termination, reluctance to receive future treatment, and continuing declining health.

Standard 3.09, Cooperation With Other Professionals

Given the nature of the intervention being proposed (i.e., a placebo while Ginger is receiving multiple therapies from a rehab team), Dr. Eidelman is ethically obligated to work with the rest of the rehabilitation team, rather than work independently, to maximize the likelihood of a successful outcome. Without a collaborative approach, any number of providers could inadvertently reinforce the continuation of psychological symptoms. An informed rehabilitation team can contribute to an overall positive outcome through their appropriate responses to Mrs. Hawthorne's expressions about her injury.

Standard 3.10, Informed Consent

Even within the context of deceptive treatment, the psychologist must still solicit informed consent for intervention. In this case, Dr. Eidelman would present more general information (e.g., work with patient to improve overall coping regarding her situation and describe what treatment will be used without identifying it as a placebo).

Standard 4.05, Disclosures

Sharing relevant information with the rest of the rehabilitation team will be critical to treatment success. Therefore this standard is upheld under the provision that such disclosure is necessary to appropriately deliver the rehabilitation psychology services toward the intended outcome of the patient's walking and coping more effectively with situational crises.

Standard 4.07, Use of Confidential Information for Didactic or Other Purposes

Given that conversion disorder in rehabilitation psychology is a fairly uncommon diagnostic category, Dr. Eidelman may choose to present this case as part of her teaching duties in the health center where she works. It would be difficult to obtain truly informed consent from Mrs. Hawthorne given that she is unaware of the placebo, the precise reason the case might be compelling to present. Therefore, Dr. Eidelman needs to be extremely careful to protect Mrs. Hawthorne's identity in this situation given the low frequency of the diagnosis and the potential for Mrs. Hawthorne to receive follow-up care at the same facility. It would be wise to eliminate or change all major identifying information, such as her name, place and date of birth, current residence, and medical identification number. It also would be wise to eliminate any link to the local rehabilitation facility.

Standard 6.01, Documentation of Professional and Scientific Work and Maintenance of Records

Dr. Eidelman needs to consider whether there is an appropriate way to document her treatment so that the deception can be inferred without being explicitly stated. This subtlety in documentation may help guard against potential future harm if the patient were to review her record or an unknowing health care provider were to raise the issue without being equipped to handle the potential repercussions.

Standard 6.07, Referrals and Fees

Dr. Eidelman must ensure her documentation to payors reasonably reflects the types of services offered. Is Dr. Eidelman ethically obligated to identify the treatment as a placebo? Although Dr. Eidelman clearly believes that a placebo is a legitimate treatment option, the insurance company may hold a bias against use of a placebo as it relates to reimbursement. Although the psychologist must document the psychological intervention presented, we are not convinced she has to identify treatment as a placebo. Consider, for example, the following note to the payor: "Dr. Eidelman provided individual psychotherapy for 10 sessions to assist the patient with coping with injuries sustained in a fall and subsequent psychological consequences exacerbated by family stress and limited coping skills." We believe this description of services is appropriate documentation.

Standard 9.01, Bases for Assessments

The differential diagnosis between malingering and conversion disorder has significant implications for treatment planning. Dr. Eidelman believes Ms. O'Malley adequately supported the diagnosis of conversion disorder on the basis of her review of the record and pertinent literature and her interviews with Mrs. Hawthorne and the rehabilitation team.

Standard 9.04, Release of Test Data

Under this standard the psychologist is obligated to release notes reflecting the patient's responses to questions during the interview process. If Dr. Eidelman or Ms. O'Malley has made notes regarding the conversion disorder or treatment, she would have to make the case that release of such information would cause substantial harm if Mrs. Hawthorne requested release of this information. Dr. Eidelman advised Ms. O'Malley to be judicious in her note taking.

Standard 10.01, Informed Consent to Therapy

Ms. O'Malley must decide what information to share with Mrs. Hawthorne that would legitimately cover the disclosure component of consent to treatment. Even in placebo treatment, she should be able to effectively cover the purpose and type of treatment, reason for consent, anticipated number of sessions, anticipated outcome, risks and benefits, alternatives, limits of confidentiality as it relates to the team, and the team's assistance in reinforcing psychological interventions. (Note: Fees were covered by the business manager.)

Standard 10.10, Terminating Therapy

Because there is a clear end point for rehabilitation, the psychologist must address termination issues early in the rehabilitation process.

Institutional and Legal Concepts That May Apply

Standards for disclosure of information have, to a certain extent, been based in case law in which patients have challenged the providers' level of disclosure. However, there has been an evolution in the focus of informed consent, moving from what the provider has disclosed to what the patient understands and authorizes. (Beauchamp & Childress, 2001, discuss informed consent in some detail.) This shift is somewhat problematic in placebo-based treatment involving deception but nevertheless places the emphasis where it should be, on the patient and not the provider. To be consistent with legal principles, the psychologist using deception must be able to make a reasonable professional argument that she is being fair to the patient and that the circumstances warrant such an action based on both professional standards of practice and the best interests of the patient.

Relevant Context and Key Stakeholders

Dr. Eidelman is confident in the diagnosis and believes that with the implementation of an appropriate treatment plan Mrs. Hawthorne can regain the use of her legs and potentially avoid needless treatment in the future. Therefore, her decision seems fairly straightforward, although the team has legitimately questioned whether the rehabilitation setting is the appropriate one in which to treat Mrs. Hawthorne. Once agreement is reached to treat Mrs. Hawthorne on the rehabilitation unit, there is no residual team conflict that would preclude moving forward with the placebo-based treatment plan. Ginger's spouse, who stopped drinking in support of his wife when she was hospitalized, actively participates in Ginger's care; he is unaware the treatment is placebo based.

The following parties were considered in executing the treatment plan.

Patient (Ginger Hawthorne). Mrs. Hawthorne has tried to hold her family together for years. With the most recent family stresses, however, Mrs. Hawthorne reached the breaking point. She seems quite distraught over her personal circumstances but hopeful that she and her family will get through these rough times. She does not have any previous psychiatric history and has not submitted any type of claim against the drug center for their lack of attention to step safety. Mrs. Hawthorne is convinced she has lower extremity paralysis but is also optimistic that the rehabilitation team can help her walk again.

Primary Psychology Team (Psychologist Dr. Roberta Eidelman and Postdoctoral Fellow Patty O'Malley). Dr. Eidelman is a seasoned rehabilitation psychologist who on rare occasions has had to manage rehabilitation patients with conversion disorder. Ms. O'Malley has never seen anyone with conversion disorder despite her recent VA psychiatric hospital rotation. She has training in stress management, hypnosis, and general psychological intervention with people undergoing significant health changes. Dr. Eidelman and Ms. O'Malley concur on diagnosis and believe the best outcome for Mrs. Hawthorne will likely be reached if she remains on the rehabilitation unit. Dr. Eidelman reasons that Mrs. Hawthorne would not have responded as well to a psychiatric placement because it is inconsistent with Mrs. Hawthorne's current frame of reference (i.e., Mrs. Hawthorne firmly believes she is paralyzed), making quick mobility recovery less likely. However, Dr. Eidelman and Ms. O'Malley must work together to ensure that they provide Mrs. Hawthorne with the precise information needed to facilitate treatment efficacy. Their allies are the rehabilitation team members. They realize if the team does not come together, the plan will fail.

Rehabilitation Team. The rehabilitation team has a good working relationship, with each member sharing the same general philosophy of maximizing patient independence. It is this underlying value system that has brought them together to try to help Mrs. Hawthorne improve her health. To the extent that Mrs. Hawthorne engages in the rehabilitation process, the team will continue to have confidence in their decision to have her remain in inpatient rehabilitation.

Family (Husband Rollo, Son Archie, and Mother Beatrice). Mrs. Hawthorne's family situation stabilized significantly shortly after her accident. Her husband stopped drinking when his wife's fall made Rollo realize that he could lose her in a tragic instant. Although out of work, he is exploring the possibility of consignment jobs to get through the economic downturn. Ginger's mother has opted for an assistive living facility while Ginger is recovering. Although Beatrice cannot afford this long term, she feels this temporary plan will allow Ginger to get back on her feet (no pun intended). Ginger's son has not visited because he is in a 30-day inpatient drug rehabilitation program at the place where she slipped and fell. She has spoken with Archie on the phone and continues to be very concerned about his recovery. Overall, despite their emotional and financial stress, the family seems to be coming together to support Ginger.

Case Resolution

Develop Intervention

Dr. Eidelman proposed a coordinated pharmacological, psychological, and physical treatment plan. Although Dr. Eidelman took the lead, she worked closely with the team to design the initial placebo-based protocol. The intervention involved the following basic elements: (a) placebo pill, (b) physical therapy exercises targeting leg strength and mobility, and (c) psychotherapy incorporating hypnosis.

Implement Plan

The team implemented the following protocol: Dr. Yee informed Mrs. Hawthorne that a pill had been developed to treat her unique type of spinal cord injury. He emphasized that the pill was a wonderful discovery because it was very effective if the protocol was followed correctly. He then prescribed a placebo pill that Mrs. Hawthorne took twice a day and explained that Dr. Eidelman would review the overall treatment plan with her. Dr. Eidelman, with Ms. O'Malley observing, met with Mrs. Hawthorne to lay out the entire protocol. She explicitly stated the timeframe in which Mrs. Hawthorne should experience movement in her legs and the walking distance she should be able to accomplish each day after that point. The physical therapist then reinforced these points with Mrs. Hawthorne. Mrs. Hawthorne participated in daily physical therapy, which used passive exercises initially and then active exercises once Mrs. Hawthorne regained some movement to enhance those gains. Mrs. Hawthorne kept a graph of distance walked. The change in exercises was used to indirectly emphasize the patient's progress along with direct reinforcement through the walking log. Ms. O'Malley provided daily psychotherapy to address stressors that might slow Mrs. Hawthorne's progress. Hypnosis complemented the psychotherapy and focused on stress management skills and posthypnotic suggestion to reinforce the impact of other treatment. Ginger's spouse Rollo was encouraged to review Ginger's graphed data. Team members not directly involved in Mrs. Hawthorne's care reinforced gains as appropriate.

Case Disposition

Mrs. Hawthorne was discharged 10 days after the initial case conference, as planned. She was walking the distance predicted and indicated feeling good. Although still a little shaky and slow on her feet, she indicated being very proud of her recovery. The medical social worker identified a caregiver support group and community resources to assist Ginger with her mother's needs. The family has yet to receive a bill from the drug rehabilitation center.

Additional Commentary

Placebo-based therapy has been shown to affect both physiological (e.g., heart rate) and psychological (e.g., mood) processes and has been used to treat a variety of health concerns, such as depression and chronic pain (Kirsch, 1997; Morris, 1997; Spiro, 1997; Turner, Deyo, Loeser, Von Korff, & Fordyce, 1994). However, its mechanisms of action are only beginning to be understood, and Harrington (1997) offers several good discussions of potential contributors to explain the placebo response. Some authors have argued that the term placebo is too generic, whereas others have argued the term is inappropriate (e.g., because a treatment effect occurs). In addition, the choice to use deceptive treatment can prove to be a place of ethical departure among disciplines. As Weijer (2002) notes, Canada's Tri-Council Policy Statement indicates placebo control groups are inappropriate in clinical trials in which standard therapy is available. In addition, Boyle (1997b) and Jonsen, Siegler, and Winslade (1998) have argued that deception such as use of a placebo is highly problematic in the physician–patient relationship, and they discuss very specific circumstances under which deception should be considered. Jonsen et al. note, for example, that one required condition in which deceptive use of a placebo is ethically justified is when the patient insists on a prescription. Clearly, this condition may or may not be relevant to psychological intervention. Deception certainly is not without its risks and warrants heightened responsibility to protect the patient's rights and welfare.

The psychologist must act in a responsible manner toward both the patient and the rehabilitation team. In this case, the psychologist cogently argued that the rehabilitation milieu created the necessary environment to allow the patient to feel supported and to perceive the interventions offered as highly relevant to her situation. In addition, the treatment corresponded with a reduction in perceived family stress that may have been the initial psychopathological trigger. These factors came together to create a powerful enough influence to break the dysfunctional pattern into which the patient had entered. The psychologist also recognized that if the patient had been discharged initially, the end result might have been a much longer course of treatment and thus, increased use of health care services. This case is used to illustrate that deception holds a very important, albeit narrow, place in psychological practice.

CASE 3.4
WHEN THE TEAM AND FAMILY DISAGREE: INCORPORATING FAMILY BELIEFS AND VALUES INTO TREATMENT

Tina Bell was an 18-year-old college freshman at State Teachers College when she sustained a C-4 (fourth-cervical vertebra-level) complete tetraplegia in a snowmobile accident. Tina experienced a complicated acute medical course in the regional community hospital, including a pulmonary embolus and numerous urinary tract infections. It was almost six weeks post injury before she was transferred to the Flat Mountain Rehabilitation Center in West Virginia. Tina was accompanied by her parents, three brothers, and many friends, a social milieu that was to continue throughout her two-month stay in rehabilitation.

During the initial portion of Tina's admission, she showed inconsistent effort in the treatment process. Several family conferences early in her stay revealed that the Bell family was convinced Tina would fully recover. They were content to wait until that day arrived. In addition, when the rehabilitation team provided Tina with encouragement or redirection, the family characteristically responded in an overprotective manner. Minnie Bell, Tina's mother, was the *only* identified caregiver. Tina's father and brothers were uncomfortable providing care, shunting that responsibility to Minnie. This behavior mirrored behavior in the Bell home where Minnie was the sole homemaker, receiving minimal help from the men in the family.

Only rarely did Minnie give correct responses to questions from the staff regarding care issues that had previously been taught. When the team asked Minnie to perform skills she had been taught, her characteristic response was to sidestep doing anything under observation. Her excuses ranged from sudden illness to "manufactured" off-campus appointments. The team's care teaching was not complete even after a month of trying.

The nurses were once again trying to catch Minnie Bell. Minnie, on the other hand, was walking quickly toward the door of the rehabilitation center. The two concerned therapists dogging her had, until a few minutes earlier, been trying to teach her care techniques. Minnie's arms were waving in the air as if to ward off buzzing insects. "Don't bother me anymore about that stuff. I've got so much on my mind. And now I have to get home to make dinner for my family." Looking hastily at her watch, "Oh my, I'm late!"

One of the therapists pleaded, "Please, Mrs. Bell, at least schedule a time with us to complete the teaching!"

As she reached the door, Minnie Bell turned briefly and smiled, "I'll see you next time I drop in to visit my daughter. We can talk then." That said, she lurched suddenly through the doorway, ran to her nearby pick-up truck, and sped off in a cloud of dust. The frustrated therapists turned to each other and said in tandem, "Tina's in trouble! Let's call the psychologist again."

The psychologist, Dr. Louise Buckett, had met separately with Tina and Minnie on multiple occasions. Her opinion was that both were acting in accord with family tradition. Despite the family's insistence on minimizing Tina's situation, they were a cohesive, mutually supportive group. There were no signs of animosity within the family, and everyone accepted the traditional roles the men and women held. Dr. Buckett cautioned the team against imposing their values on the Bell family. However, she also stated that the team must do all it could to ensure that Tina's health care needs were being adequately met.

At the next team conference meeting, the physical therapist announced that he had discharged Tina from treatment for lack of progress. This sentiment was echoed by the occupational therapist. The remainder of the team had been unaware that this change in program status had occurred and that it had been documented in the patient's chart a few minutes earlier.

Relevant Ethical Principles and Standards

Principle A: Beneficence and Nonmaleficence

Dr. Buckett needs to determine how to work within the context of the family's social structure to maximize Tina's benefit from rehabilitation and prevent SCI complications. Challenging the familial network under the guise of beneficence (i.e., Minnie needs assistance from additional caregivers, Minnie must learn the prescribed care regimen) can backfire badly, resulting in more harm through rejection of all services and disruption in the family system. The psychologist serves a critical role in facilitating team cohesiveness so that effective family interaction can occur.

Principle D: Justice

The patient has a right to adequate care and services, even if her condition prevents significant, measurable physical recovery. Given the recognition of the importance of family involvement in rehabilitation toward the long-term health and safety of a patient to be discharged home, family goals are highly valued in achieving a just outcome for Tina. However, the team must face the issue of splits among providers regarding appropriate use of resources directed toward the patient and family.

Principle E: Respect for People's Rights and Dignity

The psychologist believes the family value system is operating strongly with respect to Tina's and family members' participation in rehabilitation. The values and beliefs of the patient and family need to be honored, even if the team disagrees with those values.

Standard 3.04, Avoiding Harm

Dr. Buckett is responsible for providing direction to the treatment team, patient, and family to prevent foreseeable harm to the patient and family. If the patient or family makes a decision that will likely result in increased risk of harm to Tina, the psychologist is obligated to discuss that risk so that the patient can effectively weigh the consequences.

Standard 3.09, Cooperation With Other Professionals

Dr. Buckett needs to engage appropriately in team problem solving to reestablish team cohesion once splitting among providers occurs. Team cooperation toward achievement of appropriate patient and family goals is a hallmark of rehabilitation standards of care.

Standard 3.10, Informed Consent

The patient and family must be fully informed about psychological service provision within the framework of the rehabilitation process. This necessarily encompasses a description of how the psychologist works with the rest of the team to serve the patient, including helping the team resolve conflicts with families.

Standard 4.02, Discussing the Limits of Confidentiality

The patient and family are made aware of the circumstances under which confidential information is shared, that is, when there is actual or perceived harm to the patient and others. The perceived risk of harm to the patient in this case is significant. Therefore, Dr. Buckett and other team members bear the responsibility for monitoring safety and alerting protective agencies should care problems arise after discharge. This role must be reviewed with the patient and family.

Standard 10.02, Therapy Involving Couples or Families

Because Tina is 18 years old, she has the right to cooperate with or refuse her mother's participation in psychological intervention and her broader rehabilitation program. Because both are intimately involved in the rehabilitation process, careful delineation of their separate roles needs to be explained and accounted for by the psychologist.

Standard 10.10, Terminating Therapy

As the discharge date approaches, the psychologist must meet with the patient and her mother to discuss termination of inpatient intervention. She should design any planned outpatient follow-up to minimize loss to continuity of care.

Institutional and Legal Concepts That May Apply

Negligence is a concern in this case given the difficulties encountered with patient care teaching. This term refers to failure to exercise such care as would normally be expected by reasonable practice standards. The rehabilitation facility may be held negligent if the patient is knowingly discharged to a dangerous home environment. The rehabilitation team considered discharge to the home an adequate placement for protecting the patient's safety. Some states also have neglect statutes that apply to identified caregivers who provide inadequate care to persons with disabilities. This latter concept might apply after discharge if the family fails to provide adequate care.

Relevant Context and Key Stakeholders

Minnie Bell runs the family household. She has nursed many sick family members back to health over the years. The family has implicit trust in her care capability based on her past performance. Mrs. Bell does not question her role in her daughter's care, as she will handle the responsibility when the time comes. Nonetheless, Mrs. Bell has problems learning care according to established rehabilitation standards especially when she is monitored. Interestingly, Mrs. Bell is the one person who identified signs of autonomic dysreflexia in her daughter during one of Tina's one-day acute hospital workups for blood pressure instability. Autonomic dysreflexia is a potentially life-threatening process of autonomic nervous system activation that boosts blood pressure to dangerous levels if not treated quickly. Minnie immediately alerted nursing staff to the dysreflexia incident.

The Bells are unwilling to consider a subacute rehabilitation program to allow Tina and the family more time to adapt to the difficult care-planning process. In response to a question regarding potential emergencies occurring in the home that required more than one person's assistance, the family (including Minnie) stated that Minnie could recruit other women in the area to provide help. Their belief is that men simply should not perform personal care on women. Tina has not embraced the "middleman" role between the team and family that many patients adopt, that of evaluating team teaching in the context of the family milieu and taking an advocacy stand to meet her personal needs.

The rehabilitation team is aware that their goals regarding family mastery of skills and discharge planning are not being successfully met. In fact, the nature of Tina's disability allows only minimal physical improvements during the acute inpatient rehabilitation admission. The primary goals for the admission revolve around family teaching in preparation for Tina's return home. Given the family's lack of engagement, specific disciplines begin to split from the rest of the team, making independent decisions to discharge the patient.

The following parties played key roles in case resolution.

Patient (Tina Bell). Tina reports being aware that her mother has not measured up to the team's expectations regarding learning her care. However, Tina is reluctant to admonish her mother about her care when she observes her not performing up to the team's standards, and she is not particularly concerned because of Minnie's previous track record of successfully handling the family's health problems. She is likely not fully aware of the risks she faces if her mother's care abilities fall short of adequate.

Mother (Minnie Bell). Minnie feels that she is doing her best and would be doing better if the team would stop bugging her about all those little details. She is convinced, by virtue of her past experience, that all will be well once Tina returns home. "Caregiver" is Minnie's identity within the Bell family. She visits Tina daily and is attentive to her everyday social needs. Minnie is embarrassed when the team asks technical questions of her that she does not fully understand.

Bell Family. The family tradition has been for the men to work and the women to organize and run the household. Indeed, Tina's attendance at college had been hotly debated while she was a senior in high school, but Minnie and her daughter won the argument. The only potential problem the Bell men envision at home is Minnie's ignoring food preparation, cleaning, and other tasks, in the service of caring for Tina. They volunteered that some of their distant female cousins would be willing to help with household chores until Tina recovers. The family is not willing to consider subacute rehabilitation because of the potential for further disruption to the family unit; Minnie's daily attendance in rehabilitation and the occasional visits from her father and brothers are disturbing enough. They conclude that the team is worrying needlessly about Minnie's ability to care for Tina, almost to the point of insult.

Psychologist (Dr. Louise Buckett). The psychologist performs multiple roles. First, and foremost, Dr. Buckett acts as Tina's psychologist, addressing cognitive, behavioral, and emotional needs. The psychologist believes that Tina is invested in getting better but that a strong family system contributes to inconsistent rehabilitation performance. She believes the patient's mother is well intentioned and that both Minnie and Tina have a better understanding of Tina's care than is immediately apparent. However, she is concerned that they are afraid to ask for help from the team for fear of "excessive meddling" in the established family network. Dr. Buckett also functions as the team's "social conscience," challenging her colleagues to remain sensitive to social and emotional factors affecting the patient within the context of both the rehabilitation center and her family system. She is frustrated by the discharge actions of PT and OT, completed in the absence of team consultation. Dr. Buckett believes a negative situation could escalate quickly (i.e., inconsistent information given to the family and further team splitting) if early team resolution regarding partial discharge is not addressed.

Rehabilitation Team. The team members regularly see their care expectations being violated by Minnie. Repetitive teaching has simply led to a plateau in Minnie's caregiving accuracy and to her increasing discomfort with the team's corrective feedback. The team has raised several questions with each other. Can the team, in good conscience, let Tina go home when they are convinced her care will be compromised? What is the effect of unilateral discontinuation of treatment on team dynamics? Is lack of team consensus a legitimate position from which to make program decisions? What is the medical–legal position of the team vis-à-vis fragmentation of opinion in the patient's medical record, particularly if Tina is harmed?

Rehabilitation Facility (Flat Mountain Rehabilitation Center). The facility holds the responsibility for providing a quality rehabilitation program that satisfies both accepted standards of professional practice and the patient's and family's reasonable needs. A potentially risky discharge may satisfy the family's expressed preference for the patient to return home, but it also challenges the facility practice standards. That being the case, the facility also is in the dilemma of having a discoverable medical record indicative of a division of professional opinion about a patient's status and discharge. A resolution is required regarding treatment and the purpose of the medical record as simply an aggregate of individual discipline data and opinions versus a consensus-driven record documenting an integrated program, including discharge decisions.

Case Resolution

Establish a Family Teaching Plan That Incorporates the Strength of the Mother–Daughter Relationship

With discharge imminently looming, Dr. Buckett helped the team realize that they had to use a different strategy to engage Minnie in care training. Therefore, they decided to involve Tina and Minnie in an intensive, daylong review of care teaching. Tina was given the task of guiding her mother through the steps of each care technique while varied team members stood back as monitors. The team planned to intervene only if patient risk was significant. Only one instance of team assistance was required, as Tina proved to be an adequate director of her care, and Minnie listened readily to her daughter.

Establish a Discharge Plan That Addresses Safety Concerns

The team used a three-pronged approach to address their safety concerns related to discharge. First, they arranged for nurses from Flat Mountain Home Health Care to visit the rehabilitation facility for care orientation specifically designed to meet Tina's needs. Dr. Buckett, along with the social worker and rehabilitation nurse, alerted the home health nurses to the problems discovered during Tina's rehabilitation stay regarding family dynamics and risks to care. They agreed to work closely with Minnie and Tina, reinforcing proper care techniques. The team introduced the home health nurses to Minnie and her daughter during their one-day teaching session, emphasizing that continuity of care was a priority.

Second, Tina was scheduled for follow-up with the Flat Mountain Rehabilitation Center spinal cord injury clinic earlier and more frequently than the norm. These appointments were to serve as an external monitoring agent to identify medical concerns and progress, such as changes in skin condition, bladder and bowel function, respiratory status, and neuromuscular recovery. In addition, the clinic's interdisciplinary team could address case management, psychological, and social needs of the patient and family. The Bell family was encouraged to show up for these alternate week appointments as a unit, rather than just the patient and mother.

Finally, the team struck an agreement with the home health agency that, if their nurses detected significant uncorrected care problems in the Bell home, they would immediately contact Flat Mountain Rehabilitation case management. If such a contact was made, and concerns were expressed during the spinal cord clinic follow-up visits, the rehabilitation case manager would then contact Adult Protective Services to investigate for possible neglect.

Conduct Post Hoc Debriefing

Dr. Buckett elected to initiate an ethics committee consultation after the patient was discharged. The foci of the consult were unresolved issues related to patient safety and the effectiveness of team communication and coordination of care. The facility ethics committee chose to involve a professional ethicist to boost objectivity in the deliberations.

The external ethicist provided the team with the opportunity to explain its modus operandus in clear, unambiguous terms. Several team members explained the predicament they faced when some therapists discharged the patient in the medical record prior to the patient's actual discharge home. Essentially, once some therapies were discontinued, the patient's admission had been prematurely terminated within the bounds of Medicare regulations. This situation did not serve the patient's need for the execution of a well-coordinated discharge plan to protect the patient's health and welfare. Therefore, specific disciplines had to respond quickly with a discharge plan that did address such concerns.

The process of analyzing the flow of events with Tina allowed the team to troubleshoot the adequacy of team communication and coordination of care throughout the admission. They put into place agreed-upon steps to improve communication. Importantly, the ethics committee supported Tina Bell's discharge plan. They applauded the plan's attention to safety and the contingency-based staged patient safety monitoring while respecting the patient's right to self-determination. The latter aspect of the program was praised for its sensitivity to the Bell family's values and traditions.

Case Disposition

Tina Bell was discharged home with the recommended follow-up plan in place. Her mother and the rest of the family were delighted at the prospect of her returning home so that they could minister to her in their own way. The team held its collective breath.

Minnie Bell proved to be a consistent and competent caregiver for her daughter. She accepted the support given by the Home Health Care nurses. Within the borders of her home, she relaxed and reassumed her role as "household manager," absorbing the details of care teaching and carrying them out in a routine manner. Tina's follow-up visits were marked by team comments about the stability of her medical status. Additionally, they were impressed with the fact that Tina's social support network had succeeded in getting her into the community on a frequent basis.

Six months after her discharge, Tina began visiting individuals with new spinal cord injuries in rehabilitation. She also presented her story to the community as part of a spinal cord injury education program sponsored by the rehabilitation center.

Additional Commentary

This case illustrates the powerful role families play in the rehabilitation process. Rehabilitation professionals commonly operate under the working assumption that families are a legitimate and integral part of the team. Families not only provide emotional support but also may be first line caregivers, necessitating routine contact with the rehabilitation team. Legally, however, the individual recognized as the prioritized proxy may not be the individual most likely to be involved in providing care and making decisions. This presents no conflict when families support one another but can get very sticky when families disagree on the patient's needs or when team members align with one family member over another. Competent patients have the right to choose their caregiver whom the team must respect unless suspected abuse is at issue.

This case also serves to illustrate that a coordinated team responding sensitively to the family can substantially affect a patient's rehabilitation progress. In the case of spinal cord injury, effective family teaching can promote patient health and serve to prevent future secondary complications commonly associated with SCI. Strasser, Falconer, and Martino-Saltmann (1994) discuss the interprofessional relationships among members of the rehabilitation team. Interestingly, they postulate that physical therapists may view themselves as less dependent on the team process, which may be one variable at work in this case leading to PT's making a discharge decision separate from the team. The psychologist's sensitivity to interpersonal dynamics at play across disciplines can possibly facilitate team communication and coordination. Clearly, team cohesion is integral to upholding ethical responsibilities with families in the rehabilitation milieu and contributes to the successful implementation of needed interventions to protect patients' safety and optimize their independence. In this case, the team finally came together and recognized a specific family value system and structure affecting rehabilitation efforts. By realigning expectations to better match the family's system, rehabilitation goals became more achievable. In general, respect for a family's values and culture can facilitate positive outcome (Elliott & Rivera, 2003; Sharma & Kerl, 2002).

CASE 3.5
ACCOMMODATING QUESTIONABLE PATIENT PREFERENCES

Vonda Price, a 72-year-old married woman, needed strengthening and endurance building after having undergone an exploratory laparotomy, small bowel resection (related to ischemia), and hernia repair. Her rich medical history included morbid obesity, non-insulin-dependent diabetes mellitus, coronary artery disease, coronary artery bypass graft (two years earlier), and hysterectomy. Vonda always had a sickly air and had been emotionally sheltered by her family for decades. She was married to a retired judge whose reputation as an ultraconservative proponent of litigation was known throughout the state. The final and most challenging aspect of Mrs. Price's situation was attitudinal. She refused to be treated, cared for, or attended by people of color.

Mrs. Price had been transferred to Yellow Springs Metro Rehab from her rural community medical center during the holiday season. Vonda's 37-year-old daughter, Alfa Price, accompanied her and stated that she was going to stay with her mother for the duration of her admission. As it turned out, Alfa served as Vonda's spokesperson in all matters. Within five minutes of entering the rehabilitation center, Alfa demanded to see the director. In a spirit of customer relations, Nola Smythe (the therapy manager) agreed to meet with Alfa.

During that initial contact, Alfa fired her first verbal salvo, "Let me set the record straight." Alfa spoke in a loud voice that had the aural overtones of a cat being dragged through a pile of broken glass. "My momma will not be touched or talked to by any *colored* person. I will interview and approve other staff who might be Asian or other kinds of immigrants." Before the shocked Nola Smythe could respond, Alfa added, "My daddy, the judge, said that I'm perfectly within my rights to protect my momma." That said, Alfa removed a spiral bound notebook and pen from her oversized purse, opened the flap, and waited to record Nola's response.

As is common in rehabilitation facilities, Mrs. Price's admission to Yellow Springs Rehab was heralded by a preadmission report that was sent to Ms. Smythe. This "heads-up" report detailed a precedent-setting event that occurred during the acute hospitalization. Apparently, a gynecologist who was African American had been consulted by Mrs. Price's attending physician to do a pelvic exam and a cervical cancer screen based on a positive family history. When the patient and her daughter raised a ruckus, the physician left the room without finishing the consultation and decided not to formally pursue the issue any further. He did report the incident to the attending physician. In the spirit of accommodation and to avoid subjecting the staff to any more verbal abuse, the facility decided not to confront the patient and daughter. From the patient's and family's perspective, that inaction represented a tacit validation of their ability to dictate attitudinally based specifics of care that extended beyond their appropriate realm of control.

Ms. Smythe decided to accommodate the patient's wishes to avoid potential problems of abuse of her staff. Therefore, the primary physical and occupational therapists, one African American and the other Jamaican, were relieved of treating Vonda. Two less experienced therapists who were Caucasian were switched from other patients to fill the vacated niches. In each case, the primary therapist was informed of the situation and willingly agreed with the accommodation to avoid unpleasant interactions with Vonda and her daughter. However, both therapists expressed consternation that such attitudes appeared to be tolerated in the facility. Interestingly, Alfa had observed and interviewed two Hispanic nurses and "okayed" their continuing care for her mother.

Alfa shadowed her mother in every daily therapy activity, writing profusely in her notebook during each session. She actively tried to pace her mother's program, insisting on frequent breaks, which disrupted the treatment schedule for the whole program. Alfa let each team member know that she reserved the right to refuse any treatment at any time. She was quite vocal and publicly dramatic when her opinions were challenged. Her behavior was beginning to have a negative effect on the other patients and families, but none of the nurses or therapists felt comfortable confronting Alfa when she overstepped social bounds. They feared a public scene that might exacerbate an already difficult situation.

A week into Mrs. Price's rehabilitation program and just before a holiday weekend, Alfa approached a covering internist, Dr. West, about nurses disturbing Mrs. Price's sleep at night when they took vital signs. Alfa wanted the monitoring held to allow her mother decent rest. The covering physician was verbally sympathetic to the situation but did not write an order changing the monitoring schedule. Later that evening, Alfa posted a sign on her mother's door forbidding vitals between midnight and 6 a.m., crediting Dr. West (who had left town for the holiday) with an order to that effect. Alfa was adamant about the (Do Not Disturb) sign and became hysterical in the hallway when concerned nursing staff questioned her about it. As a result, the covering nurses honored the sign but failed to check the chart for an order.

By Tuesday morning, the team had reached the boiling point regarding Alfa's need to control all aspects of her mother's care. They requested a consult from psychology to help them regain control over treatment decisions that could affect Mrs. Price's level of recovery. Dr. Timothy Lightfoot, the supervising psychologist, thought this situation would be a great one to test the wings of the newly christened PhD, Lucinda Grey, who had just started a postdoctoral fellowship on the inpatient rehabilitation unit. The patient and family refused direct psychology contact, stating that it was "against their religious beliefs to discuss personal matters with secular humanists." Although Dr. Grey originally breathed a sigh of relief (after feeling overwhelmed by the dynamics operating between the patient and team), Dr. Lightfoot informed her that she could still serve in a consultative role to the team.

Relevant Ethical Principles and Standards

Principle A: Beneficence and Nonmaleficence

Dr. Grey must work with the team to determine the most appropriate treatment plan while still respecting the patient's right to decline specific services. On the other hand, Alfa's choice to refuse needed care and treatment based on what she believes is in the best interests of her mother risks significant harm. Dr. Grey has the expertise to offer suggestions regarding how the team communicates with the patient and her daughter to interrupt contentious interactions with the goal of minimizing risk of harm.

Principle D: Justice

The patient is entitled to quality services and yet opts for less experienced care because of the biases she holds. Although Mrs. Price is due proper care and treatment regardless of her belief system, the psychologist has a responsibility to avoid condoning unjust practices resulting from patient biases if these practices are preventable.

Principle E: Respect for People's Rights and Dignity

The patient has a right to choose and direct her health care. This broad right has ethical and legal precedent and is highly valued. The patient also has the right to have her daughter make decisions for her. However, in deciding to honor the family's request for specific care providers, they fail to consider the therapists' rights. In addition, the manner in which Alfa exercises choice is contentious at many different levels. Respecting this patient's right to choose caregivers might be interpreted by the rehabilitation team as complicity with unacceptable racial bias. The entire team must decide the boundaries of respect for people's rights in the context of Mrs. Price's rehabilitation needs.

Standard 1.02, Conflicts Between Ethics and Law, Regulations, or Other Governing Legal Authority

Accreditation agency standards demand that patient preferences be accommodated when offering rehabilitative health care services. Yet, this patient's preferences appear to be motivated by racial prejudices that challenge the intent of established laws and rehabilitation practice standards. Dr. Grey needs to seek supervision to determine how to balance these seemingly inconsistent principles for clinical practice (i.e., supporting different patients' values vs. maximizing care).

Standard 1.06, Cooperating With Ethics Committees

The emotional volatility of this case necessitates collaboration between the providers as a team and the rehabilitation facility's ethics committee to ensure both the facility and the patient are treated fairly.

Standard 3.01, Unfair Discrimination

This case presents a reverse discrimination scenario in which the patient's biases limit effective treatment. If it is held that the patient is simply exercising her right, then the psychologist must work with the staff to prevent them from responding inappropriately toward someone who holds socially provocative views. On the other hand, the facility may be engaging in discrimination among its employees if it is sanctioning reassignment of therapists on the basis of patient prejudice. Dr. Grey must consider this possibility in deciding how to resolve the conflict between the team and family.

Standard 3.10, Informed Consent

This standard is at the core of the therapeutic relationship with Mrs. Price. To the extent that the facility and rehabilitation team fully inform the patient and her daughter about the program, they preserve both the patient's right to choose program involvement and the facility's position regarding issues like staffing and accommodation of patients' and family's needs. A clear exposition of the program's mission and goals and related patients' rights and responsibilities should exist, preferably in easily accessible form. In addition, as part of the consent process, the psychologist (and other team members) must educate Mrs. Price regarding the consequences of selecting less than optimal care options.

Standard 4.01, Maintaining Confidentiality

The importance of keeping events of this emotionally charged case from being the subject of conversation outside the clinical environment cannot be overstated. The patient's identity and case-specific information must be protected.

Standard 6.01, Documentation of Professional and Scientific Work and Maintenance of Records

Alfa's "court reporter" proclivity and threats of legal action warrant more than the usual detail in documenting clinically relevant information in the medical record. Dr. Grey, as well as all other team members, needs to include quotations and behavioral descriptions of events to capture the evolving dynamic accurately. Given the emotionality surrounding this case, the psychologist may be able to offer guidance to the staff regarding choice of language in documenting responses to demands made by the patient and her family.

Institutional and Legal Concepts That May Apply

Federal legislation that deals with discrimination has focused on the actions of public institutions, agencies, and employers and not on private beliefs. The rehabilitation facility may be subject to litigation if the reassigned employees believe such reassignment constitutes discrimination. In addition, state statutes regulating a professional's duty to care and the manner of competent practice might be compromised if harm to the patient results from the therapist reassignment.

If hospital administrators had become aware of the daughter's early actions to restrict patient monitoring, they might have considered limiting Alfa's involvement in her mother's care based on endangerment until she could demonstrate reasonable safety decisions. However, it is likely that the patient would have elected to be discharged against medical advice rather than be separated from her daughter. At that point, state neglect statutes regarding care for the elderly might have become relevant.

Relevant Context and Key Stakeholders

There is one acute inpatient rehabilitation hospital, Yellow Springs Rehab Center, within reasonable distance of the patient's home. Therefore, this inpatient team realistically is the only one available to shoulder the responsibility for Mrs. Price's care. Mrs. Price's husband, a retired judge reputed to file frivolous lawsuits, is absent from all rehabilitation activities. Alfa, on behalf of her mother, has explicitly stated their preferences for therapists. The team therefore becomes bound by at least two ethical principles in conflict. The principle of respect for autonomy supports the patient's right to refuse treatment (or in this case therapists). However, this principle conflicts with the principle of beneficence and the primary goal of rehabilitation, which is to maximize outcome. By respecting the patient's autonomy, the care provided is not at an optimal level.

However, this same principle of respect for autonomy challenges providers to respect those with values differing from their own. Whether this applies to obvious racial prejudice is unclear, but the team is extremely uncomfortable and frustrated by the family's demands, and they seek a psychology consultation to assist them. Because the patient refuses psychological services, Dr. Grey serves in a consultative role to the team. The APA (2002) Ethics Code should serve as a set of guidelines for Dr. Grey to assist professional colleagues and the rehabilitation facility in crafting appropriate responses to Mrs. Price and her daughter.

The following involved parties were considered in attempting to calm the growing dissension between the team and family.

Patient (Vonda Price). Through her passive-dependent demeanor and deferring totally to her daughter, Mrs. Price essentially abdicates decision-making authority by creating a de facto surrogate. Although she actively avoids making decisions, she does follow the therapists' instructions adequately and appears interested in passively participating in her program.

Patient's Spouse (Judge Price). Mr. Price is uninvolved in his wife's care. He participates in no rehabilitation activities despite team requests and clearly informs the team that Alfa may make any treatment decisions.

Patient's Daughter (Alfa Price). Alfa's role in the family is to protect her mother and carry out her wishes, including choosing who provides her mother's care. Although her angry, demanding interactive style produces the illusion of control over her mother's situation, in reality, Alfa's attempts to protect her mother unintentionally place Vonda in harm's way through refusal of medical monitoring. In addition, refusal of many aspects of rehabilitation treatment and support result in a suboptimal outcome. The daughter's motivation for her maladaptive behavioral style likely has roots in family dynamics that cannot be significantly affected during the short rehabilitation admission.

Rehabilitation Team. In an attempt to accommodate patient and family preferences, the team inadvertently produces a counter effect. Failure to set limits with the Prices results in a family that oversteps bounds of acceptable behavior. Without challenges to their inappropriate demands, the Prices have limited opportunity to know when they engage in risky behavior, and the team sets up their own spiral of frustration and powerlessness.

Acute and Rehabilitation Facilities. The precedent set in acute care in which the family dictated care results in similar and even more egregious maladaptive choices in the rehabilitation program. Both facilities unintentionally create an atmosphere of overaccommodation that negatively influences staff decision making and limits the family's opportunity to make more adaptive choices.

The Psychologist and Postdoctoral Fellow (Dr. Timothy Lightfoot and Dr. Lucinda Grey). Dr. Lightfoot closely supervises Dr. Grey, given the case's complexities. They clearly define their role as facilitators of an appropriate solution through consultation with the rest of the team. They have no direct contact with the patient given that she refuses psychology's services.

Case Resolution

Establish the Role of Alfa

Although Alfa's behavior clearly indicates she is making decisions for her mother, there is no clear documentation that Mrs. Price has made an informed decision to transfer health care decisions to her daughter. The patient's spouse is not empowered to make this decision for Mrs. Price, who is a competent adult. Who makes decisions needs to be evaluated during a session without immediate influence from Mrs. Price's daughter, Alfa. The psychologist failed to recommend this to the team.

Remove the Sign on the Patient's Door Preventing Care Between Midnight and 6 a.m.

When the attending physiatrist returned to work after the holiday, the sign was removed. The patient and daughter were informed of the staff's need to adhere to standards of care. Alfa (but not the patient) expressed significant anger over this change but tolerated the sign's removal.

Consultation With Risk Management and the Legal Department

Dr. Lightfoot alerted the risk manager to the patient's demands, and the manager then consulted with administration and the legal department for guidance. An ethics consult was initiated, focusing on intervening with Mrs. Price and her daughter. However, by that time, Mrs. Price's treatment program was completed, and she was to be discharged home the next day.

Develop a Discharge Plan That Includes Outpatient Monitoring

The team recommended outpatient therapy to strengthen inpatient rehabilitation gains. In addition, inherent in outpatient follow-up was the opportunity to monitor Mrs. Price's rehabilitation plan and safety after discharge. The Prices agreed to therapy, indicating they recognized its benefit to Mrs. Price's continuing recovery. However, they did not show up for their appointment.

Develop Institutional Policies Regarding Treatment Refusals Resulting in Disruption of Care

After Mrs. Price's discharge, the rehabilitation staff was significantly distressed. Dr. Lightfoot intervened with administration and arranged to hold a facility-wide "Town Meeting." The purpose was to create a forum in which the staff could actively contribute to a corrective action plan for the facility. The Town Meeting occurred one week later and was well attended by staff and management from various disciplines and services. After a brief review of the purposes of accommodation, the current preadmission process, general standards of care, and patients' rights and responsibilities, the following issues were addressed: staff members' rights to refuse to treat a patient, how to respond effectively as individuals and as a team to attitudinal biases, staffing patterns and program vulnerability during holidays, and finally, how to incorporate a constructive attitude toward these issues during new employee orientation. This facility-wide forum, facilitated by Dr. Lightfoot, served to create a constructive atmosphere in which staff and management could address attitudinal and behavioral aspects of problem solving, arriving at mutually acceptable solutions.

Case Disposition

Within 10 days of arriving home, Mrs. Price's family structure was strained. As was true during inpatient rehabilitation, Mrs. Price's spouse did not participate in her care. Alfa, who had not slept well in the rehabilitation center because of her insistence on "standing guard" over her mother, still was not getting enough rest.

Home Health Services, which had been ordered by the physician out of a sense of responsibility to the patient, arrived at the Price's home. However, Alfa refused the nurses entry, stating that she could handle her mother without any outside meddling. The Yellow Springs Metro Rehab case manager had alerted the Home Health Services social worker to the potentially risky home environment after Mrs. Price missed her first outpatient appointment. The social worker contacted Adult Protective Services for an investigation. However, before the agency could respond, Mrs. Price fell when Alfa left her unattended for just a few moments to retrieve the walker, which they had left in another room. She fractured her hip, requiring open reduction and internal fixation surgery at the local medical center.

Mrs. Price and Alfa requested a return to Yellow Springs Metro Rehab; Alfa felt that their preferences and demands had been respected, and Mrs. Price liked the therapists. However, their insurance company insisted that she be admitted to the local extended-care facility for her recuperation, and the therapists at Yellow Springs Metro Rehab could be heard to breathe a collective sigh of relief. Nonetheless, the rehabilitation facility was prepared to provide the Price family with policies and procedures regarding staffing and standards of care and to educate them about patients' responsibilities prior to agreeing to readmission.

Just before discharge from the extended-care facility, an Adult Protective Services investigator counseled the Prices to accept follow-up care from Home Health Services. The family's suspicions were ramped up when the investigator, who was African American, first arrived to interview Vonda and Alfa. However, they quickly learned that they could not avoid interacting with the agent. Reluctantly, they agreed to services when possible sanctions related to endangerment were clearly explained; even the judge could not bail them out of this one.

Additional Commentary

This case begs the question: Where does a health care system draw the boundary on respect for autonomy? This family's request to change providers because of racial bias challenges a core underpinning of the entire rehabilitation philosophy; that is, all individuals should be treated with respect. What are the social costs, and therefore, the challenges to the principles of justice and beneficence, at a facility that tolerates prejudice? On the other hand, it does not appear that making a decision to reject more competent therapists placed this family at risk of substantial harm. Mrs. Price still met her rehabilitation goals, albeit not at the level the team believed could have been reached. Given that it is unlikely the rehabilitation team would have changed any strongly held prejudices (especially during a short inpatient stay) on the basis of denying staff changes and given that the team could accommodate the change requested, it seems that a reasonable, although uncomfortable, argument could be made in support of the staffing changes under the principles of respect for people's values and promoting patients' welfare. If the change had not occurred, the patient might have rejected rehabilitation outright, resulting in the need for costlier services in the future with poorer outcomes. However, in making this choice, the facility must deal very sensitively with this issue with staff members who might perceive themselves as the targets of discrimination if reassigned to what appear to be less appropriate responsibilities. In addition, the team would have needed to explain the cost benefits of the staffing change requested to ensure informed consent to the change, even though the request was initiated by the family.

Other important issues in this case related to patient outcome are the choices Alfa made to reject standard care practices and the facility's acceptance of these changes. Multiple factors came together to increase risk to both the patient and facility under the guise of respect for autonomy. Essentially, the concurrence of a holiday weekend, coverage by pool health care staff (with a limited sense of being able to manage the patient's case), the lack of effective awareness of patients' rights and restrictions, and a determined (if misguided) family member coalesced into a potentially dangerous situation. Had a medical emergency occurred during the middle of the night without staff performing their mandated per-shift vital signs monitoring, Alfa's mother could have died needlessly, and the attending physician and hospital would have been liable. These risks are unacceptably high, particularly given that they are preventable with appropriate actions on the part of the team. Rather than allowing Alfa to disrupt normal procedures, the team should have intervened early to prevent an escalation of requests for unreasonable accommodations. Clearly, she and her mother required education on sound health care practice and boundaries of accommodation. Presenting information that might be rejected by the patient or family member clearly is preferable to avoiding an unpleasant but necessary confrontation. By focusing on resolving the situation, the team might have been able to introduce procedures that would have facilitated a more positive atmosphere of teamwork with both Vonda and Alfa should they ever need to return. In addition, these procedures might have provided a more constructive approach to dealing with prejudice. If the patient and family are clear regarding the rehabilitation philosophy supported by the institution, they can then exercise their choice whether to be admitted. The reader is referred to Kreutzer and Kolakowsky-Hayner (2000) for additional comments on both stereotypes and dealing with family conflicts in the rehabilitation milieu.

CASE 3.6
RESPONDING TO MIXED MESSAGES ABOUT TREATMENT REFUSAL (CONTINUATION OF THE FERGUS MACGONAGLE SERIES)

"Well Mr. MacGonagle, how are you doing today?" Dr. Ford Monroe's cheerful sounding greeting fell limply to the floor. Fergus MacGonagle's lack of response was consistent with his behavior since transferring to the University Medical Center's acute inpatient rehabilitation unit two days before. He tried to shut out the staff whose assessment and treatment rationales appeared to have no meaning. Fergus spoke sparsely with authority figures and then only to demand that he be left alone.

Undeterred by Fergus's passive-aggressive stance, the health psychology postdoc continued, "It's good to see that you graduated from the burn unit. You'll find that the rehab program expects a lot more activity from you as you prepare to return home." Dr. Monroe sat down next to the bed, chin resting on the raised bed rail, waiting and watching.

Fergus kept his eyes closed, unwilling to acknowledge the presence of this shrink-in-training and hoping Dr. Monroe would get bored and go away. He noted that this young know-it-all seemed to be following him throughout the hospital. Fergus had used his "silent treatment" yesterday when Dr. Amanda Torrie, the senior rehabilitation psychologist (and Dr. Monroe's new supervisor), had tried to perform her initial evaluation. She had left frustrated. This recollection prompted a minute smile, a detail not lost on Dr. Monroe as he observed his patient.

The monologue went on, "The rehab team will begin to work with you to get you up, active, and doing more for yourself. As you master new ways to care for yourself, we'll step back and let you carry the ball more and more." Pausing for a moment, Dr. Monroe carefully watched Fergus's breathing pattern to ensure that he was not asleep. Then he spoke again, "You'll begin to believe in yourself again. You'll see that your ability to do for yourself will gradually improve."

Abruptly raising his arms from the bed, Fergus growled, "With these stumps and claws? Don't bullshit me, man!" Fergus had opened his eyes, swiveling his head to face the postdoc. He stared at the young man in intense anger, thin lips parted in a snarl, mottled face flushed crimson.

Undaunted and happy for any kind of response, Dr. Monroe continued with all the calmness he could muster, "If you give us a chance, Mr. MacGonagle, we will show you how to do for yourself, with *those* arms and hands."

Fergus interjected, "I'm only here because none of you would listen. You didn't respect what I said. Let me repeat it, since you all seem to have a hearing problem. I don't want your goddamn treatment. I want to control my own life!" Anger still seething, "Why should I play your games when you don't listen to *what I say*? The last few words were yelled with such force that Fergus was overcome with a hacking cough. Dr. Monroe sat back from the bed rail. He paused, letting the silence wear on for a while.

Then he asked Fergus, voice quiet, almost a whisper, "Why did you agree to be admitted to the rehab unit when you could have opted for a skilled nursing home?"

Tears began to flow from his eyes, "Maida made that call. She sat there next to my bed, like you are now, holding Willem in her lap. She said I owed it to my grandson to make a life for myself, so I just didn't say anything." A sob escaped his lips, and Fergus's eyes closed again. He seemed to sink into himself. Dr. Monroe quietly left the room, promising to return.

Relevant Ethical Principles and Standards

Principle A: Beneficence and Nonmaleficence

The rehabilitation team, which includes the psychologist, is responsible for providing Mr. MacGonagle with treatment designed to increase his functional capabilities. The team's position regarding the patient's wish to terminate treatment is aligned with that of the burn team. Fergus's condition is not terminal, and he has experience-limited awareness of what possibilities lie ahead for crafting a meaningful life. This awareness is further limited by current psychological dysfunction. The rehabilitation team is proscribed from causing harm (i.e., being negligent through treatment withdrawal) given that they believe the patient has not yet competently evaluated the consequences of treatment refusal. On the other hand, the team must acknowledge that working with a reluctant patient could produce undesirable outcomes, such as the patient's feeling compelled to take drastic measures to regain control, placing himself at increased risk for injury and damaging his social relationships (e.g., with his spouse who advocated for his transfer).

Principle D: Justice

This principle, called into question by the patient in chapter 2 of this volume, was supported by the patient's need for acute treatment. That is, the patient and family received scarce resources that resulted in the patient's survival and early prevention of complications. Mr. MacGonagle's recovery reached a level at which he could benefit from rehabilitation, the next step in his recovery, to which he reluctantly consented with significant family encouragement. A major challenge in the rehabilitation phase is to facilitate the patient's active participation, an inherent requirement of the rehabilitation setting. If this does not occur, then resources are being inappropriately allocated to someone who refuses to accept them.

Principle E: Respect for People's Rights and Dignity

The team has elected to override Mr. MacGonagle's autonomy to provide the patient both treatment and time to gain the proper set of life experiences to make an informed choice. Given that the team believes fully informed choice is not yet possible for the patient (until the patient learns about and possibly experiences daily activities armed with adaptive compensations and emotional support), they have an obligation to involve the proxy on behalf of the patient for health care decision making. Fergus's spouse serves in this role. Maida has indicated she wants her spouse to participate in rehabilitation. However, the psychologist must consider whether Maida is making an informed decision based on what Fergus would want or on what she and the family want.

Standard 2.01, Boundaries of Competence

Dr. Monroe is involved in a supervisory relationship with Dr. Torrie, the rehabilitation psychologist. She must prepare the postdoctoral trainee to handle the nuances of the therapeutic relationship as it plays out in the rehabilitation environment. Dr. Torrie also must be prepared to evaluate and treat someone with severe burns, a relatively infrequent diagnosis in inpatient rehabilitation. To facilitate care across the continuum, a reciprocal educational relationship between the burn and rehabilitation unit psychologists would be useful.

Standard 3.04, Avoiding Harm

Drs. Torrie and Monroe are bound to avoid harming their patient, either through mistreatment or not providing needed treatment. Given the psychological contributors to Mr. MacGonagle's treatment refusals, under this standard the psychologists may be able to encourage the rehabilitation team to provide for the patient's needs, despite his demands to be left alone. However, the psychologists have to acknowledge that intentionally overriding the patient's request to decline treatment may permanently damage the therapeutic alliance.

Standard 3.09, Cooperation With Other Professionals

Without a coordinated, consistent approach to Mr. MacGonagle's treatment, it would be difficult to get beyond the apparent impasse in the patient's level of participation. Therefore, the psychologists need to work in concert with the team to engage Mr. MacGonagle in the rehabilitation process.

Standard 3.10, Informed Consent

Because the rehabilitation setting is significantly different from acute care, new consent is needed to support patient participation appropriately. A detailed explanation of the rehabilitation program may facilitate Fergus's gradually increasing fund of information regarding burn recovery and provide an opportunity to affect his involvement in treatment.

Standard 3.12, Interruption of Psychological Services

To prevent disruption of psychological services, the postdoctoral trainee moved across the continuum of care from the burn unit to the rehabilitation unit under an agreement by the supervising psychologists. Although theoretically sound, the practical application of this approach has not yet matured given the patient's current level of interaction.

Standard 4.01, Maintaining Confidentiality

Even though the patient's transfer is within the University Medical Center, the patient and his spouse need to be informed again about limits and privileges of confidentiality because of the new treatment environment.

Standard 4.05, Disclosures

The interdisciplinary milieu operating in the rehabilitation environment necessarily implies that multiple disciplines *will* see the patient's record and hold case conferences in which critical information is reviewed. It is important that the patient and his spouse understand this milieu as they make choices to disclose information. Similarly, the nature of the supervisory relationship and the sharing of confidential clinical information between Dr. Torrie and Dr. Monroe need to be explained to the patient. Finally, because Fergus was injured on the job, Workers' Compensation will be one entity to which records will be released.

Standard 4.06, Consultations

Consultations back to the burn team may be needed depending on Mr. MacGonagle's recovery. Sharing confidential information in a consultative spirit between treatment teams needs to be discussed with the patient and family.

Standard 7.06, Assessing Student and Supervisee Performance

Given the early and obvious case complexities, Dr. Torrie should consider the need for more frequent supervision than would normally be implemented.

Standard 10.01, Informed Consent to Therapy

Although the patient may refuse to participate in specific therapeutic sessions, repeated offering of interventions during the course of the rehabilitation program is appropriate given the evolving nature of his physical status and psychological response to his situation. Rapport building necessary for acquiring informed consent for treatment in this case will likely occur over multiple contacts.

Standard 10.10, Terminating Therapy

Given the ongoing challenges in burn recovery (e.g., challenges associated with familial routines, community reintegration, and continuing pain), it is very likely that outpatient treatment will be warranted after discharge from inpatient rehabilitation. Providing a mechanism to receive treatment and facilitating a connection to this mechanism are required prior to discharge.

Institutional and Legal Concepts That May Apply

Key legal concepts to be considered in this case are under what circumstances withdrawal of treatment is appropriate and the patient's right to refuse treatment. As noted in previous cases, the courts have generally held that a competent person has the right to refuse treatment. However, this case presents conflicting information regarding competence and treatment refusal. Although the patient is continuing to demand treatment withdrawal, he agreed to be transferred to the rehabilitation program rather than go to a long-term care facility, and he has accepted some therapy. The tacit agreement to be transferred and cooperating with specific therapies are inconsistent with Mr. MacGonagle's demands for treatment withdrawal. He explained the transfer as a manipulation by his family. His expressed wish not to receive treatment clashes with that of his spouse, who may be serving as a proxy. Under these ambiguous circumstances, the rehabilitation team prioritizes safety and provides care based on the patient's health care needs. The team believes that failing to provide such care may be construed as negligence. The point at which this becomes critical in rehabilitation is the juncture at which the *patient's effort* is the linchpin for successful therapy outcome. Treatments requiring passive acceptance (i.e., wound care and dressings) are less obviously involved. However, active therapies focused on activities of daily living and mobility depend on the patient's active participation to have a beneficial effect. The team must therefore decide whether to go beyond simply offering the opportunity to get out of bed and participate in therapy and actively persuading and encouraging interaction to execute due care. The psychologist must ensure the patient's depressive symptoms are addressed given their contributions to the patient's capacity to consent.

Relevant Context and Key Stakeholders

What had begun as a tragic accident at work has now morphed into a horrendous battle, not for survival but for self-identity. Fergus has been the leader, decision maker, and financial provider in his family. It is the only role he understands, and one that does not leave much room for taking account of others' feelings and opinions. After the accident, Maida and Iain took on pieces of roles Fergus previously managed as if they had been waiting for the opportunity. Maida holds onto the belief of a hopeful future for her husband, one that Fergus simply cannot fathom. He has been stripped of his natural ability to manipulate objects with skill and efficiency, and his visage has been replaced by a hairless, raccoon-eyed stranger almost unrecognizable to him and those who had known him. Internally, except for the unrelenting pain, he feels familiar sensations and experiences recognizable thoughts. However, he knows his ability to control his environment has been radically altered. This once staunchly independent man has been reduced to a patient, a case, a designated bed in a facility. The staff knows with certainty what to do to care for him, but Fergus is convinced that they do not have a clue about his perspective. They afford him generic respect, but not the kind he reserves for those whose actions he deems worthy. After all, he feels helpless, exacerbated by the unrelenting pain.

Awakening to pain is a daily routine for Fergus. He has developed the ability to discriminate dull, burning pain at rest from searing pain associated with wound dressing changes and pulling, tearing pain associated with stretching tight joints during range of motion.

Adding to this baseline of suffering is the insidious development of scar tissue and the treatment needed to prevent scar bands from binding his joints into immobility. Having heard the team's explanation of the healing process after burn injury, Fergus knows that his body is desperately trying to regenerate protective skin to cover his wounds. Along with vigorous scar massage and application of copious amounts of moisturizing lotion (scar tissue lacks natural lubrication), tight, custom-fitting elastic pressure garments are required to gain needed control over scar formation. Fergus is facing a scar formation process lasting up to 18 months. He believes he is being molded into a different being, one with which he does not particularly want to be associated.

The following parties are critical to Fergus's continuing recovery.

Patient (Fergus MacGonagle). The setting has changed, but the patient remains verbally committed to his position of treatment withdrawal. Fergus allows his wife to persuade him (with the influence of his grandson) to enter the rehabilitation program, an inconsistency in his position. However, without his active desire to recover optimally, Fergus will face early discharge for failure to improve in a treatment setting that demands increasing patient participation. His attitudinal biases continue to limit the number of staff who can positively affect his situation. He is significantly challenged by depressive features associated with altered self-concept, ongoing pain, and fears of family disintegration associated with role changes.

Family (Wife Maida, Son Iain and his Wife, Grandson Willem). The family clearly sides with the health care team regarding Fergus's treatment. Maida adeptly uses Fergus's love for his only grandchild to persuade Fergus to opt for inpatient rehabilitation rather than an extended-care facility. Additionally, she secures Fergus's promise to cooperate with the nurses and therapists so that he can return home at the end of his rehabilitation admission. Although Fergus grouses about this maneuver, he reluctantly admits to its veracity when asked by various staff. The family continues to visit regularly and adopts a "normalizing" approach to their interactions with Fergus. Iain has chosen, aided by the wise counsel of his mother and Dr. Torrie, to take a backseat during the family's initial interactions with Fergus. His history of conflict with his father might well have clouded the current issues regarding care with old emotional turmoil. Iain supports his mother's view of the recovery course.

Psychologists (Dr. Amanda Torrie, Supervisor; and Dr. Ford Monroe, Postdoctoral Trainee). Dr. Torrie is aware of Mr. MacGonagle's gender bias and welcomes Dr. Monroe to the rehabilitation team. She establishes an active supervisory relationship with him from admission onward and is comfortable with Dr. Monroe taking the primary role in intervention. She episodically meets with Fergus to reinforce their consultative approach. The two psychologists believe that Mr. MacGonagle's treatment refusal is related to his losing his sense of physical, psychological, and social identity and that he fears he would place a heavy burden of care on his spouse after discharge. Dr. Torrie and Dr. Monroe are concerned that initial psychological shock is being replaced with depression. As behavioral specialists, the psychologists have a primary role in facilitating Mr. MacGonagle's rehabilitation participation. They also are critical in determining the patient's evolving capacity to refuse treatment.

Rehabilitation Team. The underlying value system of the team has significantly affected their decision regarding treatment of Mr. MacGonagle. They embrace the belief that early treatment refusal in catastrophic injury is attributed to poor adjustment based on the patient's initial reactions to dramatic physical changes and lack of knowledge and awareness of the possibilities rehabilitation creates toward improving overall quality of life. They must continually reevaluate Mr. MacGonagle's competence to disagree with their position.

Case Resolution

Determination of the Patient's Consent

Dr. Monroe reasoned that Mr. MacGonagle would not participate in anything that appeared like a "formal" assessment process. The postdoc therefore used his already established bedside conversations to complete a functional assessment of Mr. MacGonagle's decision making resulting in treatment refusal. Through this conversational approach, Dr. Monroe confirmed the patient's anger and beliefs that nothing could help him return to a "normal" life and that his family as he knows it was going to perish as a result. He believed the patient's affective responses were significantly compromising his judgment. The patient's recent behavioral history, which included inconsistent actions in response to rehabilitation efforts, the emotional overtones noted during the interviews, and the pervasiveness of the impact of the burn injury, prompted the psychologist to consider options carefully. He believed Mr. MacGonagle was not yet at a point at which he could effectively weigh the benefits of treatment, a necessary component of informed decision making. Dr. Monroe implemented a process of periodic reevaluation as the patient progressed and maintained contact with the family.

Use of the Family

Given the patient's dysfunctional interaction pattern, formal psychotherapy was a laudable but not very workable approach to engendering adaptive behavioral change. Therefore, early on in the case the psychologists decided to intervene both directly (through Dr. Monroe) and indirectly through the family members. Additionally, both Dr. Torrie and Dr. Monroe met regularly with the MacGonagle family to support them and offer guidance regarding their focus on meeting rehabilitation program goals. Fergus had shown on two separate instances that he was willing to set aside his attitude of abandonment and work on behalf of his family. Consequently, whenever his effort in treatment waned, Maida intervened with family support strategies. In addition, as his wounds began to heal and required only the application of lotion, Maida and their children took a more active role in scar massage. With the help of the nursing staff in providing privacy, Maida used her "time applying lotion" to re-establish basic aspects of her physical relationship with Fergus.

Setting Consistent Expectations Across the Team

The performance expectations of the team focused on everyday living skills. The skills were concrete, making weekly negotiation of functional goals more easily understood and accepted by Fergus. The team also reminded Fergus of his "promise" to his grandson to work hard in the rehabilitation program, information shared among the team by the psychologists. The various rehabilitation disciplines routinely updated Fergus on his progress throughout his program in objective, practical terms related to his return to his home and community. Through this reinforcement, Fergus began to establish an increasingly independent self-care routine, manipulating objects quite deftly with his injured hands, sometimes demonstrating his skill at throwing them across the room.

Use of the Outreach Volunteer

Dr. Torrie asked Otis Mitchell to work with Fergus toward the end of Mr. MacGonagle's rehabilitation admission. Mr. Mitchell had been an inpatient in the rehabilitation program two years earlier. His burn injuries were very similar to Fergus's. Otis and his wife had successfully managed his scar formation, which had halted. He was active in visitation ministry for his church and had recently begun vocational retraining through Workers' Compensation. However, the most important reason for Otis being brought in to assist was his hope, reflected in a "there isn't any challenge I can't beat" attitude toward his recovery course and his current life. He periodically volunteered to talk to patients with burns when requested by the team, and these visits had a consistently positive effect.

Dr. Monroe escorted Mr. Mitchell to Fergus's room. Initially Dr. Monroe had Otis wait in the hallway. The postdoctoral fellow briefly spoke with Fergus, explaining the process of outreach patient contact as a routine part of the burn rehabilitation program. When Fergus began to complain loudly and express a desire to avoid such a meeting, Dr. Monroe cautioned him to speak more softly because Otis was right outside. With Maida's encouragement Fergus relented, and Dr. Monroe brought Otis into the room. Dr. Monroe then simply listened for several minutes before leaving them alone. Dr. Torrie had told the trainee to watch "the master" at work, and that is just what Dr. Monroe did.

The expression on Fergus MacGonagle's face was priceless when Otis walked into the room. Otis presented as a bald, earless, noseless African American man with a face of swirled melanin and unpigmented skin. He sported a broad smile (he'd been especially proud of the results of the stretching exercises he used to keep his mouth from scarring down). His eyes were captivating, as bright as jewels, exuding sincerity and a sense of compelling compassion.

"Well howdy Mr. MacGonagle. I'm pleased to meet you, being that we're brothers of sorts." That said, Otis extended his fingerless hands in a "handshake." He gingerly reached down and clasped the remnants of Fergus's right hand in a gentle two-handed squeeze, removing any thought of social discomfort from the introduction.

"Uh . . . I . . .um . . . I'm glad to meet you," the tentativeness in Fergus's voice made his normally gruff growl quiver almost uncontrollably. He couldn't help but stare at Otis . . . his brother in suffering . . . someone who'd been where he was.

Otis picked up on the once-over, "I see that you're comparing scars. Well that's all right by me. Did the same thing myself when I was laying in this very same bed 'bout two years ago. Doc Amanda brought in this woman with scars worse than mine." Otis leaned down, brought his scarred hand to his mouth and mugged, "But, she had this long silky brown hair. I just couldn't stop staring. Then she did the darndest thing; she whipped off that wig hat and started to laugh. I couldn't help it. I did too. We laughed and laughed, and she hadn't even said a word. I tell you, that first meeting brought me up short."

Otis had taken a seat next to Fergus during his story. He kicked back and put his hands behind his hairless head, looking up at the ceiling. He said, "You know, I'd been feeling so sorry for myself that I was sure I'd never have a real life again . . . that my wife would leave me for a real man . . . that my kids would be frightened of the horror movie I became after the burn." Otis leaned closer to Fergus, "You know, I wouldn't even look at myself in the mirror. Hell, I scared *me*!" With that he laughed . . . an infectious laugh that managed to pry a grin out of Fergus.

Otis continued, "Tell me, man, how'd you get hurt?" With that simple question, Fergus opened up, almost erupting with the desire to tell his tale to someone who would understand. He and Otis spent the next half hour swapping one-up burn stories until both of them were heard laughing in tandem. The staff passing by in the hallway smiled at the magic wielded by Otis Mitchell.

Case Disposition

Slow, steady gains marked Fergus MacGonagle's rehabilitation program. After several weeks, his affect had begun to vary more. Although he still maintained his sullen anger during interactions with team leadership, he selectively and tentatively began to relate more personally to treatment staff. His baseline mood first brightened somewhat after his meeting with Otis. This meeting was memorable.

Despite the progress made, Fergus continued to say that he had been railroaded into participating in the rehabilitation program by his family and the medical staff. He said that everyone would have been better off had he died. Further, Fergus was convinced that his return home would be a failure because of the care burden it would place on his wife and his son's family. However, Workers' Compensation agreed to pay for a part-time caregiver to assist Maida with the more demanding physical aspects of Fergus's care. This decision appeared to mollify Fergus, and he finally agreed to return home.

There were many discharge goals: scar management, wound care, upper extremity range of motion and functional skill improvement, emotional stability, and vocational evaluation and planning. Otis Mitchell offered to meet periodically with Fergus, arranging once-a-month contact at his home. Maida was strongly in favor of this relationship, a position that Fergus felt he was in no position to challenge; his wife had taken over!

Dr. Monroe arranged to follow Fergus in the rehabilitation center's outpatient clinic under Dr. Torrie's supervision. Additionally, both of them alerted the state's Department of Vocational Rehabilitation of a likely referral in the future, once the Workers' Compensation program had fulfilled its responsibilities in supporting a stable home care situation.

Finally, the two psychologists suspected that Fergus had agreed with the rehabilitation discharge plan to exit the paternalistic health care system as quickly as possible. They believed that his risk of self-harm would increase after he returned home. Coincidentally, Maida and Iain approached them to express their suspicions in the same regard. In a rare confrontation, Maida challenged Fergus with this fear on the day of discharge. She demanded that he follow up with psychology, expressing her frustration and anger in a direct manner. Maida also told Fergus that if he took his own life, the family would be left emotionally and financially destitute without their anchor. Despite being a curmudgeon, she knew that Fergus loved his family and that fact kept them on solid emotional ground. Even though he did not value his role played out through disability insurance payments, Fergus MacGonagle was still the primary breadwinner in the family. The recognition of this role would prove critical to further recovery. See chapter 4 of this volume for the continuation of the case of Fergus MacGonagle.

Additional Commentary

Competence and the involvement of proxy decision makers after catastrophic injury can present interesting challenges to health care teams trying to promote patients' welfare. Health care providers must be careful to guard against accepting patients' or proxies' decisions simply because these decisions agree with what the health care providers believe is appropriate. Patients have the right to refuse treatment even when life-saving measures are available; a health care team overriding this right must have compelling evidence that the patient does not have the capacity to make this decision or that benefit outweighs self-determination to such an extent that the providers' actions represent justifiable paternalism. In this case, it is unclear whether the patient's wife truly represented the patient's interests in agreeing with the treatment team. Some research suggests proxies do not necessarily effectively demonstrate substituted judgment because of lack of knowledge regarding the person's wishes or response to personal values, beliefs, and other variables affecting their decisions (Emanuel & Emanuel, 1992; Gerety, Chiodo, Kanten, Tuley, & Cornell, 1993; Karel & Gatz, 1996). Additionally, at least one study suggests that rehabilitation teams overstate levels of patients' impairment (Callahan & Hagglund, 1995). It seems that consent and treatment refusals by patients are sometimes challenged inappropriately under the principle of beneficence. To the extent that the patient's capacity to refuse was clearly evaluated and his rights protected in involving the surrogate, the rehabilitation team upheld ethical practice.

4

OUTPATIENT SERVICES

Outpatient settings are perhaps the most eclectic milieu in which psychologists practice. Psychologists' professional involvement with their patients can range from individual sessions to follow-up appointments occurring months, even years, after termination of regular therapeutic contact. Psychologists may offer professional services and effectively address patients' concerns as practitioners operating totally independently or as partners in simple to complex outpatient teams. Typical settings include mental health centers; outpatient clinics affiliated with acute medical, psychiatric, or rehabilitation hospitals; comprehensive outpatient rehabilitation facilities and programs; and independently operating Independent Practice Associations (IPAs) or private practices.

Psychologists increasingly serve in primary care settings in which they partner with physicians or other health care professionals to provide comprehensive care (Driscoll & McCabe, 2004; Frank, McDaniel, Bray, & Heldring, 2004; Haley et al., 1998; Sears, Evans, & Kuper, 2003; Wagenfield, Murray, Mohatt, & DeBruyn, 1993). Psychologists may bear the most significant responsibility for providing mental health services in areas that have been traditionally underserved, such as rural health care (see references for multiple readings). One of the reasons psychologists have increasingly advocated for prescriptive authority (endorsed by the APA Council of Representatives in

1996) is to improve access to the underserved (Benson, 2003; DeLeon & VandenBos, 2000; Phelps & Reed, 2004; Sammons, Gorny, Zinner, & Allen, 2000). By adding prescription privileges to their skill set, psychologists are in a position to provide more comprehensive care needed by patients presenting with emotional, behavioral, and cognitive problems in underserved rural areas in which psychologists are the front-line (Elliott & Frank, 2000; Phelps & Reed).

In contrast to the common outpatient practice in which psychologists provide direct assessment and intervention services, psychologists instead may function solely (or with other professionals) as consultants and expert witnesses or collaborators on clinical projects requiring no direct patient contact. These myriad roles reflect psychologists' increasing expertise in organizational systems. Examples are as varied as the nature of the consultant contracts and may include service as program development advisors to existing health provider organizations, external consultants to health care ethics committees, surveyors for accrediting agents, and consulting supervisors for a health care facility's existing clinical staff.

The outpatient setting is fraught with potential ethical challenges. As noted in chapter 1 of this volume, psychologists in outpatient practice may be the first line of defense for rapidly decompensating patients. The patient's presenting picture may be quite murky, given that physical manifestations of disease and disability may be intercurrent with mental health presentations. Psychologists may see patients ranging from those presenting straightforward concerns with single-stressor triggers to once-in-a-lifetime, convoluted stories of declining health and despair.

The complexity of many patients' clinical presentations argues strongly for a comprehensive primary care model of practice (Bray, Frank, McDaniel, & Heldring, 2004). To the extent that the outpatient psychologist has readily accessible connections within the broader health care community, patients will likely be better served, hopefully experiencing higher quality outcomes. For example, having a well-established contact network for implementing commitment procedures and abuse referrals will facilitate appropriate management of the patient's care, including respect for the patient's rights. In addition to knowledge of commitment procedures and patients' rights in this area, a thorough understanding of confidentiality, documentation, and disclosure is critical to ethical practice. Appropriate boundaries with patients' families must be established, and clarifying role expectations early in intervention will help facilitate appropriate ethical processes. In addition, understanding attorneys' rights of access and the appropriate release of test materials and other evaluative information to invested agents, such as attorneys, employers, and schools, will help ensure that appropriate confidentiality standards are met.

Setting clear boundaries with patients also is paramount. For example, psychologists may work with individuals who raise questions or show interest in social engagements outside of the ongoing clinical context or shortly after termination of therapy. This outpatient milieu offers the psychologist the opportunity to bring to bear all aspects of training and expertise. Psychologists simply cannot practice effectively in the outpatient setting without a competent grasp of the American Psychological Association Ethics Code (APA, 2002).

CASE 4.1
MANAGING A PATIENT'S RISK-TAKING BEHAVIOR

Wilbur James was a 51-year-old computer company executive. Everyone who worked with Wilbur knew him as a hard-driving workaholic who was a *hands-on* boss. Although many other *dot-com* companies went bankrupt during the recent and highly publicized high-tech stock market crash, Mr. James's company survived relatively intact because of his company's management and marketing strategies, strategies the company board openly acknowledged were orchestrated by Mr. James.

Many companies whose bubbles burst were now looking to Mr. James's corporation to buy them out and salvage something for themselves. Mr. James felt a great sense of social responsibility regarding the financial loss of so many he knew personally. Even his wife of 20 years, Noreen, noticed that Wilbur seemed more stressed and driven than usual to create new products to enhance the company's financial portfolio. Mr. James had hoped he could redirect this new cash flow toward buy-out options.

His longstanding primary care physician, Dr. Heather Longely, had spoken with Wilbur more than once about his high blood pressure and need to change his lifestyle to better manage his stress. However, she knew that Wilbur was not going to slow down despite her latest concern about his rising blood pressure. It came as no real surprise to Dr. Longely when she got a call from Wilbur's wife, who was in the local emergency room waiting to hear about her husband's condition. Paramedics had brought Mr. James to the ER after he experienced significant left-sided weakness at home. The CT scan showed a small right frontoparietal brain hemorrhage.

Mr. James quickly stabilized with no reoccurrence of hemorrhaging or other stroke activity. He remained in the hospital for five days because of left-sided weakness, poor coordination and balance, and mildly disinhibited behavior. Acute care nursing and occupational and physical therapy (OT and PT) showed that both Wilbur's motor and visual-perceptual problems were contributing to difficulties with self-care, sitting, transferring from one place and position to another, and walking. In addition, when they gave Mr. James directions to help him improve his technique on specific tasks, he frequently expressed his frustration by calling them incompetent.

Mr. James's recovery was excellent over the course of the next two days. The initial left-sided weakness, abnormal gait, and poor gross and fine motor coordination rapidly improved. Although neurology originally considered referring Mr. James for a brief inpatient rehabilitation stay, Wilbur was doing so well by the fifth day that he was discharged home with outpatient follow-up from OT, PT, and medicine at Dr. Longely's practice. He was told not to drink alcohol or drive a motor vehicle of any type, and make sure that he took his blood pressure medicine. In addition, he was advised to wait to return to work for at least one month, and then to return gradually, according to the recommendation of the outpatient providers. Neurology planned to follow up with Dr. Longely to ensure Mr. James's recovery continued uneventfully.

As scheduled, two weeks after Wilbur was discharged, Noreen drove him to his first medical follow-up appointment. It was immediately apparent to Dr. Longely that Noreen was upset. When Dr. Longely inquired, Noreen hesitated and then described how their home life had completely changed since Wilbur's stroke. Noreen, anxiously eyeing her husband, shared the following: "Nothing's the same. Wilbur just seems to get angry at little things; he doesn't want anyone to help him, and he does whatever he damn well pleases." Mr. James sat still, silently watching his wife.

Suddenly, anger assumed control of Noreen's narrative. "He's taken the boat out twice with a friend from work, who said Wilbur narrowly missed another boat. He tried to go back to work right after he got out of the hospital, but I guess something didn't go well there because he came home extremely frustrated." Noreen pleaded, "When I try to help, he just gets mad and leaves, driving to who knows where. I feel like I've lost my husband; he would never have ignored me before. We had a partnership . . . and now . . . that's gone."

Wilbur piped up and tersely stated, "Noreen has been acting like a mother hen ever since the stroke. I am perfectly capable of running both my own life and the company. You know, I've been in charge of my company for 10 years."

The physician acknowledged her patient's competence and desire to return to his former lifestyle. Dr. Longely also knew she needed help. She excused herself and went into the consultation room down the hall. She contacted Dr. Byron Yoletti, a local psychologist who consulted to Dr. Longely's practice. Dr. Longely then returned to Mr. and Mrs. James and told them of her psychology recommendation. Wilbur predictably groused, but Noreen was hopeful. They left the office with Dr. Longely's encouragement to honor the precautions they had been living under and await a call from Dr. Yoletti.

Dr. Yoletti's typical patient was a young woman in her 20s or 30s facing financial or familial stress. His experience with poststroke recovery was minimal. After reviewing the record and in consultation with Dr. Longely, Dr. Yoletti referred the case to Dr. Sarah Barnstorm, a psychologist who was board certified in rehabilitation and who worked at the rehabilitation hospital.

At the meeting with the psychologist, Mrs. James volunteered her tale of woe. Dr. Barnstorm felt she was hearing a familiar story, right stroke from which patient successfully recovers use of left side so he does not receive comprehensive rehabilitation. After discharge, the family, but not the patient, notes lingering problems with poor insight creating family strife, potentially crumbling marriage, poor work reentry, and poor judgment possibly coupled with perceptual problems making driving problematic and general decision making around risky behavior suspect.

Dr. Barnstorm had not even sat down in her chair when Mr. James said, "No matter what you prescribe, doctor, I'm planning on running my own life."

Relevant Ethical Principles and Standards

Principle A: Beneficence and Nonmaleficence

Dr. Barnstorm needs to balance the issues of how Mr. James can "control his own life" and continue to recover safely. If she believes she is attempting to minimize the likelihood of an undesirable and perhaps even tragic event, then she may make a strong enough case to override Mr. James's right to determine his own course of action as it relates to specific daily activities. Dr. Barnstorm needs to evaluate each domain of function separately (i.e., return to work and driving) if she is to be truly beneficent in her health care recommendations. Given Mr. James has clearly implied he wants to engage in potentially reckless activities, Dr. Barnstorm must decide if the restrictions create, on balance, more harm or benefit to Mr. James. For example, she may cause more harm if Mr. James adamantly refuses restrictive recommendations and engages in increased risk taking in response. In addition, if she solicits Mrs. James's assistance in preventing harm through restrictive actions, Mrs. James's decision to participate may have a negative effect on the couple's marriage, which already may be at some risk for decompensation. However, if Dr. Barnstorm supports Mr. James in his pursuit of activities in which she is fairly confident he will fail, she may cause harm to Mr. James by not taking steps to prevent the consequences of his actions. This may be particularly relevant, for example, in Mr. James's attempts to return to work. If he is no longer viewed as a strong, competent leader because of premature work reentry, his acceptance as a leader could not only suffer but the company's image could also destabilize.

Principle B: Fidelity and Responsibility

If Dr. Barnstorm believes Mr. James poses a threat to others on the basis of his behavioral actions, she must consider the degree to which she believes her actions will minimize the social risks involved. If the risk is high but her actions are ineffectual, it may be irresponsible to reduce the patient's autonomy.

Principle E: Respect for People's Rights and Dignity

Even if Dr. Barnstorm disagrees with his position, Mr. James, if a competent adult, has a fundamental right to refuse treatment even if that refusal results in serious harm to himself. Dr. Barnstorm must therefore consider whether lack of insight based on the occurrence of stroke is compelling enough to override the patient's stated position. She would base this decision on the patient's lack of capacity, risk to himself or others, and her ability to intervene in a manner that provides significant benefit or minimizes the anticipated risk of harm.

Standard 1.02, Conflicts Between Ethics and Law, Regulations, or Other Governing Legal Authority

Mr. James has retained his legal right to drive. Yet, under the principle of beneficence, he may not be deemed safe to drive or operate a car or boat. Dr. Barnstorm therefore faces treatment decisions that bring the principles of beneficence and respect for autonomy in conflict and whose potential solutions are inconsistent with legal precedents and guidelines. Involvement of family also can become a bit of a minefield as it relates to upholding patient confidentiality versus protecting welfare. Dr. Barnstorm will need to consider this balance as she moves forward in this case (i.e., the extent to which family involvement is critical, even if against the wishes of Mr. James).

Standard 2.01, Boundaries of Competence

Dr. Yoletti transferred this case to Dr. Barnstorm, believing that it would require professional skills he did not possess, an action that is consistent with this standard. A reasonable alternative to transfer may have been to work under Dr. Barnstorm's supervision and consultation. This is an appealing alternative when geographic distance prevents the type of transfer implemented in this case. Telehealth strategies might also come into play if Dr. Barnstorm intervened or consulted remotely. Appropriate encryption and safeguards regarding confidentiality would be crucial if this strategy were selected.

Standard 2.04, Bases for Scientific and Professional Judgments

Dr. Barnstorm has a body of empirical literature on which to base her understanding of Mr. James's poststroke presentation. In addition, she can rely on professional practice standards in weighing actions consistent with the principle of beneficence that may conflict with respect for autonomy when the direct scientific evidence supporting her contention of risk is limited, such as in boat-accident risk.

Standard 3.04, Avoiding Harm

If Dr. Barnstorm makes a paternalistic decision to intervene, this action should be based on the belief that it will prevent or lessen harm or minimize risk even if harm ultimately results. She will need to weigh what she believes the probability and magnitude of harm are, based on her professional expertise and training (and when available, scientific data regarding risk probability).

Standard 3.09, *Cooperation With Other Professionals*

As Mr. James's primary care physician, Dr. Longely will monitor Mr. James's status after the psychologist signs off the case. Therefore, enlisting Dr. Longely's help may prove to be very useful regarding long-term adherence to any psychology recommendations and in comprehensively understanding premorbid and current medical factors contributing to the patient's presentation.

Standard 3.10, *Informed Consent*

The patient's capacity to give informed consent has not yet been established. How Dr. Barnstorm proceeds will rest to a great extent on whether she believes Mr. James has the capacity to decline services that are viewed as promoting his welfare or protecting him from foreseeable harm. Because both Mr. and Mrs. James are the clients, consent from both for psychological services must be sought.

Standard 4.02, *Discussing the Limits of Confidentiality*

Because Dr. Barnstorm is ethically obligated to protect confidential information, she must clearly review the limits of what she is willing to keep confidential as it relates to consultation with Dr. Longely in particular. Conversely, if she is unwilling to release information regarding the patient and his spouse, she must convey this to Dr. Longely. For example, she may have specific details regarding Mr. James's failure at work that she does not feel are directly relevant to the decisions being made or she does not feel at liberty to discuss on the basis of the patient's and family's request.

Standard 4.05, *Disclosures*

If Dr. Barnstorm wants to discuss any assessment data with key third parties, such as Mr. James's work colleagues, Dr. Barnstorm has to believe Mr. James can give consent for these disclosures and must then acquire that consent. Under this standard, she also may disclose confidential information without such consent to prevent harm, if disclosure is permitted by law.

Standard 4.06, *Consultations*

Given the impact of the stroke on Mr. James's daily life as perceived by his spouse, a reliable source, it is likely that the majority of information garnered about current function will be relevant to the physician monitoring the progress of this patient. However, the psychologist must be continuously vigilant about what is and is not necessary and relevant to share, even with the referral source.

Standard 6.04, Fees and Financial Arrangements

Mr. James has a successful company and so has the financial resources to cover any agreed-on fees. However, the psychologist is in somewhat of a *catch-22* regarding when to discuss fees. Given that she is initially uncertain about Mr. James's capacity, it is reasonable to include his spouse in a discussion of fees for service. Once capacity is clear, reassessment of the patient's understanding and acceptance of fees is necessary.

Standard 9.04, Release of Test Data

Dr. Barnstorm has to face the possibility that Mr. James could rescind his consent to release assessment data once the results are known. The psychologist has to respect this decision unless there exists convincing evidence to override such a decision.

Standard 9.05, Test Construction

Because no specific examination exists for assessment of risk, Dr. Barnstorm must rely on her own professional knowledge and existing empirical literature to determine an appropriate set of questions to fit Mr. James's situation.

Standard 9.08, Obsolete Tests and Outdated Test Results

Given the tremendous proliferation of research on stroke and capacity assessment, Dr. Barnstorm has to ensure her methods are up-to-date.

Standard 9.10, Explaining Assessment Results

Whether or not Mr. James accepts treatment recommendations, including activity restrictions, may depend to a great extent on his confidence in the psychological assessment. The psychologist must be careful to relate the assessment to Mr. James's future success and stability without overinterpreting data not clearly related to Mr. James's stroke.

Standard 10.02, Therapy Involving Couples or Families

The psychologist believes that both Mr. and Mrs. James are critical to effective implementation of the treatment plan. Therefore, she has to clarify at the outset that she considers both of them her clients and that she wants to be able to share all evaluative information with both partners.

Institutional and Legal Concepts That May Apply

As previously discussed, in recent history, legal decisions in American society have generally preserved the right of a competent adult to make decisions for himself or herself even if harmful. Therefore, a health care provider must be able to present a very compelling argument before making a decision whose end result is the reduction of a patient's right to self-determination and privacy. Unfortunately, complications of serious health conditions, such as stroke, create murky legal water and present true moral dilemmas that involve carefully weighing whether the principle of beneficence as it is practically applied justifies compromising respect for autonomy. For example, states regulate who can and cannot drive and typically have medical review procedures for individuals who have incurred a significant change in their health. After a stroke, a person still possesses a valid driver's license unless it has been revoked, so the psychologist may have no legal standing to tell Mr. James not to drive given that there is no national standard for clinical driving assessment (Schultheis, Hillary, & Chute, 2003). This recommendation is instead based predominantly on the ethical decision-making process. The psychologist needs to understand state guidelines regarding patient evaluation for recision of a license to reestablish congruence between her ethical and legal–social responsibility. In addition, familial involvement is not legally sanctioned unless the patient is shown to be incompetent in one or more areas of decision making or gives consent for the family to participate in care. In this case, the limits of understanding one's situation may present a practical question of whether the patient has capacity to make a truly informed decision.

Relevant Context and Key Stakeholders

Mr. James had a stroke doing what he loves, being a hard-driving, successful individual who cares about his company, his colleagues, and his family. The stroke has placed the family and his company in turmoil. The psychologist has to assess the impact of the stroke indirectly (on social and financial welfare) and directly (on Mr. James's psychological and physical health), particularly given that this type of medical insult can occur concurrently with aging effects on cognition (MacDonald, Hultsch, & Dixon, 2003). To do so effectively, Dr. Barnstorm has to understand Mr. James's health status and his preferences. She is obliged to weigh carefully the bioethical principles of beneficence, nonmaleficence, and respect for autonomy. In addition, she has to consider the principle of justice as it relates to her social responsibilities if Mr. James expresses interest in engaging in risky activities that may prove harmful to others. Dr. Barnstorm has the opportunity to garner other professional resources to assist her, both at the rehabilitation center and with Dr. Longely.

The following individuals were critical to case resolution.

Patient (Wilbur James). Mr. James not only thrives on both the power and the success afforded by his position as CEO but also feels a great sense of responsibility to his employees and customers, most of whom have met him.

Because Mr. James has always been a hard-driving individual, he has been intimately involved in all major company decisions and has a very difficult time giving up control. The impact of the stroke, particularly his impulsive behavior, poor safety judgment, and rejection of his wife's assistance, threatens his entire persona and negatively affects his relationship with his wife and colleagues. During the initial psychology session, he seems unwilling to change his expressed behavior to control his life and make decisions independently of his wife.

Psychologist (Dr. Sarah Barnstorm). Dr. Barnstorm has extensive professional experience but must be careful not to bias her interpretation of Mr. James's presentation on the basis of "that familiar ring." Her working assumption (based on the interview and presenting symptoms) is that Mr. James needs familial assistance to understand and cope with the effects of his stroke; therefore, Mrs. James should be involved in any plan developed. She also believes, on the basis of her knowledge of stroke rehabilitation, that Mr. James can expect additional symptom improvement beyond the current level experienced. This knowledge will weigh into her treatment planning.

Patient's Spouse (Noreen James). Noreen James has been at her husband's side since his stroke. She is very frustrated by the negative changes she has witnessed in her spouse. She feels rejected by him and does not know how to help. However, she is willing to do whatever it takes to help her husband maximize his recovery.

Physician (Dr. Heather Longely). Dr. Longely is only peripherally involved in the case as Dr. Barnstorm proceeds. She fully supports the psychological intervention and has had a good working relationship with the psychologist who already consults to her practice. She expects to be fully informed regarding the treatment plan for Mr. James and plans to play a key role in monitoring that plan.

Case Resolution

Seek Consent and Conduct a Neuropsychological Evaluation

To determine the effects of the stroke on Mr. James's cognitive function, Dr. Barnstorm ordered a comprehensive neuropsychological evaluation conducted by a psychometrist. When soliciting consent for this evaluation, she included both Mr. and Mrs. James. Given that Dr. Barnstorm was not confident of the evaluation's outcome, Mrs. James would be the next legally recognized individual who could make decisions on Mr. James's behalf. Mr. James was initially reluctant to agree to assessment but was then challenged by his wife. She intimated that he must suspect he would not do well. She basically used his own need to demonstrate competence to compel him to agree. The neuropsychological examination supported visual-attentional and organizational problems, poor planning, difficulty with abstract reasoning, and mildly disinhibited responding. Both verbal and visual recall and fine motor coordination were average, although perhaps lower than would be expected given Mr. James's level of education (master's degree) and avocation.

Conduct a Functional Assessment

The neuropsychological exam was helpful in understanding the component skills that comprise Mr. James's risk-taking behaviors (e.g., general reasoning and visual-perceptual skills). However, Dr. Barnstorm did not consider this exam sufficient in assessing Mr. James's ability to reject any treatment and in determining risk because of its lack of specificity. She therefore conducted a complementary functional assessment that included three parts. First, she asked Mr. James very specific questions regarding his understanding of his capabilities, his level of awareness of risky behaviors he had already engaged in, alternative actions he might have considered, and the potential consequences of each. Second, she referred Mr. James for an in-car driving evaluation through a program jointly offered by the psychology and occupational therapy departments at the outpatient rehabilitation center. Third, she conducted an in vivo work evaluation along with the rehabilitation counselor.

The results of the functional assessment indicated that Mr. James could state the potential consequences of his actions (i.e., that he could hurt someone boating or driving and could do more harm than good in returning to work), but he was adamant that these events would not happen to him because of his vigilance. He expressed that he did not see the need to contemplate alternative plans and refused to do so when encouraged to try. When confronted with the difficulties already observed by others, he minimized these observations. Mr. James was able to state the risks of lack of follow-up to his stroke and of not following his medical regimen.

The in-car evaluation suggested that he had continuing mild problems with visual inattention and impulsivity with lane changes. His reaction time and ability to follow directions (even though he had never done so before his stroke) were fine. The therapists believed that with further resolution of the noted deficits within the next one to two months Mr. James would be able to begin driving.

The results of the work assessment revealed what had happened the day he came home frustrated. Apparently, Mr. James had incorrectly interpreted a report on the profit margin of a new product line and had called the other company to begin negotiating a deal when his partner came in and stopped him. He did not acknowledge the mistake but instead blamed the "bad numbers" on an employee who had developed the spreadsheet. The partner indicated this impulsive deal making was highly uncharacteristic of Wilbur.

On the basis of the results of the assessment, Dr. Barnstorm concluded that Mr. James did not appear to have the capacity for treatment refusal as it relates to driving or return to work because he did not clearly understand the consequences of his behavior, which he should have been able to understand given his education and experience. In the case of return to driving, she reasoned that although the likelihood of harm was low (accident may not occur), the risk was so high (if accident occurred injury was likely to patient or others) she needed to intervene. In the case of return to work, the risk and magnitude were less clear until Dr. Barnstorm learned of the incident at work. However, as discussed in the next section, she chose to manage this concern while Mr. James did, in fact, return to work. In the final area of concern (managing health care decisions), Mr. James appeared to have the capacity to make health care decisions regarding management of the medical aspects of his stroke.

Review Results and Treatment Plan With Patient

Wilbur was incensed at the results of the psychological evaluation; however, he remained for the entire session as Dr. Barnstorm reviewed each recommendation with him and Noreen. Dr. Barnstorm began by emphasizing that Mr. James was very early in his recovery and that she clearly expected further gains, particularly given the recovery curve to date. She expressed her belief that he would be able to return to both work and driving but that he would have to use his determination to help him reach those goals. Dr. Barnstorm recommended (a) a driving reevaluation approximately one month after occupational therapy addressed impulsivity and visual inattention, (b) a work reentry plan, and (c) psychotherapy.

The vocational plan included Wilbur's returning immediately to his place of employment. The rationale was that Wilbur would likely choose to go to work anyway, and it would be very difficult for anyone to prevent him from doing so. Therefore, the least restrictive intervention was to attempt to have him agree to work part time with a job coach who would address the impact of his cognitive and behavioral deficits on his work responsibilities. He was to work only a few hours a day (3–4 hours at first), and he would review organizational projects assigned with the psychologist in biweekly meetings. Psychotherapy was recommended weekly initially to address coping issues and role changes in the family.

Enlist Assistance of Dr. Longely

Dr. Barnstorm solicited the medical paperwork required to prevent Mr. James from driving. She asked Dr. Longely to complete this paperwork and to discuss the reason for it with Mr. James. Dr. Longely would also be the one deciding when to sign medical release papers for Mr. James to return to work. Therefore, working closely together on Mr. James's level of progress was critical.

Case Disposition

Dr. Barnstorm used the fact that Mr. James could lose his license as a motivator to agree to therapy focusing on driving skills. Mrs. James kept the car and boat keys to prevent an impulsive action by her husband to operate a motor vehicle independently. Regular boating trips were arranged with a friend who also had a boat so that the social enjoyment around this hobby was not lost. The paperwork was never filed with the Department of Motor Vehicles because the health care team expected Mr. James would be able to drive before that paperwork would be processed. This turned out to be correct.

Mrs. James was critical in convincing her husband to attend psychotherapy. Although initially not well engaged, over a two-week period his insight related to his deficits substantially improved, and he more actively participated in the entire treatment plan. His marriage stabilized as both he and Mrs. James improved their knowledge and coping skills regarding the impact of the stroke on their lives. However, they continued to struggle with Mr. James's loss of status at work and therefore, his self-esteem. Mrs. James felt she had to provide much more emotional support than anticipated, and she struggled to balance her needs with his. The effects of stroke commonly challenge familial structure and role identification, as Mr. and Mrs. James were experiencing (Palmer & Glass, 2003).

Work reentry remained the most problematic area. Mr. James refused a job coach, but he did agree to work closely with his executive vice president, John Davis. Mr. Davis was the one who stopped Mr. James from making the bad deal with another company. Dr. Barnstorm met with Mr. Davis to discuss the cognitive concerns, the impulsive behavior, and recommendations regarding structuring Mr. James's workday. Mr. Davis convinced Mr. James to start slow and to let one of the vice presidents handle all executive board meetings until he received medical clearance to come back to work full time. Although the psychologist could have forced the issue of not being medically fit for work, she chose to let Mr. James experience failure with the hope that this would have a positive effect on his low level of insight regarding his work performance. However, problems continued with inconsistent planning, impulsive behavior, and temper outbursts. Dr. Longely prescribed tegretol to manage his affect, and Dr. Barnstorm increased therapy sessions to one time per week for four weeks, at which point Mr. James appeared to stabilize. Eventually, Mr. James stepped aside as CEO (was actually voted out), but remained on the board.

Additional Commentary

To justify her paternalistic approach, Dr. Barnstorm had to show that Mr. James's capacity was compromised in some manner and that the consequences of respecting his autonomy would be risk of substantial harm. To determine this, Dr. Barnstorm had to carefully assess what Mr. James understood regarding the consequences of his decisions. If he recognized the consequences and still chose to drive or return to work prematurely, he might be making an informed, albeit unwise, choice, which is his right to make. Dr. Barnstorm would have to respect this right.

This case illustrates several important points. First, capacity is not simply a dichotomy with incompetence. It is a functional assessment that is focused on specific areas of decision making. Second, risk–harm assessment must necessarily incorporate capacity as well as patient preferences as part of the cognitive equation. It must also consider the likelihood that any intervention on the part of the provider will make a difference. Third, a provider should not override the patient's right to self-determination based solely on the benefit gained unless the likelihood of substantial harm is grounded in evidence that extends beyond clinical opinion. In addition, the alternative that is the least restrictive of the patient's autonomy should be favored. Banja (1994) criticized health care professionals for being overly paternalistic and clearly argued that the burden of demonstrating that patients' actions reflect excessive risk rests with the provider. In this case, there was clear risk (based on the patient's actions and reports) and potentially substantial harm, which provided justification for the psychologist's actions.

CASE 4.2
RESOLVING REQUESTS FOR THIRD-PARTY OBSERVERS

P. J. Shrugg, a 37-year-old woman, was referred by her primary care physician for an outpatient comprehensive functional capacities evaluation (FCE) two years post multitrauma injury, which included a mild traumatic brain injury (TBI). Dr. Iris Blufeld was to perform the psychological assessment portion of the FCE, funded through Workers' Compensation, in her clinical assessment laboratory. Dr. Blufeld was affiliated with Methane Springs Health Center in Solaris, Florida. The timing of the evaluation was linked to Ms. Shrugg's vocational rehabilitation intervention plan.

Two years earlier, Ms. Shrugg was driving a delivery van owned by her employer, Whiffenkauf Fertilizer Company, when she was T-boned at a rural intersection by a John Deere tractor. The driver, who was not injured, had slid through a stop sign. Because the weather was stormy and visibility poor, the driver was not cited. Ms. Shrugg was in a coma for 16 hours. She had a Glasgow Coma Scale (GCS) score of 7 at the scene and 9 in the ER at Rattlesnake Creek Community Hospital in Solaris. The GCS scores improved steadily throughout the first day in the intensive care unit (ICU), and then the patient awakened, amnestic for the accident but otherwise not confused. A neurobehavioral screening measure administered in the ICU by a consulting psychologist revealed lower than average scores only on the memory portion of the exam. Neuroimaging revealed no hemorrhagic lesions and no midline shift. No further neuropsychological assessment was performed. The neurological diagnosis was mild TBI with a good recovery anticipated.

The next morning Ms. Shrugg underwent surgery for her orthopedic injuries, including both a lower and an upper extremity fracture (left upper arm open reduction internal fixation non-weight-bearing and right ankle external fixation). Recovery was uneventful. Ms. Shrugg was transferred to a subacute program in a nursing home in nearby Brighton, Florida, for orthopedic management on the fifth day postinjury. Four days later, she went home. P. J. received outpatient speech therapy for several weeks to address mild episodic memory dysfunction. Having reached her goals, she returned to work at the fertilizer plant six weeks postinjury.

In the intervening two years, Ms. Shrugg lost her job at the fertilizer plant because of problems with attendance, distractibility, and temper management. She had tried in vain to hold down similar delivery jobs but could not consistently maintain her attendance. Additionally, she got into altercations with both fellow workers and supervisors. Temper dyscontrol, a problem that had only mildly affected her social and family life before the accident, had begun to spill over into her work. Ms. Shrugg had previously repeatedly refused psychological intervention sponsored by the Department of Workers' Compensation (DWC) to assist with job stability. At the time of the outpatient evaluation, Ms. Shrugg was unemployed, living only off disability payments. This sole source of income was under utilization review by the DWC system.

The day before the psychological evaluation, Dr. Blufeld received an unannounced visit from Ms. Shrugg's attorney, Jackson Grant, JD, PhD (counseling psychology degree, not licensed to practice). The gist of the introduction was that Dr. Grant had observed the physical portion of the FCE, and he wanted to be included in the psychological assessment.

Dr. Blufeld objected, "Dr. Grant, I have serious reservations about the unpredictable effects of in-person observation on my patient's performance. Those effects might not be adequately controlled in the testing session, making the data invalid."

Dr. Grant countered, "Come, come, Dr. Blufeld, surely you don't suggest that I would distract my client?" Pausing for a moment, the attorney added, "You are aware, doctor, that I too am trained as a psychologist."

Dr. Blufeld responded, as calmly as she could, "I am aware that you've had psychological training, and I assume that you are knowledgeable regarding issues of test validity. However, I seriously doubt that my generating questionable data would help your client."

Reconsidering his position, Dr. Grant smiled broadly and offered, "I understand your concerns, doctor. Let me counter by arranging a digital video recording of the test session. Jamie, my video technician would have to set it up, but once the recording was started he could leave."

Before the psychologist could continue voicing her objections, the lawyer leaned forward in his seat, arms spread in a pleading gesture and added, "My client's behavioral performance during testing will be offered into evidence to demonstrate the seriousness of her continuing debilitation." Then, the emotional tone of his voice changed. Dr. Grant sat back, crossed his legs, and adopted the air of a confident but determined adversary, "As a matter of course, I will also monitor your test administration technique for adherence to standardized procedures." Abruptly smiling again, the attorney finished, "Dr. Blufeld, I must inform you that I have the approval of Judge Knoll to obtain such a record; he will be sitting on this case."

Relevant Ethical Principles and Standards

Principle A: Beneficence and Nonmaleficence

Dr. Blufeld is aware that the presence of an observer, including a recording device, is a deviation from the standardized administration procedures on which interpretations are based. These deviations could threaten the validity of the test results, thus harming Ms. Shrugg's chances for receiving appropriately targeted services. The observation, for example, could increase Ms. Shrugg's inattentiveness, resulting in an overestimation of disability. Dr. Blufeld must guard against preventable actions that jeopardize a valid test session. Therefore, if she believes harm outweighs the benefit of permitting an observer or recording device, she should take reasonable steps to prevent such observation.

Principle B: Fidelity and Responsibility

Dr. Blufeld has a responsibility to cooperate with other professionals and institutions to the extent needed to serve Ms. Shrugg's best interests. However, because Dr. Blufeld has a social responsibility regarding test management as well as an obligation to manage conflicts counter to Ms. Shrugg's best interests, she must determine whether to challenge the attorney's and judge's position.

Principle C: Integrity

If Dr. Blufeld believes that providing the psychological assessment under the conditions of observation jeopardizes Ms. Shrugg's best interests, she must consider whether she is making an unwise commitment to provide such an evaluation.

Principle D: Justice

Dr. Blufeld needs to ensure the integrity of the test materials for valid future use with other individuals. Is test integrity threatened because a recording device is present? Similarly, inappropriate test interpretation (by not addressing observer influences) can result in unjust allocation of resources to Ms. Shrugg, who might receive incorrect or unnecessary services. If a test observer ultimately is allowed, Dr. Blufeld needs to clearly address the observer's effects on Ms. Shrugg's performance.

Standard 1.01, Misuse of Psychologists' Work

Introduction of a recording device increases the potential for misinterpretation of test data by untrained individuals. Dr. Blufeld needs to take reasonable steps to reduce the chances of her evaluation being misused.

Standard 1.02, Conflicts Between Ethics and Law, Regulations, or Other Governing Legal Authority

If Dr. Blufeld's ethical obligations conflict with legal demands, she must attempt to resolve the matter responsibly, adhere to the requirements of the law, or withdraw from the case.

Standard 3.09, Cooperation With Other Professionals

Dr. Blufeld has a responsibility to work with other involved parties to establish an acceptable compromise that satisfies everyone's needs. In doing so, Dr. Blufeld is obligated to educate the attorney and judge regarding her reservations on the basis of consensual professional opinion about observation of psychological testing.

Standard 4.01, Maintaining Confidentiality

If a legal request exists that conflicts with what Dr. Blufeld believes is appropriate protection of records (i.e., test materials or data), under this ethical standard she must take reasonable steps to put safeguards in place to maximize confidentiality. This should occur prior to releasing test data under the circumstances of the legal mandate.

Standard 4.03, Recording

If recording of the psychological assessment occurs, Dr. Blufeld must ensure that appropriate consent has been obtained. A signed release should not be considered sufficient; Dr. Blufeld needs to ensure the patient understands the risks associated with any recorded material (e.g., limited test validity, qualified interpretation, availability of detailed record of performance that is not typically accessible by others, and potential effect on expert testimony).

Standard 4.05, Disclosures

Dr. Blufeld must respect Ms. Shrugg's right to privacy and confidentiality and must disclose any test summaries or recorded material only as dictated by informed consent of the patient and the law in this case.

Standard 6.01, Documentation of Professional and Scientific Work and Maintenance of Records

Dr. Blufeld must document any deviation from standardized procedures in her professional record to both facilitate future accurate use and allow replication if needed.

Standard 9.03, Informed Consent in Assessments

At this point, the client's position regarding testing is unclear. Dr. Blufeld must inform Ms. Shrugg of the potential risks of any deviations from standardized testing procedures, especially those associated with the presence of observers. Dr. Blufeld can tie these concerns to Ms. Shrugg's previously exhibited behavior (i.e., temper dyscontrol and inattentiveness). Threats to privacy and confidentiality also must be discussed in this context, particularly with recording the evaluation and release of materials to outside parties. Dr. Blufeld must be careful to present the facts and not excessively influence the patient's decision on the basis of the psychologist's own biases regarding observation.

Standard 9.04, Release of Test Data

Ms. Shrugg's test data must be safeguarded except from those to whom she authorizes release and those allowed access by law. By consenting to observation or recording, she would be consenting to at least limited disclosure of her raw test data.

Standard 9.06, Interpreting Assessment Results

Dr. Blufeld must report any reservations about the accuracy of the results obtained with nonstandardized test administration, such as with observation. She must thoroughly consider and observe the potential impact of Ms. Shrugg's behavioral pattern, including temper regulation problems and distractibility, on test completion.

Standard 9.11, Maintaining Test Security

Dr. Blufeld needs to anticipate that the attorney may follow up the assessment session with more intrusive requests, such as release of test protocols. Without a court order, Dr. Blufeld must not release test materials, such as manuals, instruments, or stimuli. In addition, recording an evaluation, depending on restrictions placed on the use of such recordings, may violate this standard, particularly as it relates to test questions.

Institutional and Legal Concepts That May Apply

Copyright laws obviously affect the release of test materials under nonadjudicated circumstances. Observation and recording laws are not as pervasive. In a few states, the right to have independent examinations observed or recorded has been determined by statute. In other cases, a judge may make the determination. Three possible goals in making such requests are (a) to ensure that an appropriate and fair examination is performed; (b) to ensure appropriate client participation; and (c) to vividly demonstrate to the court the nature and extent of the plaintiff's cognitive, emotional, or behavioral difficulties. The goals of recording Ms. Shrugg's evaluation are both to ensure appropriate testing procedures and to use the recordings as evidence in a legal disability proceeding.

Relevant Context and Key Stakeholders

Dr. Blufeld called the DWC for clarification regarding the evaluation request. The in-house attorney noted that in recent years, functional capacity evaluations have been routinely observed and videotaped when requests have gone through Judge Knoll's court. Because the physical portion of the FCE has been observed, the attorney now has the expectation of viewing all sections of the evaluation. Dr. Blufeld knows that having an attorney with doctoral training in psychology as an observer does not likely pose a threat to test security. However, the attorney is not an active member of APA and is not licensed to practice psychology in the state. Dr. Grant is requesting the observation in his role as attorney, not as psychologist. Although Dr. Grant is familiar with and could respect the APA Ethics Code, he is not technically bound by the Ethics Code to safeguard such test materials. The psychologist also is aware of the social facilitation literature that, although not identical to the testing situation, indicates that having an observer present can influence test results (Guerin, 1986).

The following parties were considered when determining steps needed to protect the patient's welfare and the integrity of the testing situation.

Patient (P. J. Shrugg). P. J. appears willing to go along with her attorney's plan for evidence gathering. She sees the case and her attorney as the keys to maintaining her disability income. She is unaware of the risks inherent in observed psychological evaluation and relies on the psychologist to provide a balanced view of the benefits and risks.

Department of Workers' Compensation. The DWC attempts to follow policies and procedures regarding provision of client services. The agency is sensitive to the political situation vis-à-vis the judge and implications for future clients' cases. The DWC does not want to challenge Judge Knoll's decision regarding observation given that psychological evaluation is part of the FCE.

Attorney (Dr. Jackson Grant). Dr. Grant desires to present legal arguments and evidence that strengthen Ms. Shrugg's case for disability. He also wants to gather evidence regarding a potential challenge to the competency of testimony (i.e., the psychologist's ability to administer tests), if needed. He approaches this from a knowledgeable perspective. There exists a procedural precedent within the Methane Springs Health Center: He had free and unchallenged access to observational data from the physical portion of the FCE.

Psychologist (Dr. Iris Blufeld). Dr. Blufeld wants to fulfill her contractual role to the DWC by providing valid test results based on accepted testing standards. She has limited familiarity with the literature on third-party observers. She desires to protect patient confidentiality and to ensure informed consent. She is concerned that observation and recording increase the likelihood of problematic patient behavior occurring, compressing the patient's true capacity to perform.

Court (Judge Knoll). Judge Knoll allows the plan of the attorney to go forward, persuaded by the argument that observational evidence is important in documenting level of impairment, which directly bears on the upcoming legal proceeding.

Facility (Methane Springs Health Center). Because facility administrators allowed observation of the physical therapy component of the FCE, they seem to endorse such a practice standard. However, the managers have not been educated on the differences in physical and psychological evaluation environments, and they have a stake in protecting the clinical environments of their employees from external influence. Any policies and procedures related to external observation of clinical activities should have been reviewed for consistency across disciplines, which has not occurred.

Case Resolution

Clearly Identify the Issues

Dr. Blufeld identified the primary issues to be considered as (a) the need to safeguard test materials to minimize opportunity for subsequent misuse; (b) the potential impact of deviation from standardized test administration procedures on comparisons of examinee's scores to those of normative groups; (c) the potential, but ill-defined, impact of the observers on Ms. Shrugg's performance, particularly given her behavioral history; (d) threats to her privacy should recordings of her performance become available; (e) the potential risk and benefit to Ms. Shrugg of having the court see first-hand the severity of her deficits; and finally (f) the importance for both the patient and the DWC of cooperating with Dr. Grant and Judge Knoll.

Determine Professional Position

Dr. Blufeld reviewed several prominent sources of literature (see the section Additional Commentary in this chapter), which generally supported her position to prevent third-party observation.

Clarify Ms. Shrugg's Consent

Dr. Blufeld met with Ms. Shrugg prior to testing to ensure she understood the ramifications of her originally signed consent form. Ms. Shrugg, as a competent adult, had to be informed of the issues being discussed, including both the potential benefits and the drawbacks of her testing being observed or recorded. She consented to the observation.

Depending on her degree of cognitive impairment, Ms. Shrugg might not fully appreciate the potential benefits and risks and may feel pulled in opposing directions, thus resulting in increased emotional distress. If that had been the case, Dr. Blufeld may have argued for a delay in the evaluation in order for procedural challenges to be settled and for Ms. Shrugg to consider appropriate social support in evaluating her decision.

Clarify Position With the Attorney and Court

Dr. Blufeld had to make known her reservations about having the psychological evaluation observed or recorded, educating all parties on the reasons for her reluctance. Dr. Grant had already demonstrated a willingness to negotiate the manner in which the observation would occur by modifying his request from direct observation to video recording. It was possible that he would negotiate further given that Dr. Blufeld conveyed an appreciation of Dr. Grant's needs for gathering case information. Dr. Grant was willing to do so, as noted in the Case Disposition section in this chapter.

Contact the Test Publisher

The psychologist contacted the test publisher (holder of the copyright) to inform the company of possible inadvertent release of secure test materials and procedures. The publisher's legal department contacted the judge for consultation prior to the hearing date to express concerns regarding potential copyright infringement.

Offer Alternatives for Observation

Dr. Blufeld offered to demonstrate her competence in administering tests without compromising the evaluation. She suggested an alternate technique: allow video recording of functionally oriented tasks that would perhaps have more face validity to the court than observing Ms. Shrugg trying to learn "meaningless" words. This approach would allow the court to see whether she struggled to perform tasks that most individuals would find routine.

Case Disposition

Dr. Blufeld met with Attorney Grant and Judge Knoll. She explained all of the relevant considerations, supported by the position papers and guidelines available from professional organizations. Dr. Grant, being trained as a psychologist, was aware of many of the issues but not all of them. He had not considered some of the potential alternatives that Dr. Blufeld presented. Judge Knoll was impressed by the degree that Dr. Blufeld seemed to have done her homework on the issue and admired her conviction. He agreed that her proposals had merit.

Together, the trio of professionals developed a plan to observe the clinical interview portion of the evaluation and have test results and reports peer reviewed. They agreed to then have Dr. Blufeld engage Ms. Shrugg in psychological tasks of the psychologist's devising for video recording to illustrate to the court the patient's success or difficulty on functional tasks. Dr. Blufeld and Dr. Grant then met with Ms. Shrugg and described the plan, including potential benefits and risks, allowed her the opportunity to ask questions, and sought her consent, which was provided.

Additional Commentary

If there had been a refusal to negotiate further, Dr. Blufeld would have considered seeking a court order to protect the recording per the reasons previously explained, with the recording returned to her following completion of legal proceedings. If the court did not agree to this type of stipulation or ruled that a third-party observer could be present during the examination, Dr. Blufeld might have offered counsel the option to observe an interview. She might also have subsequent testing records reviewed by a qualified psychologist to form opinions. If the attorney and court were still unwilling to accept any of the offered compromises, Dr. Blufeld would have needed to decide whether to refuse to complete the evaluation.

This case illustrates that disagreement can exist between psychological and legal interests regarding the appropriateness of observing or recording psychological evaluations. Furthermore, there is some disagreement within the profession of psychology. Part of the disagreement between psychologists and attorneys and courts has been due to a lack of education about the reasons psychological evaluations should not be observed or recorded (e.g., justice to future users and situational influences). The other part of the disagreement within the ranks of psychologists has been due to the relative paucity of studies examining the effects of observers on test performance.

Recent literature on the topic has generally supported the inappropriateness of third-party observers (Sweet, Grote, & van Gorp, 2002). Constantinou, Ashendorf, and McCaffrey (2002) found that having a recording device present during neuropsychological testing had a negative effect on cognitive test performance. Further, position papers by professional organizations reinforce the inappropriateness of having involved third parties observe medico-legal psychological evaluations (American Academy of Clinical Neuropsychology, 2001; National Academy of Neuropsychology Policy and Planning Committee, 2000). Although the section of the APA Ethics Code related specifically to forensic activities was deleted, specific standards were dispersed throughout the 2002 Ethics Code in relevant sections. Finally, the "Specialty Guidelines for Forensic Psychologists" (Committee on Ethical Guidelines for Forensic Psychologists, 1991) and the *Stan-*

dards for Educational and Psychological Testing (American Educational Research Association, American Psychological Association, & National Council on Measurement in Education, 1999) remain excellent resources for concerns such as these.

Of course, nothing is absolute. Third-party observation is sometimes necessary to serve specific subpopulations such as people with sensory deficits who use interpreters. Legitimate situations will arise that challenge the scope of acceptable practice (Wilde et al., 2002). Competent psychologists, like Dr. Blufeld, will approach these situations in a deliberate, thoughtful, and ultimately defensible manner using available resources and practice standards to clarify their position.

CASE 4.3
RESPONDING TO PATIENTS WORKING THE SYSTEM

Skip Ronson, a 26-year-old driver for a large parcel delivery company, was injured the week before Christmas while loading his truck. He had placed a package on one of the truck's higher shelves when he lost his balance, fell backward, and strained his back. He also bumped the back of his head against another cardboard box. Skip did not experience any dizziness, confusion, or loss of consciousness, but coworkers observed him complaining of considerable back pain. An ambulance was called, and Skip was taken to the local emergency department. It was a familiar ride, as this was not the first work-related accident Skip had experienced.

To be sure, Skip was upset by his injury; it promised to keep him out of the Southern California Holiday Classic, a competitive surfing tournament. He had been training since the Thanksgiving Surfing Championships, in which he placed just outside the group of elite professional competitors. It was Skip's dream to someday win such a tournament and sign a lucrative contract with a surfwear sponsor. Then, he could spend the next 20 years traveling the world in search of the perfect ride. Now, Skip's dream had to be postponed. Skip was also upset that he might miss the holiday overtime required to serve all those shopping procrastinators.

In the emergency room, Skip underwent X-rays of his lower back. He was diagnosed with "likely soft tissue damage," prescribed a mild narcotic analgesic for pain, encouraged to follow up with his primary care physician, and sent home. Later that week, he saw his primary care physician, Dr. Del Ray. Dr. Ray conducted a thorough interview and physical examination.

During the interview, Skip tearfully reported a myriad of problems, "Dr. Ray, I can't begin to tell you the problems this new injury has caused; much worse than last time. If only I hadn't gone in to work . . ." Dr. Ray inquired, "I didn't notice anything unusual in the hospital discharge summary. What types of problems, Skip?"

Without a moment's pause, Skip continued, "Well, sometimes I can't feel my feet. And my hands tingle and burn. I drop little stuff now and then . . . you know . . . pens, eating utensils . . . that kind of stuff." He paused, dramatically gathering himself.

"Yes, go on," Dr. Ray encouraged, dutifully taking notes, eyes frantically scanning Skip's chart for some hint of neurological etiology.

Skip added, "My head hurts, not just where that box cracked my skull but all over. I can't sleep. Just thinking about that terrible fall and the pain . . . it freaks me out!" The physician looked up from the chart. Skip's eyes opened wide, reminding Dr. Ray of a frightened child.

Skip continued, "My memory . . . what were we . . . Oh yeah, my memory is shot. I can't learn anything new. Just yesterday, I forgot why I'd gone to the grocery store. It took me 20 minutes, some heavy-duty caffeine, and a glazed donut to figure out why I was there." Pleading with his physician, voice trembling, "Dr. Ray, I think I'm losing my mind and body. I'm really scared!"

Dr. Ray attempted to console his distressed patient, writing an additional prescription for a benzodiazepine to treat anxiety. He assured Skip that he would communicate his reported health concerns to the professionals to whom he was planning referrals. Skip thanked Dr. Ray for his thoroughness. The physician referred Skip to various specialists with whom Skip had worked after a previous back injury a few years earlier.

Once home from Dr. Ray's visit, Skip made appointments with his physical therapist, acupuncturist, massage therapist, chiropractor, neurologist, orthopedist, psychologist, and most important (to Skip anyway), Susan Moore, an attorney who had successfully litigated his previous accident. Ms. Moore worked her magic once again, this time with Workers' Compensation. The Workers' Compensation case manager, who was relatively new and overly sympathetic to the woes of her clients, provided written authorization for all of Skip's treatment. This decision ultimately resulted in her spending the new year looking for a different job.

After securing Workers' Compensation's authorization for services, Skip contacted Sanford Beech, the clinical psychologist who briefly saw him for pain management after his first injury. Dr. Beech was glad to hear of Skip's successful recovery during the intervening years and stated that he was glad to see Skip again, even under such trying circumstances. Given Skip's dramatic description of what happened at work, Dr. Beech felt it was important that he conduct a very thorough evaluation.

Dr. Beech obtained and reviewed Dr. Ray's records, conducted his own clinical interview, and administered a battery of tests. During the clinical interview, Skip endorsed nearly all of the symptoms about which Dr. Beech inquired. (In fact, the only symptom he did not endorse was sexual dysfunction, a symptom to which he replied, "Dr. B, this surfer dude's a hang ten.") The psychologist also administered personality and cognitive tests. Despite voicing pain and distress, Skip appeared to put forth good effort on the tests.

On the standardized self-administered personality inventory, Skip endorsed numerous items rarely endorsed by most patient populations. He also indicated experiencing numerous somatic symptoms along with high levels of anxiety.

Cognitive testing revealed greater item failure than Dr. Beech would have anticipated based on the nature of the accident. For example, on a list-learning task, Skip initially did well, but his performance declined on subsequent learning trials. Delayed free recall was average, but cued recall was severely impaired. Yes and no recognition was average, but Skip missed four on a forced-choice recognition component. Other apparent "inconsistencies" were noted throughout the test battery. Although Dr. Beech did not question Skip's apparent suffering, to be thorough, he administered a specific measure of response validity that involved immediate recall and graphomotor reproduction of shapes. Skip performed with 100% accuracy on that measure.

Dr. Beech reported back to Skip's primary care physician, attorney, and the Workers' Compensation carrier that Skip had sustained a mild TBI, post-traumatic stress, and an emotional adjustment disorder as a result of his work-related accident. He reported that the inconsistencies noted on certain tests reflected Skip's brain injury, physical pain, fatigue, emotional distress, and the possible effects of pain medications. He pointed to Skip's performance on the response validity measure to support his position that Skip was not malingering or otherwise fabricating or exaggerating symptoms. Finally, Dr. Beech estimated that Skip had an 80% permanent disability and was in need of immediate psychotherapeutic treatment. A separate plan for treatment was submitted along with the evaluation.

On receiving Dr. Beech's report, the new (and more experienced) claims representative at the Workers' Compensation carrier scheduled Independent Medical Examinations (IMEs) with all of the disciplines Skip saw as well as some Skip had not yet considered. After reviewing the evaluative data, Dr. Sally Slade (an IME psychologist) disagreed with Dr. Beech's opinion. She reported to Workers' Compensation that she believed Skip was malingering. She cited his test-response inconsistencies, the dramatic difference between his self-report and neurological findings, potential financial gain, and the scientific literature to support her position.

Relevant Ethical Principles and Standards

Principle A: Beneficence and Nonmaleficence

The disagreement between the psychologists' interpretations has significant implications for support or denial of a multitude of services and can also reinforce a particular response pattern by the patient. Although Dr. Beech conducted an objective evaluation of Skip's cognitive and emotional functioning, he may have inadequately interpreted evaluative data, contributing to inappropriate service provision. In addition, providing an estimate of both the degree and the permanence of a disabling condition at an acute stage in the natural course of recovery may have perpetuated the patient's dysfunctional behavioral pattern (i.e., sick role and seeking excessive services). Dr. Slade has a responsibility to reevaluate Skip before rendering an opinion, particularly given her suspicions and the implications of the diagnostic label of malingering on continuation of specific services.

Principle C: Integrity

Dr. Beech has an obligation to present Skip's psychological status accurately. He is culpable to the extent that he commits to provide services for which he is not adequately professionally prepared.

Principle D: Justice

Inadequate consultant reports may result in valuable limited health care resources being misallocated. Dr. Beech has a responsibility to represent his skills appropriately and to use psychologists with an understanding of the interplay between postconcussive behavior and pain complaints to prevent both misguided use of resources and damage to the credibility of psychology for future client referrals.

Standard 1.04, Informal Resolution of Ethical Violations

If Dr. Slade believes Dr. Beech is practicing outside his areas of competence, she is obligated to raise her concerns with Dr. Beech. If Dr. Beech responds appropriately, these concerns should be resolvable without formal review.

Standard 2.01, Boundaries of Competence

Dr. Beech is a clinical psychologist with focused expertise in chronic pain management. He lacks neuropsychological training. His reliance on a relatively insensitive measure of response validity and his inadequate interpretation of the rest of the cognitive and psychological test data suggest that either he is unknowingly ill-prepared to perform such evaluations with this population or his integrity is in question.

Standard 2.04, Bases for Scientific and Professional Judgments

Dr. Beech's conclusions should hold up to the scrutiny of the scientific literature regarding malingering. In this case, he would be hard pressed to present evidence from the psychological literature to defend his conclusions about Skip's cognitive and emotional functioning.

Standard 3.04, Avoiding Harm

Dr. Beech's mishandling of the evaluation, either intentionally or unintentionally, negatively affects Skip and the health care system. Dr. Beech has (a) inadvertently overpathologized someone with a questionable clinical presentation and (b) unknowingly reinforced a patient's manipulative, disingenuous, and illegal maneuver to obtain financial advantage and misuse health care services. Conversely, Dr. Slade must be reasonably confident in her interpretation of malingering given this term can have powerful and negative consequences for someone seeking health care. In addition, the patient's reported symptoms are not necessarily easily ruled out, and some may require treatment. If Dr. Slade only focuses on malingering, the patient may be denied needed services.

Standard 3.10, Informed Consent

As part of seeking informed consent, Dr. Beech and Dr. Slade must review the nature of the psychological evaluation. This does not require a direct reference to malingering but should include a statement indicating that tests are included to identify reduced patient effort and response consistency, which could affect the recommendations.

Standard 6.06, Accuracy in Reports to Payors and Funding Sources

Dr. Beech's report contains statements that an independent peer reviewer might find inaccurate or misleading. Such statements may complicate funding decisions.

Standard 9.02(a), Use of Assessments

Dr. Beech appears to have chosen appropriate measures and is presumed to have administered and scored them in a manner consistent with standardized procedures. However, he has not taken into account the timing of his evaluation or the potential effects of medication on cognitive function. He also may not have interpreted the results in a manner consistent with the research on which the measures were developed or on the findings of subsequent studies with relevant populations.

Standard 9.06, Interpreting Assessment Results

Dr. Beech appears, appropriately, to have taken into account the context in which the evaluation was performed, including the obvious secondary gain opportunities. However, instead of examining how this context influences his judgment, reduces the accuracy of his interpretations, and affects his behavioral objectivity, he appears to use the information to bias his opinions in favor of Skip and himself (if subsequent therapy is funded).

Institutional and Legal Concepts That May Apply

If Dr. Beech has intentionally filed inaccurate reports and submitted bills based on those reports, he is engaging in fraudulent behavior. However, allegations of such behavior are difficult to prove. Objective peer reviewers would likely disagree with Dr. Beech's analyses of the data as Dr. Slade did. However, there exist sufficient confounds in mild TBI and pain management literature (Nicholson, Martelli, & Zasler, 2001) to allow the practitioner to defend his behavior on the basis of differing philosophical opinions regarding the nature of the condition at issue and the uniqueness of the individual patient. Little is likely to be done legally to dissuade Dr. Beech from continuing this course of behavior. However, Dr. Beech would need to demonstrate he is practicing within his boundaries of competence, which is questionable. His inadequate assessment led to a diagnostic conclusion that could be considered a therapeutic error. In reality, the Workers' Compensation carrier may be unsophisticated in the subtleties of test interpretation and will either accept the questionable interpretation or refer the claimant for an independent psychological examination. However, Workers' Compensation could put into place procedures to identify a systematic pattern of ordering reevaluations to determine whether the costs associated with these evaluations are preventable (e.g., secondary to preventable error).

Relevant Context and Key Stakeholders

Six years earlier, while working for a competing delivery company, Skip had been struck by a truck as it slowly pulled away from the loading dock. He had bent down to pick up a dropped pen, obscuring him from the driver's view. As soon as the tire had run over Skip's left foot, pain signals reached Skip's brain. He screamed in pain and promptly stood back up, his back directly in the path of a piece of lumber hanging over the edge of the truck bed. It was clearly not Skip's day as he broke several bones. His luck brightened, however. As the result of litigation, Skip limped away with a sizeable settlement and spent the following two years surfing back to health along the coast of Baja, California. He learned there was money to be made when injury strikes. However, in his current situation, there appears to be minimal support for the plethora of services sought.

The following individuals were critical in weighing case information.

Patient (Skip Ronson). More than anything, Skip loves to surf. His personality neither recognizes nor accepts delayed gratification. Given the choice, he would prefer to surf in the Holiday Classic than to endure the long medicolegal process to award the money needed to retire to Fiji. His back pain, which is very distressing to him, has a physical basis. Not surprising, Skip prefers hefty doses of narcotic analgesics and anxiolytic (benzodiazepine) medication, finding that he is less upset when dosing in liberal amounts. He also notices that he has increased fatigue, mental slowing, and attention and memory problems on the medication, a linkage he fails to mention during the psychological evaluation. He may benefit from psychotherapy to address his adjustment-related dysphoria.

Psychologists (Dr. Sanford Beech and Dr. Sally Slade). Dr. Beech administers an adequate test battery and dutifully documents the symptoms Skip reports. Because of a combination of limited professional experience and a desire to help his patient and please the attorney, Dr. Beech attributes Skip's cognitive problems to hitting his head on the cardboard box. In addition, he rationalizes data inconsistencies and relies selectively on findings that support his conclusions. Dr. Slade, an experienced examiner, believes Dr. Beech's conclusions are incorrect. The inconsistencies in Skip's reported presentation and testing are simply too great not to consider malingering. Dr. Slade is angry at Dr. Beech for misrepresenting psychology.

Workers' Compensation Case Manager. The more experienced replacement case manager is distrustful of Dr. Beech's opinions on the basis of his previous experience with him. Because of Dr. Beech's connections to the medical consultants recommended by Dr. Ray, she is also distrustful of those other professionals. As a result, she schedules Skip for IMEs for all disciplines representing services Skip is receiving. She also adds physiatry and cardiology to establish a broader medical baseline from which to assess possible future claims.

Case Resolution

Conduct a Comprehensive Evaluation and Interpret Data

To sort malingering from other diagnoses one must collect data from multiple sources. Dr. Beech collected data via interview, chart review, and diverse test administration. He failed to make himself aware of information on normative performance with various populations. In addition, he repeated no portions of the examination to determine stability of responding, sometimes an issue in TBI and in acute pain management with narcotics. Dr. Beech reasoned that Skip's TBI must account for the inconsistencies in reporting given the validity scale results. However, Dr. Slade believed Dr. Beech did not appropriately weigh the context in which this evaluation was requested (i.e., Workers' Compensation claim and acute treatment in progress) and did not reconcile noted and marked inconsistencies in the data with available literature. In contrast, by taking these steps, Dr. Slade (on reviewing existing data) was confident in her finding that Skip was malingering. However, her focus on the label of malingering negatively biased the agency's decision regarding medical and psychological treatment for Skip's recurring back pain.

Provide Report to Appropriate Personnel

Dr. Beech and Dr. Slade appropriately reported findings to the Workers' Compensation carrier, the attorney, and to Mr. Ronson.

Plan to Contact Dr. Beech Regarding Inadequate Evaluation

Because Workers' Compensation was considered Dr. Slade's client, they believed they maintained influence over Dr. Slade's actions related to the case. Dr. Slade did not have consent from Mr. Ronson or the carrier to contact Dr. Beech, and further contact with the patient was prohibited. Dr. Slade discussed her concerns with the case manager and then spoke to the claims supervisor. Both stated that she should let the matter drop, as they were satisfied with the results of the IME. Besides, they did not want any suits for libel or defamation of character brought against the agency. Despite her distress over the bias evident in Dr. Beech's work, Dr. Slade felt her hands were tied and did not contact Dr. Beech.

Case Disposition

As typically happened with Dr. Beech's patients, the IME psychologist (Dr. Sally Slade) concluded that Skip Ronson was malingering and, therefore, was not in need of further cognitive or emotional evaluation or treatment. Consistent with Dr. Slade's recommendations, further psychological services for Skip were denied. By misattributing Skip's symptoms in an attempt to assist him, Dr. Beech's actions ultimately harmed his patient. One by one, IMEs resulted in the termination of Mr. Ronson's other medical services as well. He continued to receive the analgesics and anxiolytics through his primary care physician and his managed care health insurance. On the basis of the results of all of the IMEs, the disability case was dropped. Retirement plans sank, Skip Ronson opted to return to work, now driving under the influence of a risky combination of prescription pain medications. Dr. Beech was considered an eager-to-please plaintiff's expert and continued to receive referrals from the opportunistic attorney, Sue Moore.

Additional Commentary

Malingering can sometimes occur in the context of a very complex symptom presentation. It is important that the psychologist not minimize symptoms or make broad generalizations by assuming that all symptoms are the result of intentional misrepresentation of one's health for some secondary gain. To do so could result in an incomplete intervention and likely reoccurrence of the presenting problem. Comprehensive assessment and team management are key to offering an appropriate treatment plan to the overall benefit of the patient with complex symptomatology. In addition, correct diagnosis of malingering can prevent inappropriate distribution of resources toward undeserving individuals, supporting the bioethical principle of justice. Conversely, incorrect diagnosis can violate the principle of nonmaleficence by depriving deserving individuals of needed services, resulting in physical and psychological harm. Clinicians working with reha-bilitation populations must be aware of the possibility of malingering; must use techniques to adequately examine response validity; and must examine their own motivations, perspectives, and potential biases (Deiden & Bush, 2002; Sweet & Moulthrop, 1999). Failure to do so is suggestive of ethical misconduct.

Unfortunately, malingering can be challenging to identify in work-related-injury populations because it can overlay with symptoms supported by clear diagnostic evidence (Vanderploeg & Curtiss, 2001). In addition, situational demands can significantly affect patients' performance, which is particularly relevant for patients with mild TBI (Martelli, Bush, & Zasler, 2003). Provider knowledge of mild TBI can also overshadow the impact of pain on cognitive function (Nicholson et al., 2001). A comprehensive bat-tery in which converging sources of data are used is critical (Bordini, Chaknis, Ekman-Turner, & Perna, 2002). Clearly understanding any social and finan-cial system factors that might be underlying motives for feigning symptoms contributes to the differential diagnosis. In some cases, results of both effort and ability testing may be ambiguous, and greater reliance must be placed on nonpsychometric data (e.g., FCEs). One set of authors offers interesting com-mentary on the influence of coping style on pain perception and insurance adjusters' decisions to award compensation for disability claims (MacLeod, LaChapelle, Hadjistavropoulos, & Pfeifer, 2001). However, the data presented in this case would have led most clinicians to one conclusion, one that Dr. Beech did not embrace.

Had Dr. Beech confronted Skip about his suspicious response profile, Skip may have been open to reasonable treatment alternatives. Instead, Skip was denied needed services and was working under dangerous conditions. Dr. Slade contributed to this negative situation by placing her focus exclusively on the TBI question, ignoring the back injury and assuming malingering required no intervention other than confrontation. In addition, Dr. Slade failed to take reasonable steps to resolve the conflict with the DWC regard-ing Dr. Beech's professional competence, thereby jeopardizing future clients' welfare and the reputation of psychology.

Both psychologists' actions could be considered therapeutic errors. The collective cost of various types of errors is staggering. The Institute of Medi-cine (Kohn, Corrigan, & Donaldson, 2000) summarized data suggesting pre-ventable adverse events cost $17 billion per year. In addition, Dovey (2002) reported that errors in primary care differ from those in hospitals but are no less disconcerting. Of 330 errors reported by family practitioners in one study, approximately 14 % were clinical knowledge or skills errors such as misdiag-nosis and inappropriate treatment decisions. (Those remaining were attrib-uted to systems errors.) In addition to human error, adverse work conditions (e.g., high workload, inadequate supervision, inadequate fiscal resources, poor communication, and rapid change) may contribute to medical mistakes

(Rosner, Berger, Kark, Potash, & Bennett, 2000; Vincent, Taylor-Adams, & Stanhope, 1998). Taken together, these results clearly have implications for psychologists and highlight the importance of both practicing within one's areas of competence and being vigilant in weighing sufficient data to draw reasonable conclusions. The results also reinforce the importance of ensuring appropriate operational procedures to minimize the presence of systematic contributors to therapeutic error, such as inadequate communication, excessive caseloads, and insufficient test materials. A recent position paper by the National Academy of Neuropsychology includes recommendations for using appropriate operational procedures in the context of IMEs (Bush, Barth, Pliskin, Arffa, Axelrod, Blackburn, et al., in press). Psychologists need to be aware not only of the ethical issues involved in cases that they take but also of the laws and regulations that govern certain types of cases such as those involving Workers' Compensation (Cox, in press).

CASE 4.4
RETURN TO WORK AFTER CATASTROPHIC INJURY:
IMPLICATIONS OF THE AMERICANS WITH DISABILITIES ACT
(CONCLUSION OF THE FERGUS MACGONAGLE SERIES)

The loud voice carried its message of emotional torment through the sound deadening insulation of the outpatient clinic door. Several staff passed by in the hall, rolling their eyes toward Dr. Monroe's office. Each knew who the scheduled patient was without needing to ask.

"I *hate* this body!" Fergus MacGonagle then spewed a string of invectives that called into question a host of topics ranging from bodily functions to spiritual beliefs. For added intensity, he banged the remnants of his well-healed hands on the arms of his chair, wincing in pain. He added, eyes fiercely staring at the postdoc, "If you'd let me die early on, I wouldn't have to live this curse!"

The sad expression in the eyes of Dr. Ford Monroe prompted another outburst from Fergus. "You should see the look on your face, doc . . . pitiful. What I see is pity . . . pity for this sorry-ass burn victim sitting across from you. Admit it!" Fergus leaned forward toward the postdoctoral psychologist trainee with a lopsided sneer plastered on his scarred, asymmetric face. "You've really got nothing to offer someone like me in that shrink's magic bag, do ya? A poor slob who's had his whole life stripped away, along with most of his skin that wasn't already vaporized." Mr. MacGonagle threw himself back into the chair, eyes closed, fighting tears of anger and frustration.

After a time Dr. Monroe answered, "You're a perceptive man, Fergus. You correctly identified sadness on my face. The only problem is that you've colored your perceptions of my emotions to fit your skewed, world view of misery."

Noting the beginnings of a questioning look by the tilt of Fergus's head and intensity of his eyes (Fergus was wearing an opaque burn mask), Dr. Monroe continued, "You see, I do feel sadness when I talk with you. It's sadness driven by the fact that you've given up on yourself." Staring directly into Fergus's eyes, "I see a man sitting across from me who has so much talent locked up inside that he's in danger of imploding . . . talent that used to play out through your skilled hands directly into the materials you crafted. Talent that others clearly admired and wanted to copy." He paused again, waiting for Fergus's curiosity to spur him on. Dr. Monroe did not have to wait long.

"So what? What's your point, doc?"

Dr. Monroe went on, "Talent that could be expressed again, in new ways, innovative ways that you've worked very hard to ignore, dismiss, wish away. That's why I'm sad."

Holding up the two clawed digits he retained, Fergus yelled, "How the hell am I gonna set up and run a milling machine with these?" Suddenly, he let loose a barking laugh, oozing with sarcasm, "I can tell you've never been near a machine shop, buddy. Any snot-nosed kid would know that you just can't do the job without fingers."

Dr. Monroe abruptly turned and picked up the phone on his desk. He dialed the front desk of the outpatient clinic and spoke quietly into the receiver. Fergus was again nonplussed by Dr. Monroe's seemingly tangential behavior. "Who ya calling? Doc, we're talkin' here! This is my dime."

Dr. Monroe turned back toward his patient, poker-faced, hand held up, palm toward Fergus, "Hang on a minute. I've got a surprise for you." At the knock on the door, Dr. Monroe said loudly, "Come on in." When the door had opened, he said, "I've been discussing return-to-work issues with our mutual acquaintance."

Otis Mitchell quickly entered the room, smiling broadly and reaching out toward Fergus with one of his patented double-hand squeezes. Otis said, "Hey Fergus, my man, how are you doin'? Never would've recognized you in your rassler get-up. Then again, I was there myself, not so long ago." Fergus had to smile despite himself. He responded to Otis, "Otis, it's been a long time, my friend." The friendly appellation surprised the postdoctoral fellow.

Dr. Monroe jumped in while the momentum was in his favor, "Fergus, I happened to see Otis before your session and had asked if he was still getting together with you. When he mentioned that he hadn't seen you in a while, I invited him to stop by."

Fergus was about to cry foul when Otis interjected, "Hey Fergus, guess what? I'm getting on-the-job training. Vocational Rehab set it up." Taken off guard, Fergus asked, "What are ya training to do?" He seemed genuinely interested.

Otis sat down in an empty chair next to Fergus. He angled the chair toward his compatriot and said in all earnestness, "You're the one who inspired me." Fergus was again taken aback. Otis went on, "Talking to you about your machine shop job, I got real curious about how those computer controlled machines operated." Smiling even more broadly, he said, "I even went down to your old shop and asked the guys to show me around. They thought I was some kind of nut until they learned that I knew you. Then, they were real comical, fallin' all over each other to show me the shop setup. My old computer installation experience came in real handy. I asked a bunch of computer questions and actually understood the stuff they showed me about how the machines were controlled."

Otis had Fergus's attention now. This was familiar territory for Fergus, *his* territory. Otis continued, animated, "Your boss wasn't too enthused about my interest in job training. He got one look at my *totally analog* hands and decided that I was too much of a safety risk to be messin' around with digitally controlled machining equipment."

At that point in his story, Otis nodded toward Dr. Monroe, "Doc here had told me about the Americans With Disabilities Act, so I knew that I had some rights when it came to employment. I told your boss that I had some valuable information that just might help a friend get his job back. Then, I shook his hand and left, real sudden. Just left him floppin' on the line." Otis let loose with his toothy grin, "Shoulda seen the look on his face as I left!"

"I'll be damned, Otis! You've got more nerve than a bartender at an Irish wake!" Fergus then became more serious, "Hold on, man! No matter what you saw at the shop, there's no way you or I could do a quality machining job without fingers . . . no way." The old familiar anger began rising again.

Otis laid his palm gently on Fergus's arm for both comfort and emphasis. "You're looking at your old job through the eyes of an artist. One hell of an artist, judging by what your shop buddies said about you, but one hidebound in tradition. That, along with your *one-man-against-the-world* attitude, is blinding you to possibilities." Otis pressed down on his friend's arm with a light pressure, and said, "I, on the other hand, don't know beans about how the cutting edge and gears of a milling machine work. But I *do* know about how a computer can control such a machine. I can do the data entry with the help of adapted tools to set up a simple job. I just need an assistant to maneuver the billet into the right position and remove the piece when it's finished."

Standing up and mugging a prideful stance, Otis said, "With the help of my Voc Rehab case manager, I started training at one of your competitor's shops two weeks ago! *And*, I'm kicking butt."

Both Otis Mitchell and Ford Monroe looked expectantly at Fergus. He sat stiffly in his chair, a far-off look in his eyes, shaking his head ever so slightly. "Well I'll be . . ."

Relevant Ethical Principles and Standards

Principle A: Beneficence and Nonmaleficence

Risk for emotional disturbance, such as posttraumatic stress disorder and general difficulty coping with social reintegration, commonly increases after hospital discharge for patients with severe burns (Patterson & Ford, 2000). Fergus MacGonagle's veiled threats of self-harm, given his personal perspective of helplessness, must be addressed in the context of prevention. Overall, as Fergus has moved from inpatient to outpatient treatment, the psychologists have focused on optimizing rehabilitation gains by helping Fergus achieve emotional stability and creating appropriate linkages for successful community adaptation, including return to work. The psychologists have chosen to attempt to do this through connection to Otis Mitchell.

Principle E: Respect for People's Rights and Dignity

Although the psychologist has observed hopelessness and anger, Fergus's reactions are buffered when realistic hope is presented. Dr. Monroe accepts these increasingly inconsistent events as evidence of the patient's evolving readiness to make health care decisions competently. Under this principle, the duty to protect and provide for the patient's best interests must be balanced with the patient's ability to make autonomous choices regarding health care. This delicate balance is evident in Dr. Monroe's decision to consult Otis Mitchell without Fergus's reaffirming earlier permission but then providing Fergus the opportunity to reject this intervention.

Standard 2.05, Delegation of Work to Others

As Dr. Monroe follows Fergus through the continuum of care, his supervisor (Dr. Torrie) must update him with clinical information pertinent to the specific treatment setting and the patient's anticipated recovery course, which faces new challenges at each transition.

Standard 3.04, Avoiding Harm

The psychology supervisor and her trainee continue to face the patient's verbalized hopelessness and wish that he had not survived acute care. They must determine whether formal monitoring mechanisms (e.g., probing for cardinal symptoms and family observations) need to be in place with the team to provide warning of impending danger and identify significant affective or attitudinal changes over time.

Standard 3.09, Cooperation With Other Professionals

Dr. Monroe has a responsibility to identify and cooperate with appropriate external resources that can contribute to the patient's recovery within his medical, social, and vocational network. These may include surgical contacts (e.g., plastic reconstructive surgeon to assist with preparing the patient for surgery and setting realistic expectations regarding surgical outcome), Department of Vocational Rehabilitation (DVR), his former employer, Workers' Compensation, home health, and his family, with a shifting focus toward reestablishing a daily routine.

Standard 4.02, *Discussing the Limits of Confidentiality*

The caveat of duty to protect when danger to self or others emerges needs to be explained to Fergus in this new treatment setting.

Standard 4.06, *Consultations*

Given the case's complexity, Dr. Monroe knows that ongoing consultation is necessary. He needs to determine how to involve the patient's support agencies directly and indirectly in the treatment program. He also needs to ensure that the patient is aware of the intent of these professional connections.

Standard 10.01, *Informed Consent to Therapy*

Knowing that he was going to continue to provide treatment to Fergus in the outpatient setting, Dr. Monroe acquired consent prior to the patient's leaving the inpatient setting. He needs to reestablish consent to involve Fergus's family in treatment planning and implementation given Fergus's improving capacity.

Standard 10.02, *Therapy Involving Couples or Families*

Although this case involves only occasional formal family therapy, the involvement of family members in routine data sharing, behavioral observation data gathering, and reinforcing recommendations from the psychology staff needs to be discussed with the patient and involved family members in the context of moving from the inpatient to outpatient milieu.

Standard 10.10, *Terminating Therapy*

Dr. Monroe needs to prepare Fergus appropriately for the possible emotional dynamic of termination once goals are met. As part of this process, it may be useful to discuss ongoing agency support given that health care system involvement is likely for an extended period of time.

Institutional and Legal Concepts That May Apply

It remains an open question as to any litigation (e.g., damages and compensation) Fergus might bring against the company in connection with his work-related injury. He has not mentioned securing an attorney to either Dr. Monroe or his employer. When asked directly about that issue, Fergus states that the company has taken care of the medical bills through Workers' Compensation. He is reluctant to challenge the company legally because of his hope to eventually return to some kind of employment. The machinist's trade is all he knows, so he does not want to limit his options in the future by setting up an adversarial relationship with his employer.

Relevant Context and Key Stakeholders

Evolving Medical Condition

Fergus MacGonagle continues to face a changing set of medical circumstances. His scar management is a continuing challenge, and as summer has set in, the custom-fitted compression garments (including a face mask that makes him look like a professional wrestler) provided by Workers' Compensation are very uncomfortable to wear in the heat. The recommended wearing time is 23 hours per day. Because the sweat glands in the skin of his upper body are significantly altered, heat dissipation is a problem. Fergus has to stay in air-conditioned environments most of the day, which is an unpleasant burden. However, this discomfort is offset by Fergus's desire to remain in the house rather than risk being stared at on the street in his *superhero suit*.

Fergus is also approaching the time when reconstructive plastic surgery is planned. He hopes the corrective procedures will allow him to regain some semblance of a human appearance, especially on his face and head. He has discussed the surgery with Otis Mitchell, who chose to forgo further medical procedures because of potential cardiac complications (related to his medical history). Instead, Otis made up his mind to help others adapt to his new look by addressing their unspoken questions first. His friendly, no-holds-barred demeanor puts people at ease, and his charm invariably wins the day. Fergus does not appear to possess such charm.

Family Issues

Maida MacGonagle has consistently managed Fergus's recovery at home. She plans daily activities around the house, including chores. Maida provides transportation for her husband's health care appointments. In addition, she arranges for Iain's young family to share family dinner twice a week. Fergus, although reluctant to admit it, very much enjoys the company of his grandson. Although it initially took the better part of an hour to convince Willem that his grandpa was inside the spandex compression garment, he quickly became accustomed to playing with the *real Batman*. The young boy's boundless energy captivates Fergus during every visit, and Fergus never tires of Willem's pressing him for more variations of Bat hero games.

After two months at home, Maida's practiced eye notices that Fergus only brings up his hopelessness and wish to die in situations that lend themselves to such discussions, during therapy with Dr. Monroe or visits with the family minister. These rants have become an abstract, intellectualized exercise for Fergus. Maida also observes that Fergus has drifted back into his premorbid sleep–wake cycle (early to rise, early to bed), although continuing pain sometimes awakens him. He maintains an activity-oriented daytime schedule. Even though the scope of his activities is restricted, Fergus takes charge of accomplishing his assigned chores.

Maida has interpreted these changes as signs of improved coping, with which Drs. Torrie and Monroe agree. Not surprising, when the issue of improvement is broached in joint patient–family psychotherapy sessions, Fergus grouses that Maida's persistent optimism could make the Armageddon look like a picnic. Nonetheless, it seems that fundamental changes in Fergus's emotional baseline are occurring, supported by therapist and family observations, despite his adamant minimization of their significance.

The following resources and associated information were considered in case resolution.

Patient (Fergus MacGonagle). Fergus is showing increasing disparity between his verbal reports (uniformly negative) and his social behavior (incrementally more positive). He continues to set himself up in a conceptually and emotionally unassailable position of unique experience that no one can possibly understand. However, when not in a situation that triggers defensiveness or one that gives him the opportunity to harangue his listeners, he relaxes and successfully engages in social diversions. Finally, Fergus has opted for reconstructive surgery and continues to endure the compression garments, both adaptive behaviors.

Family (Wife Maida, Son Iain and his Wife, and Grandson Willem). Accustomed to Fergus's difficulty expressing affection, the family persists in providing him the opportunity to show his emotions indirectly. Regular interactions with his grandson and gradually taking on increasing household maintenance responsibility inject meaning into Fergus's daily existence. The family takes solace in the fact that Fergus has been smiling more since his return home. Maida and Fergus have not yet become sexually active but have gradually increased their touching behavior.

Psychologists (Dr. Amanda Torrie, Supervisor; and Dr. Ford Monroe, Postdoctoral Trainee). Dr. Monroe continues to work with Fergus primarily in the context of his social environment. Although he has less influence over his treatment environment than when Fergus was an inpatient, the patient's network of social supports has increased since his return home, and Dr. Monroe incorporates that network into Fergus's treatment. Drs. Torrie and Monroe consider it a primary goal at this point to convince Fergus to accept a DVR evaluation. They enlist Otis Mitchell's help to challenge Fergus's assumptions regarding potential job training. They suspect that what superficially appears to be an insurmountable barrier (Fergus's belief that he is unemployable) is really fear turned outward. They believe Otis's competitive challenge will be too hard for Fergus to resist given other positive signs of coping.

Agencies (Workers' Compensation and DVR). Workers' Compensation has supported a safe and secure home care plan by providing part-time-attendant services to Maida at Fergus's discharge from inpatient rehabilitation. Although this service was discontinued after the first month at home, the extra help gave Maida breathing space to organize the household routine. The disability income allows the family to survive, while still linking economic responsibility to Fergus, a crucial factor in his self-identity. This support will continue through Fergus's reconstructive surgeries and recovery (a period of seven months).

Although not yet engaged, the DVR (through the Ticket-to-Work Program, Social Security Administration, 2001) offers a critical service to assist Fergus MacGonagle in returning to a productive life.

Employer (Fabrication Shop Owner). The owner, although supportive of Fergus's recovery, is very reluctant to take Fergus back to his old job. He believes the loss of all but two digits will prevent Fergus from producing the quality of work for which he is known. He is concerned that failure in attempting to return to work would be emotionally devastating for his former employee. In addition, the owner does not want the increased liability of potential reinjury via unsafe operation of equipment.

Outreach Volunteer (Otis Mitchell). Otis is the one person Fergus MacGonagle cannot dismiss as being unable to *walk in his shoes.* The fact of Otis's very similar burn injury and resulting disability stare Fergus in the face at every contact. Otis, ever the positive opportunist, is making the most of this situation. He is more than willing to join the psychologists in leveraging an adaptive future for Fergus MacGonagle because he likes the old curmudgeon! The kicker is that Otis, inspired by Fergus's stories of his days as a machinist, is training in that "undoable" occupation!

Case Resolution

Coordinate Care With Appropriate Personnel and Agencies

As his formerly unassailable position of hopelessness was dismantled by people and events around him, Fergus reluctantly opened up to possibilities for his future. He gave permission for Dr. Amanda Torrie and Dr. Ford Monroe to work with the DVR case manager. Therefore, Dr. Monroe contacted the DVR and arranged a visit to Fergus MacGonagle's workplace to evaluate the work site and negotiate a retraining program with his boss. The DVR Ticket-to-Work program coordinator then took responsibility for assessing Fergus's work-related potential, funding a work-hardening program, engaging in work retraining and placement, negotiating with his employer through incentives (i.e., salary offset during a work trial period and reducing liability during retraining), and providing a workplace evaluation including ergonomic accommodations and training of a job assistant. These services adaptively confronted Fergus MacGonagle's assertion that he could not be employed and further diminished his position of hopelessness.

Address Employer's Concerns

Fergus's rights under the Americans With Disabilities Act (ADA) were explained in a constructive light that calmed the employer's initial reticence to participate. The specific details regarding reasonable accommodations were discussed in the context of computer-assisted job performance and availability of an aide for final task completion. The employer's incentives available through DVR further sweetened the pot. The employer himself indicated that the business would likely benefit from Fergus's return, no matter what his eventual role. The fact was that customer loyalty had waned during Fergus's absence, and the employer wanted to boost business volume. Fergus's decision to eschew legal fisticuffs in his Workers' Compensation case had opened the door to a welcomed return.

Implement Work Reentry

A 90-day retraining program was devised that incorporated a job assistant as was done in Otis's situation. Dr. Monroe coordinated with the DVR to monitor Fergus's reentry. After some initial problems in establishing a stable working relationship between Fergus and his assistant, the training program progressed slowly but smoothly. Fergus, in a follow-up session with Dr. Monroe, admitted rather freely that he had underestimated his own ability to adapt to the challenge. He also allowed that Otis had been right in the matter of return to work but threatened the psychologist with grievous bodily harm if he ever passed this admission along to his friend.

Educate the Family on the Rights of Patients With Disabilities Under the Americans With Disabilities Act

Dr. Monroe knew that Maida had been a strong advocate of Fergus's from the beginning of his treatment. Because of her pivotal role in both Fergus's coping and community reentry, it was important that she be educated on the Americans With Disabilities Act so that she could appropriately advocate on her husband's behalf for other services he might require in the community.

Case Disposition

Fergus's coworkers were glad to have the master machinist back. However, his perfectionistic nature proved too much for several job assistants over the next six months. His limited ability to fine-tune a product after he was dissatisfied with its quality ended more often than not in frustration and hurt feelings. Fergus's work did not meet his own expectations of efficiency and quality. Nonetheless, the business was again growing, and Fergus felt more comfortable schmoozing with his old regular customers. They quickly looked past the scarred surface and dealt with their trusted ally.

The quality of Fergus's work and his frustrations with it became the focus of psychology booster sessions for several months. Together with Fergus and his boss, the psychology team devised a workable solution spontaneously volunteered by the employer. Fergus was promoted to the position of manager of design and quality control. This newly created position combined Fergus's strengths in spatial conceptualization, knowledge of the shop's operational capacity, customer service, and his commitment to quality fabrication. Although his coworkers initially grumbled at being held to Fergus's expectations for quality in their final product, they realized that the business (and their job security) would ultimately benefit. Fergus MacGonagle continued in that position until his retirement. Maida became a community watchdog for ADA violations.

Additional Commentary

The Fergus MacGonagle case presented across chapters was used to illustrate how a psychologist can address stated treatment refusals and lack of appropriate engagement in the therapeutic process while still respecting the patient's rights and dignity. Patients sustaining severe burns have a complicated and long path to recovery, which can raise ethical issues at every turn. For a more comprehensive discussion of immediate and long-term recovery after severe burn injuries and the challenges that psychologists face, the reader is referred to Patterson and Ford's (2000) work.

In this case, Fergus is at a critical juncture—attempting work reentry. The Americans With Disabilities Act of 1990 offers legislative support for persons with disabilities by requiring reasonable accommodations (e.g., work adaptations) for successful work reentry. Developed to prevent discrimination against people with disabilities and to promote participation in society, it covers five areas, including employment, public services, public accommodations, transportation, and telecommunications (Bruyere & O'Keeffe, 1994). Although it was considered by many to be landmark civil rights legislation, over time the Americans With Disabilities Act has been interpreted rather narrowly by the Supreme Court (Gostin, 2003). A recent article summarizing the limited research on knowledge regarding the Americans With Disabilities Act suggests that those primarily affected by it, such as employers, lack an understanding of the implications of the act. However, this research is weak, and the authors offer a new knowledge survey that can help determine educational needs (Hernandez, Keys, & Balcazar, 2003). Clearly, psychologists need to have a thorough understanding of the Americans With Disabilities Act to be effective advocates for their patients' vocational reentry and to meet their professional responsibilities under the principles of beneficence and justice.

5

SUBACUTE AND LONG-TERM CARE

Long-term care settings traditionally have had a smaller psychology presence than inpatient and outpatient settings (DeAngelis, 2002). These settings have commonly served individuals who can no longer safely live independently or be cared for at home by loved ones. In addition, they have served the needs of those requiring attendant care without the ability to pay or locate an attendant. However, we believe there are four factors that have been converging to create a significant need for psychologists to play a more visible role in the long-term care process. These factors are the exponential growth of the U.S. senior population; the difficulty providers have differentiating mental health needs from the aging process, resulting in misdiagnosis of psychological contributors to health problems; the location of subacute rehabilitation in extended-care facilities; and the shift in the definition of quality care in long-term care settings from a focus on structure to a focus on process (Wallace, Abel, Stefanowicz, & Pourat, 2001). For example, outcome measures such as psychological well-being are now included in federal nursing home regulations (Ettner, 2001; Wallace et al., 2001). In addition, De Angelis highlighted the importance of psychologists' becoming more involved in end-of-life care. As these facilities increase their prominence within the health care continuum, psychologists need to advocate for health care reimbursement revisions and models of care responding to the trends in the types of health care needed. (For a discussion of skilled nursing facility [SNF] payment systems, see Hagglund, Kewman, & Ashkanazi, 2000.)

In the long-term care setting, psychologists often are viewed as independent providers accessed through consultation rather than as part of the primary team delivering care. There is significant opportunity to interact with other health care professionals, particularly nurses and nurses' aides, social workers, physicians, and community support networks, such as hospice staff. Psychologists may be asked to perform one-time cognitive, behavioral, or psychological evaluations or offer individual, family, or group therapy services.

The long-term care setting, by its very nature, presents psychologists with both challenging and emotionally charged ethical issues. End-of-life choices, pain management for those who are terminally ill, cognitive status changes related to aging versus medical conditions, and respecting the rights and preferences of older citizens are issues psychologists face in this setting every day. Unlike other practice settings, psychologists sometimes work with families even more than they work with patients. Family and friends provide 70% to 80% of care requested by older individuals with disabilities (Wallace et al., 2001). In addition, family involvement in caregiving may help moderate the grieving process if the family's loved one dies (Connor & Adams, 2003). Thus, family and friends are key partners for the psychologist offering services. Psychologists provide therapeutic intervention and education to families as they struggle to cope with diverse issues such as medical and psychological changes that are confusing; the reality of "losing" a loved one; the family's role in advocating for their loved one's rights when no one seems to be listening to the patient; navigating community support systems; and learning to serve their surrogacy or proxy responsibilities appropriately, including taking care of their own psychological health.

As is the case in other settings, psychologists must familiarize themselves with institutional policies and protocols affecting the regulation and monitoring of patients' behavior, such as restriction of patients' rights when safety is a concern (e.g., use of pharmacological or behavioral restraints). It is within the context of these policies that the American Psychological Association Ethics Code (APA, 2002) may sometimes come into conflict with expected institutional practice. Psychologists consulting in long-term care also must understand both federal and state issues regarding the rights of patients versus those of surrogates and proxies. In addition to general rulings applying across populations, policies exist that are specific to the primary population served in long-term care, the elderly, and psychologists must be aware of these policies and statutes as well. For example, psychologists need to be familiar with state law regarding elder abuse reporting. In the United States, elder neglect and abuse is estimated to affect between 700,000 and 1.2 million older adults, but only 1 in 10 cases is reported (Fulmer, 2003). Fulmer offered a brief review of the Elder Assessment Instrument, designed to identify elder abuse or exploitation. This instrument has not yet been tested in the long-term case setting, providing an opportunity for psychologists to apply their research training to a significant clinical need in the long-term care environment.

Psychologists practicing in long-term care must demonstrate special sensitivity to the unique issues faced by older individuals in the American sociocultural context, such as subtle discrimination that can play out in practical health care decision making. Psychologists must be committed to social advocacy on behalf of the elderly, as this advocacy is embedded in the everyday practice of psychologists in long-term care.

CASE 5.1
SERVING THE PATIENT WHO IS TOTALLY INCAPACITATED

Fidelis Akimbe had been the kind of man most people would pass on the street without notice. Mr. Akimbe had no time for marriage or children, as his life's goal was to digest the literary legacy of humankind. Every day of his adult life, except Sundays when the repository of knowledge was closed, he could be found in the city library intently pouring over books, manuscripts, periodicals . . . anything he could lay his hands on. His goal to read the library's entire holdings left little time for real-life interaction with other people.

Fidelis lived in a small furnished apartment within walking distance of the library. He did not have a television, computer, or radio. He ate two meals per day in the same small café located midway between his apartment and the library. The owners of the Book Lovers Café knew him only as the quiet, unassuming man who frequented their establishment and tipped the wait staff generously. His parents had been people of means when they emigrated from northern Africa with little time to spend with their only child. Thus, Fidelis had been raised by a British nanny. She had instilled in his thirsty young mind the wonder of the written word. Untold vistas simply awaited the opening of a book cover. Fidelis pursued his goal with single-minded determination. Then, in an instant, everything changed.

On a cold blustery day, a cardiac arrest threw Mr. Akimbe rudely to the sidewalk as he made his way home from the library. An alert pedestrian initiated manual cardiopulmonary resuscitation while simultaneously sending a friend to call 911. Still unresponsive and in need of rescue breathing, Mr. Akimbe was rushed by ambulance to nearby Pleasant Valley Hospital. En route to the hospital, the emergency medical technicians administered oxygen-enriched bag breathing and then applied electric shock to Mr. Akimbe's stilled heart. The second shock stimulated Fidelis's heart to begin its own sustained rhythm. He was admitted to the intensive care unit (ICU) in a deep coma and connected to an electromechanical ventilator.

Later that evening, Mr. Akimbe had one brief period of cognitive clarity. Several ICU nurses were in attendance when he awakened, eyes fluttering. He scanned the faces of the strangers and equipment arrayed around him in a confused panic. At first, Mr. Akimbe tried to speak, but the ventilator's oral tubing prevented anything but clumsy mouthing. Frantically, he tried to extubate himself but was restrained by the alert nursing staff. Then, one of the critical care nurses rushed to a nearby storage cabinet to retrieve a letter–number board left on the unit several months earlier by a consulting rehabilitation psychologist for just such occasions. When the device was presented to Mr. Akimbe, his eyes brightened. He began excitedly stabbing at the letters, at first, in a seemingly random manner. Then, a repeated pattern emerged. The letters D . . . O . . . R . . . C . . . A . . . S were clearly spelled out. One nurse wrote down the letters. Mr. Akimbe looked expectantly at the faces surrounding him but saw no hint of comprehension.

The first reaction of the nurses was that Mr. Akimbe was trying to communicate in a foreign language. They worried aloud that he didn't know English, but Mr. Akimbe then spelled out the word *friend*. Next he spelled out the word *Dorcas* again, looking expectantly at the sea of faces. Their puzzled expressions remained until a passing critical care resident glanced at the written word, recognizing it as an uncommon but classical Greek name. When he voiced that opinion, Mr. Akimbe nodded emphatically. Then, Mr. Akimbe frenetically began stabbing at numbers on the communication board. Before a coherent series could be produced, Mr. Akimbe experienced a grand mal seizure, his eyes rolling upward and his body wracked by violent tonic-clonic jerking. The seizure was quickly quelled by an injection of phenobarbital through his IV port, but sadly, Mr. Akimbe did not awaken again from his coma. An EEG on Day 2 revealed an equivocal pattern of cortical activity. Two weeks passed and there was no improvement in Mr. Akimbe's condition, and there were no inquiries as to his whereabouts.

Pleasant Valley's protocol required that a family member be notified to make decisions on behalf of a patient who is incapacitated, consistent with state law. Unfortunately, no family contact information was found in Mr. Akimbe's personal effects, and no other clues to his family existed. No one knew the identity of the mysterious Dorcas. Given his medical status and his prognosis, treating staff, reacting with personal feelings about quality of life, questioned the continuation of life-sustaining measures. The nursing staff's new case manager, Rachel Skinner, consulted the facility's ethics committee to help determine Mr. Akimbe's fate. Dr. Esther Morales, a health psychologist with 15 years experience in hospitals and skilled nursing facilities, chaired the hospital's ethics committee. Dr. Morales had the burden of respectfully looking into Fidelis Akimbe's life to assemble the right people and facilitate appropriate steps to determine whether life support would be continued.

Relevant Ethical Principles and Standards

Because the APA Ethics Code is founded on broad, widely accepted ethical tenets representative of societal values, it can provide guidance in situations not strictly within the realm of the profession of psychology. This case offers the opportunity to apply the principles and standards to a broader decision-making process.

Principle A: Beneficence and Nonmaleficence

The act of providing thoughtful, properly directed decision making on behalf of the patient is a critical benefit. The patient's welfare is protected, and this principle is upheld if the patient's wishes are followed. However, when a patient's wishes are unknown and no surrogate is available, health care team members are left with (a) their best judgment, largely influenced by prevailing medical indicators for recovery on which to base immediate decisions, and with (b) legal processes to establish a guardian ad litem. However, this court-appointed patient representative is also likely to heavily consider the opinions of the health care team. If Mr. Akimbe is believed to be in an irreversible, persistent state, avoiding harm may require the providers to prevent futile extraordinary care by recommending action to disconnect the ventilator.

Principle B: Fidelity and Responsibility

The final health care decision maker has to exercise honesty and truthfulness in shouldering the responsibility for ensuring an appropriate decision-making process occurs on behalf of Mr. Akimbe. In addition, the decisions of Dr. Morales and the ethics committee may affect the level of trust the hospital places in her and, thus, provider willingness to seek the consultation of the ethics committee in the future.

Principle D: Justice

If Mr. Akimbe receives treatment considered to be futile, then expensive, costly, and scarce resources are being used in an unjust fashion. However, if there is medical evidence to suggest Mr. Akimbe has a reasonable chance of improvement, the health care providers must decide what they believe represents an appropriate and equitable distribution of resources.

Principle E: Respect for People's Rights and Dignity

To uphold this principle, the providers must recognize the dignity and worth of Mr. Akimbe even though he is in an unresponsive state. They do so by respecting his right to self-determination through attempting to understand his wishes.

Standard 2.01, Boundaries of Competence

To exercise her duties as chair of the ethics committee, Dr. Morales must ensure she understands both organizational policies affecting management and disposition of Mr. Akimbe's care as well as relevant state laws and federal rulings that affect Mr. Akimbe's right to life-sustaining measures and the facility's right to choose to continue or discontinue maintenance procedures.

Standard 3.03, Other Harassment

If Dr. Morales or other members of the ethics committee do not attempt to determine Mr. Akimbe's wishes, they have inadvertently taken action that is demeaning because they have failed to respect his wishes.

Standard 3.04, Avoiding Harm

The ethics committee must engage in reasonable steps to discover what the patient would want in his current situation (i.e., cortical function equivocal and minimal chance of recovery). Otherwise, decisions are being forced on the patient simply because he cannot represent his own wishes. Although the patient may not be able to experience harm, from both an ethical and a legal standpoint, the committee has not taken reasonable steps to avoid harm.

Standard 3.05, Multiple Relationships

Dr. Morales must clearly define her role as the chair of the ethics committee. If she is also a consulting psychologist in the hospital and consults with the providers involved in this case, she has entered into multiple relationships. This could create a conflict if she is unduly influenced by those provider relationships, compromising her objectivity to make a fair decision on Mr. Akimbe's behalf. If this were the case, she would need to consider recusing herself from the committee.

Standard 3.09, Cooperation With Other Professionals

Dr. Morales must cooperate with both the ethics committee and the providers involved in monitoring Mr. Akimbe. In addition, if a guardian or significant other came forward, Dr. Morales would need to involve that individual in the decision-making process to best serve Mr. Akimbe. There are clear professional and statutory requirements that multiple stakeholders be involved in the health care decision-making process. Dr. Morales must ensure that she communicates with and solicits information from all appropriate personnel.

Standard 3.10, Informed Consent

Mr. Akimbe did not need to give his consent to receive treatment at the accident site or in the emergency room because of the life-endangering situation in which he was found. However, once someone is stabilized, his consent needs to be solicited. Until appropriate consent is received or qualified authorities make a determination regarding his care, the providers will continue to provide life-sustaining measures under the principle of justifiable paternalism.

Standard 9.01, Bases for Assessments

The ethics committee must be careful not to make assumptions regarding Mr. Akimbe's health status and prognosis without appropriate medical information. Dr. Morales must recognize and acknowledge the limits of scientifically based information in predicting recovery from states of unconsciousness.

Institutional and Legal Concepts That May Apply

Although definitions vary somewhat across various states' statutes, persistent (permanent) vegetative state (PVS) involves an irreversible condition of unconsciousness in which there is an absence of voluntary action and cognitive behavior and an inability to communicate or interact purposefully with the environment (Cranford, 1988). Individuals in a PVS, like Mr. Akimbe, require someone else to make decisions on their behalf. There are three types of potential decision makers for PVS patients, a surrogate, a proxy, or a court-appointed guardian (Moseley, 2000). A surrogate decision maker is responsible for health care decisions when the patient is unable to make them. A surrogate decision maker is appointed by advanced directive or oral declaration and is presumed to speak for the patient. This legal status is based on the idea that the surrogate would know the patient's desires because he or she was specifically named by the patient. A proxy decision maker is chosen from a hierarchical list of persons usually related to the incapacitated person as defined by state statute. A proxy decision maker is recognized if there has been no previously appointed surrogate or guardian. A proxy must produce clear and convincing evidence that he or she speaks for the patient. In the case of either a surrogate or a proxy, the appointed decision maker must base health care decisions on *only* the wishes or best interests of the patient not on the surrogate's or proxy's own values and beliefs. If neither a surrogate nor a proxy is available, the court may appoint a guardian on the patient's behalf. The process for doing so varies by state but may require a health care provider's petition requesting such an action.

Regardless of who represents the patient, two primary standards for decision making have been widely discussed in the literature, the best interests standard and the substituted judgment standard. The best interests standard is intended to represent the best interests of the patient under the present circumstances. This decision-making rationale is open to potential bias or abuse when the decision maker identifies with the decision or emotional valence of the circumstances rather than considering only the patient's best interests. This standard is not universally supported in state law. The substituted judgment standard is based solely on deciding what the patient would have done under the current circumstances if capable of making such a decision. This standard is more commonly accepted in state statutes.

If a patient is identified as being in a PVS, then the patient's representative must be involved in deciding whether to withdraw life-sustaining measures. In the case of a court appointed guardian, the guardian, usually in agreement with the physician of record (and often with the consultation of an ethics committee), can approve withdrawal of life support in the best interests of the patient. However, the best interests standard in such cases remains controversial (see Dresser & Robertson, 1989, for an excellent discussion on this topic).

Relevant Context and Key Stakeholders

Mr. Akimbe has sustained a severe cardiac arrest resulting in the need for artificial life-sustaining measures. There apparently is no family member available to serve as the patient's proxy. In fact, the critical care case manager initially thought that the diminutive stranger might be homeless when his personal effects contained nothing beyond tattered Social Security and library cards, a nondescript key, and $16. That belief changed when a concerned Dorcas Panopoulos began calling hospitals after Mr. Akimbe failed to show up at the library too many days in a row. A sensitive but rather naïve hospital case manager referred Ms. Panopoulos to the Pleasant Valley facility, where she received the tragic news.

Dr. Morales requested to meet with Dorcas Panopoulos given that she appeared to be the only link to Mr. Akimbe's life. Dr. Morales first asked Ms. Panopoulos to describe her relationship with Mr. Akimbe. Ms. Panopoulos described Fidelis Akimbe as the brother she never had and explained that he had once told her how satisfied he was to have met someone who did not think his "life's work" was just plain weird. Eventually, Ms. Panopoulos invited Mr. Akimbe to share holiday celebrations with her, her husband Spiros, and their three children. Mr. Akimbe began to look forward to holidays as he never had before. Ms. Panopoulos smiled as she described how Mr. Akimbe had shared his love of books with her children, who loved to have him read bedtime stories. His uncharacteristically dramatic reading style and the hint of a proper British accent delighted them. Everyone, including Mr. Akimbe himself, considered him part of the family even though their contacts were infrequent.

Dr. Morales then specifically asked Ms. Panopoulos about Mr. Akimbe's wishes regarding extraordinary life-sustaining measures. Ms. Panopoulos could not recall ever hearing him mention the topic. However, she did remember Mr. Akimbe once boasting that he was a "cash-and-carry" kind of guy. He never had any credit cards, was not in debt, did not own a car, and had neither a family physician nor health insurance. At the time, Ms. Panopoulos had laughingly accused Mr. Akimbe of being downright un-American. She ruefully regretted that she had not talked her friend into receiving annual physicals. The psychologist then encouraged Ms. Panopoulos and the case manager to gather any information that might relate to Mr. Akimbe's wishes about health care preferences. Dr. Morales' strategy was to attempt to survey the patient's environment for any evidence of these wishes. In addition, she inquired whether Ms. Panopoulos might be willing to consider serving as Mr. Akimbe's proxy if no family members presented themselves. Thus far, Ms. Panopoulos appeared to be the only one who had a meaningful relationship with the patient. She replied that she would carefully consider this weighty responsibility after speaking with her family.

Ms. Panopoulos shared Mr. Akimbe's address and offered to retrieve his mail from the apartment with the help of the building superintendent, whom she had met multiple times. In the pile of assorted junk mail and bills gathering under the apartment door slot, Ms. Panopoulos found a letter from a law firm and a bank statement. She returned to the center and gave the letter to the attorney on Pleasant Valley's Ethics Committee. The contents of the law firm letter revealed an impressive quarterly financial statement from a stock fund administrator. In contacting the fund administrator, the committee learned that Mr. Akimbe only had a correspondence relationship with the firm, which had served his now deceased parents. Apparently, no other Akimbe family members existed.

The trust firm declined any decision-making role given that they only had cursory contact with Mr. Akimbe. They did suggest, however, contacting his bank to see if he had stored a will, advanced directive, or any other documents that might shed some light on this difficult situation. When contacted by the case manager, the bank denied access to the safe deposit box reserved in the name of Fidelis Akimbe; it was a tantalizing find but one that was beyond the committee's reach.

The following parties were involved in influencing Mr. Akimbe's fate.

Patient (Fidelis Akimbe). The reclusive, self-reliant gentleman never anticipated needing the help of another person. Now, he is helplessly dependent and using scarce and costly resources without certainty of recovery. The only potential clue to discerning Mr. Akimbe's wishes is locked in an inaccessible vault.

Friend (Dorcas Panopoulos). Unrelated to Mr. Akimbe (but his only friend), Ms. Panopoulos is faced with an agonizing decision concerning whether to serve as Mr. Akimbe's proxy to determine withdrawal of extraordinary life-sustaining technology. She finds little solace in the "best interests" and substituted judgment standards the psychologist has shared with her. Mr. Akimbe never really shared his personal perspectives regarding treatment withdrawal with Ms. Panopoulos and her family. His head was always spinning with the thoughts of authors he had recently read. She had no idea that he had no living family members or that she would be asked to take responsibility for a life and death decision regarding her friend.

Psychologist and Ethics Committee Chair (Dr. Esther Morales). Dr. Morales does not have a professional relationship with Mr. Akimbe. However, she has an ethical responsibility as a representative of Pleasant Valley Hospital to ensure that the health care decision-making process is properly carried out. Mr. Akimbe's reclusive nature leaves the psychologist little to go on regarding his wishes. She also feels the need to offer support to Dorcas Panopulous, who is facing the realization of losing her friend.

Hospital Ethics Committee and Legal Department. As consultants on the case, these two resources with expertise in ethics and law are available to assist in the formulation of the process for decision making.

Business Agents (Stock Fund Administrator and the Bank). The stock fund company has had a direct business relationship with Mr. Akimbe's parents. Unfortunately, the firm has had no direct contact with Mr. Akimbe, having always corresponded through their stock fund beneficiary since his parents' death in an automobile accident 30 years earlier. Mr. Akimbe's bank is protecting the property of their client entrusted to their vault. Only a probate court order can open the safety deposit box.

Case Resolution

Determine Patient Capacity and Anticipated Recovery

Dr. Morales called an ethics committee meeting to address the decision-making issue. The neurologist indicated that the results of serial EEGs established that the patient was totally incapacitated without likelihood of recovery. Therefore, the committee determined that Mr. Akimbe (as a previously capacitated individual) was now incapacitated and needed a health care proxy decision maker.

Determine the Existence of a Surrogate or Establish a Proxy Decision Maker

Dr. Morales has been the chair of the ethics committee for three years. She is very familiar with the need to establish an appropriate proxy for Mr. Akimbe if no family can be located. Because no surrogate had yet been established, Dorcas Panopoulos, the only person who had any sustained relationship with the patient, was the sole credible choice for proxy decision maker without going to a court-appointed guardian. Accordingly, Ms. Panopoulos and her husband were formally approached by Dr. Morales. Ms. Panopoulos consented to take on the role of proxy on behalf of her friend.

Attempt to Gather Credible Materials That Might Establish the Patient's Wishes

The ethics committee consulted the hospital's law firm for guidance regarding the safety deposit box. The outcome of that contact was a petition by the hospital (with agreement by Ms. Panopoulos) on behalf of their patient to the probate court. The hospital asked the court to order that Mr. Akimbe's safety deposit box be opened given the patient's dire situation and his state of incapacity. The court granted the petition, and the bank complied with the court order to release the contents of the safe deposit box to the court's representative.

The box contained old income tax records and a last will and testament. A statement printed on the outside of the sealed envelope containing the will read, "To be opened upon the occasion of my death." The envelope was signed by Mr. Akimbe and dated almost four years earlier. There was no separate advanced directive, a discovery that was consistent with Mr. Akimbe's avoidance of anything medical aside from health-related texts occasionally perused. It had now been six weeks since Mr. Akimbe had become unresponsive. The most recent EEG interpretation was "no significant cortical activity." The consulting neurologist speculated in the medical record that the patient had experienced an embolic shower to the cortex around the time of his myocardial infarction. The lack of cortical activity was compelling regarding consideration of removal of life-sustaining measures under the principle of justifiable paternalism.

Meet With Proxy to Determine Decision Regarding Mr. Akimbe's Care

Dr. Morales arranged a meeting among the principles in the case. In attendance were members of the Pleasant Valley Ethics Committee, the physician of record, a representative of the legal department, and Dorcas Panopoulos and her husband. As soon as the meeting got underway, an opportunity to gain legal insight arose.

Dr. Morales's opening statement referred to making decisions in the patient's best interests. The Pleasant Valley attorney immediately interjected the statutory necessity of using the "substituted judgment" rather than "best interests" standard of decision making. The hospital's attorney clarified the distinction and instructed Ms. Panopoulos in this regard to ensure that she clearly understood her role of deciding what Fidelis Akimbe would have wanted, independent of her own values. Once Ms. Panopoulos demonstrated clarity on that matter, the meeting proceeded.

Ms. Panopoulos was asked to describe in detail her relationship with Mr. Akimbe. Questions dealt with the timeframe of the relationship, the frequency of contact, the nature of their interactions that might characterize Mr. Akimbe's beliefs and values, and any specific instances Ms. Panopoulos recalled in which Mr. Akimbe mentioned his wishes regarding health-related issues. Neither Ms. Panopoulos nor her husband could recall Mr. Akimbe's mentioning his personal health status or his beliefs and values regarding either a comatose or a persistent vegetative state. However, both volunteered numerous recollections of Mr. Akimbe's life's work of 8 digesting the contents of the library's holdings before he died. They vividly recalled Mr. Akimbe's stating that, if he could not perform his life's work, his existence would be meaningless. It was that last statement that gave the group direction.

The attending physician was then asked his opinion about his patient's condition, specifically the possibility of recovery. The physician responded that, to the best of his professional knowledge on the basis of available data, Mr. Akimbe's coma was irreversible. He was being kept alive by the ventilator.

Finally, the question about discontinuing the ventilator was put to Dorcas Panopoulos. With her husband gently holding her hand, Ms. Panopoulos paused, head down and eyes closed. Then she raised her head and looked around the table at the assembled group of professionals. Finally she said, in a surprisingly strong voice, that she believed Mr. Akimbe would want the life support discontinued. His sole stated purpose in life was to read humanity's literature. Absent that ability, her dear friend had no reason to go on living.

Case Disposition

Later that day, life support was withdrawn from Mr. Akimbe. He passed away peacefully several minutes later. Dorcas Panopoulos took Dr. Morales up on her offer of referral for emotional support to assist in the grieving process.

Several months later, a court-appointed executor contacted the Panopoulos family. He presented them with a letter that explained their inclusion in the estate of one Fidelis Akimbe. Despite a court-ordered investigation, no other family members had been located. Accordingly, the Panopoulos family had been left the money remaining in Mr. Akimbe's stock fund after the expenses of his estate were settled. Fidelis Akimbe had indeed adopted Ms. Panopoulos and her family.

Additional Commentary

Coma in which cortical activity is present must be distinguished from PVS in weighing life-altering decisions, such as withholding or stopping treatment. Persistent (permanent) vegetative state is characterized by an individual who has lost cortical function but not necessarily brain stem function. It is this reflexive activity that can confuse families regarding the likelihood of recovery, making very difficult choices for loved ones even more heart wrenching. The psychologist can play a critical role in both educating and supporting families or other surrogates through this sometimes very lengthy process. (See Karel & Gatz, 1996, for a discussion of potential factors influencing treatment decisions.)

If no proxy had been located on behalf of Mr. Akimbe, Dr. Morales, in her role as ethics committee chair, would have been obligated to recommend that Pleasant Valley seek a court-appointed guardian. More typically, however, family members are available and serve as proxies if there is no previously recognized surrogate decision maker. Most states designate proxy authority in a specific order, such as guardian, spouse, adult child, parent, and sibling. Psychologists as well as other health care providers must ensure that they contact the legally recognized proxy rather than the most immediate or accessible family member. It is then the responsibility of the proxy to both protect the patient's welfare (i.e., from futile treatment that does not allow minimal participation in one's life) and the patient's wishes (based on known values of the patient, previous statements regarding hypothetical traumatic events, and the need for life-sustaining procedures). It is neither the psychologist's nor the ethics committee's decision regarding what to do. It is the proxy's right to represent the patient's wishes. If it were determined that the individual would have likely wanted treatment to cease, this right should be respected according to Supreme Court rulings upholding the individual's right to terminate life support. In the Nancy Cruzan case (1990) in particular, the court found that states have a right to set conditions on the burden of proof regarding what the patient would have wanted. Therefore, if a proxy can show he or she represents the patient's intended advanced directives, this proxy decision would be constitutionally protected. A summary of relevant court cases is provided by Gostin (1997).

CASE 5.2
DIFFICULT BEHAVIOR AND THE PERCEPTION
OF INCOMPETENCE

"Hey Dr. Finney, we've got a good one for you today!" Wanda, the unit clerk, smiled over the top of her computer at the psychologist who had just arrived on the unit. Dr. Sonata Finney had consulted with the Golden Years Rest Home and Subacute Rehabilitation Center for several years. She accepted the proffered patient chart and retired to the consultation room to review it. Dr. Finney had a challenging case waiting in the wings, one she had to address immediately.

Johannes Svendsen, a 77-year-old gentleman who had recently undergone total right hip arthroplasty, was the focus of the consult. He was a reluctant new resident of Golden Years. Ever since his admission three days earlier, Mr. Svendsen had been giving the staff grief over a variety of topics. Being somewhat aloof, he preferred solitude to congregate dining and only wanted to participate in therapy "when the spirit moved him." He had run several technicians from the room when blood samples were requested. The blood work was important as Mr. Svendsen was only one-month post cardiac pacemaker implantation. The most recent episode in his short but checkered career as a patient occurred the day before. Mr. Svendsen was on the telephone with his cardiologist discussing how to adjust the pacing rate of his implanted pacemaker by sending a telephonic command to it. All Mr. Svendsen had to do was place the phone receiver over the implanted unit, and the automatic system would adjust through the electronic command tone. However, after several unsuccessful attempts at accurate receiver placement, Mr. Svendsen hung up on the physician, loudly stating he refused to participate in "silly games." The conclusion of the frustrated cardiologist was that his patient was depressed and confused and should be medicated before making another attempt to adjust the pacemaker. The cardiologist readily shared this conclusion with Mr. Svendsen's attending physician, Dr. John Baron, who consulted psychology to rule out "a dementing process."

Entering the patient's room, Dr. Finney found Mr. Svendsen lying in bed, facing away from the door. As she approached the bed she heard, "All right, that's far enough! I thought I told you to leave me alone!" The patient had mastered the art of yelling without moving an inch.

"Excuse me, Mr. Svendsen, I haven't met you. I'm Dr. Finney, the consulting psychologist. I've been asked by your physician to perform an evaluation." Sonata Finney waited a few moments for some kind of reaction from her reluctant patient. When no retort was forthcoming, she added, "I understand from your chart that you hail from the Midwest. I'm from Ohio myself."

After a moment's delay, "Figures that quack physician *would* dig up an Ohioan to see me. You'd think that the least he'd do is conjure up a Minnesotan." That said, Mr. Svendsen rolled over in bed and squinted at the psychologist, unexpectedly producing a thoroughly charming smile. The elderly gentleman gestured at the chair next to his bed, "Come on over here and take a load off, young lady."

He regarded the psychologist for a few moments, and then said, "So ole Doc Baron thinks I've gone bonkers, huh?" The charming smile hadn't diminished a centimeter.

"Mr. Svendsen . . ." Dr. Finney began.

"Why don't you just call me Joe," the patient interrupted.

The psychologist continued, "Okay, Joe . . . I'm here to conduct an evaluation to check your thinking skills like reasoning and memory and to get a better idea of how you're coping."

Before she could explain further, Mr. Svendsen growled, "Now why the hell would I want to cooperate with such nonsense? Wait a darned minute . . . Did my children put you up to this?" The charming smile had vanished, replaced by a frown and an accompanying suspiciousness.

Dr. Finney, taken aback by the abrupt change in her patient's manner, said, "Mr. Svendsen, I've never met your children, and they haven't tried to contact me. Dr. Baron asked me to perform this evaluation. He wants to make sure that you are able to make your own health care decisions."

Mr. Svendsen stared off into space and said, "You know they dumped me here against my will . . . those money-grubbing kids of mine. They're plotting to take away my money and my land and dump me in some black hole to rot."

Relevant Ethical Principles and Standards

Principle A: Beneficence and Nonmaleficence

Dr. Finney must be careful not to make judgments or express opinions to Mr. Svendsen about his capacity based only on her behavioral observations without the advantage of a clinical interview or psychometric assessment. Mr. Svendsen has good conversational skills, which can sometimes mask underlying cognitive pathology. Conversely, his apparent obstinacy may or may not be consistent with a dementia or poor coping significant enough to compromise capacity. The psychologist must consider working with the staff to prevent them from drawing conclusions regarding the patient's capacity based solely on behavior they perceive as difficult. Either error (cognitive-language or behavioral) could cause harm to the patient through premature conclusions about his mental status, resulting in an inappropriate determination of the need for medical supervision or intervention for behavior labeled as disruptive and creating unjust allocation of staff time. (See Souder & O'Sullivan, 2003, for a discussion of time staff members spend managing disruptive behavior.) In addition, Dr. Finney must guard against coercive action to obtain the patient's agreement to an evaluation the patient may want to refuse.

Principle B: Fidelity and Responsibility

As part of her data gathering, Dr. Finney has the opportunity to consult with other staff who have observed Mr. Svendsen completing health care tasks and making other health care decisions. The social worker might be a particularly valuable resource in the latter area. Converging data can bolster the psychologist's findings.

Principle E: Respect for People's Rights and Dignity

The provision of psychological services may allow the patient to enjoy his right to make free choices regarding health care and management of personal resources. There is a question of whether this patient's rights were violated in the transfer to Golden Years prior to the assessment. However, if Mr. Svendsen does not engage in the assessment, in a manner similar to his refusals to cooperate in other procedures, the psychologist will be unable to offer an opinion regarding the potential violation of consent.

Standard 1.02, Conflicts Between Ethics and Law, Regulations, or Other Governing Legal Authority

Dr. Finney focuses on the task-specific application of capacity in performing an evaluation to demonstrate the patient's cognitive and emotional status regarding decision making. However, the legal action (described in the Institutional and Legal Concepts That May Apply section of this chapter) focuses solely on the emotional condition of the patient during certain events. This incongruence, which could result in different conclusions regarding capacity, needs to be resolved.

Standard 2.03, Maintaining Competence

The psychologist must maintain awareness of the current literature regarding both cognition and aging and psychopathology and aging (e.g., depression); legal statutes in her state (e.g., incompetence and potential elder abuse by family); and ethical standards regarding assessment, including potential adaptations required (e.g., for fatigue given health status) and age-appropriate norms for testing.

Standard 3.09, Cooperation With Other Professionals

Dr. Finney will need to work with the other providers to establish appropriate follow-up procedures for Mr. Svendsen based on the outcome of the assessment. She also may work with staff and the patient to address behavioral difficulties depending on the nature of her consultant role. If capacity is established but Mr. Svendsen continues to refuse necessary treatment, Dr. Finney may help the team engage the patient by identifying associated coping concerns and developing a coordinated treatment plan. However, if capacity is not established, Dr. Finney may ask the team to participate in serial reassessments of Mr. Svendsen's cognitive and emotional function as well as make environmental modifications to enhance patient functioning.

Standard 4.05, Disclosures

Dr. Finney has to inform Mr. Svendsen that the test interpretation and her conclusions will be shared with the treatment team. In addition, if she discovers that legal action may become relevant, she needs to inform the patient of the possibility of the evaluation being legally discoverable.

Standard 9.01, Bases for Assessments

In addition to weighing the patient's medical treatment (e.g., medications and conditioning), the psychologist must consider cognitive (e.g., a dementing process), emotional (e.g., anxiety, depression, and adjustment disorder), social (e.g., familial stress), and contextual (e.g., change in environment) contributors to the patient's current irritable presentation. Therefore, her evaluation should be comprehensive enough to account for each type of factor.

Standard 9.03, Informed Consent in Assessments

The psychologist has to ensure that her patient comprehends the nature of the service she is providing, including the intent, methods, accompanying risks and benefits, and the implications of the data generated by the evaluation. She needs to explain that she will use the test results not only to render an opinion regarding capacity but also to work with the team to address emotional or behavioral concerns supported by the evaluation (if permitted within her consultant role).

Standard 9.10, Explaining Assessment Results

The results of testing should be presented in their relevant context (i.e., capacity to make decisions).

Institutional and Legal Concepts That May Apply

Outside the legal arena, the term *capacity* is used instead of the term *competence*. A person is capacitated if he or she can (a) understand fundamental health information related to the decisions being considered; (b) weigh the risks, benefits, and alternatives to judge the situation; and (c) make and communicate a voluntary (uncoerced), stable choice. The burden of proof falls to the person trying to prove incapacity, *not* on the patient. The preceding terms in italics are "threshold" concepts in that they are task specific rather than global constructs applying across all situations. As discussed in previous chapters of this volume, it is important to specify under what conditions and for what decisions the person is incapacitated. Importantly, a person is not incapacitated simply because he or she refuses medical care or disagrees with a proposed treatment (Beauchamp & Childress, 2001).

Elder abuse statutes also could be relevant in this case if the patient's children willfully and inappropriately deprived their father of his independence or money. In addition, self-neglect could be an issue if an extensive pattern of unwillingness to obtain medical care were established (Levine, 2003). However, capacity and free choice clearly intersect with this concept.

Relevant Context and Key Stakeholders

Johannes Svendsen was the operational definition of a self-made man. He had not finished high school when he enlisted in the army during World War II. While serving in the infantry, he completed his GED and learned that his social acumen could be put to good use. Early on, he aligned himself with the unit's wily supply sergeant. Learning to ply his trade, Joe Svendsen quickly rose in rank, replacing the existing sergeant who was shipped home after becoming seriously ill. Joe was known as the *magician*, the man who could "procure" any needed equipment, parts, services, and support. The officers and enlisted personnel who depended on those supplies quickly learned not to press Joe about his operation. He simply made what was needed "appear," hence the well-deserved "magician" moniker.

After his stint in the military, Mr. Svendsen enjoyed traveling throughout the Midwest, selling everything from clothing to farm equipment. However, his real success came when he entered the tire business. He discovered that he could triple the company's growth by targeting specific high-volume products based on customer demographics and dealer needs. His company's stock rose, and over the next two decades Joe Svendsen rocketed through the ranks of the company, eventually becoming president. He was widely known as an honest but gutsy infighter. When he finally retired at age 70, Mr. Svendsen had amassed a sizeable fortune and several valuable plots of land in his native Minnesota.

Along the way, Mr. Svendsen married and had twin children, Thor and Helga. He was not home much because he loved the mobility of the business and just could not stay in one place. The marriage fell apart after seven years. His ex-wife was given uncontested custody of the children, whom he rarely saw. His son and daughter remained estranged from him for most of their adult lives. Both children had experienced failed marriages in their early 20s. Neither had completed college nor held a steady job after several half-hearted attempts. However, when Thor and Helga reached the age of 25, the interest from a generous trust fund established at the time of the Svendsen's divorce provided for their daily needs.

Only recently had Thor and Helga reentered Mr. Svendsen's life. At first, the re-union between father and children had been amicable, and during this time, Mr. Svendsen jointly appointed his children power of attorney for his health care. He began to enjoy their visits, feeling guilty at having abandoned them during their formative years. He hoped that he could begin to make up for lost time. However, declining health dogged Mr. Svendsen over the subsequent two years. A chronic cardiac arrhythmia had worsened to the point that he needed the implanted pacemaker. Arthritis also took its toll, necessitating Mr. Svendsen's present hospitalization and rehabilitation after his total hip joint replacement surgery. When his health problems arose, the twins quickly assumed control, making decisions without sufficient input from their father.

Both Thor and Helga repeatedly asked Dr. Baron to declare their father incapacitated during the current Golden Years admission on the basis of their belief that he was dementing. As evidence, they cited his expressions of anger associated with his debilitated state and fear of losing his personal freedom and the foul language that flowed freely in response to the Golden Years health care team's requests for his program participation. His animated rejections of necessary procedures and apparent difficulty following a pacemaker instruction also raised concerns among the staff. Mr. Svendsen's take on this turn of events, shared with Dr. Baron, was that the staff could not deal with someone who actually demanded things or made decisions contrary to theirs and that the twins were manipulating him in an attempt to wrest control of his finances. He believed he needed to get back home to guard the possessions for which he had worked tirelessly throughout his life. Those possessions represented a tangible badge of success in a life marked by a series of hard-fought battles, a process that Johannes Svendsen had thoroughly enjoyed.

The following individuals and information were considered in attempting resolution.

Patient (Johannes Svendsen). Mr. Svendsen has recently undergone two significant health care procedures. Being a fiercely independent man, he deeply resents the care-recipient role expected of a medical patient and has little patience for the health problems he has accrued over the years. However, he is not able to ignore them as he had done earlier in his life. His temper, demandingness, and rather impulsive behavior have warranted the concern of the health care team at Golden Years and his children. He believes his children are trying to manipulate his finances by limiting his rights.

Children (Thor and Helga). The twins have reentered Joe Svendsen's life after years of estrangement. They have lived on the money provided them by their parents. They are pushing for a declaration of incompetence from the medical community, but it is unclear if their motivation is nefarious, as Joe claims. Thor and Helga have had the opportunity to observe their father at home and to form judgments regarding his physical and cognitive status. Currently, they are taking an active role in health care decisions without consulting him. It is this insensitive and assertive stance that has earned them the ire of their father.

Psychologist (Dr. Sonata Finney). By virtue of her role as consultant to Golden Years, Dr. Finney is invested in providing Dr. Baron a balanced view of her patient's health care decision-making capacity. She has significant experience associated with age-related cognitive decline, emotional problems in the elderly, and differential dementia diagnoses. Despite no established therapeutic relationship, Dr. Finney has to convince Mr. Svendsen to cooperate with the evaluation. She also is aware that her patient's children are seeking a declaration of incapacity from Dr. Baron.

Attending Physician (Dr. John Baron). By requesting a psychology consult, the physician is responding to the concerns of the patient's cardiologist, his subacute program staff, and the patient's children regarding Mr. Svendsen's cognitive and emotional status. Referring patients to Dr. Finney for evaluation is a routine part of his practice. He has come to rely on the psychologist for valuable information regarding diagnosis and current patient functioning. He is reserving judgment regarding capacity until he has more data on which to base his decision.

Case Resolution

Clarify Consultation Request With the Physician

Dr. Finney left Mr. Svendsen's room to talk further with Dr. Baron about his suspicions regarding a nonspecific dementing process. It was during this conversation that Dr. Baron mentioned the twins' demand to declare their father incapacitated. Data favoring some kind of protective action on behalf of the patient rested in Mr. Svendsen's impulsive rejection of the cardiology intervention, his almost daily harassing of the staff, and general lack of cooperation with medical procedures. The physician explained he was deferring his decision until he had additional concrete information from the psychologist on which to act.

Solicit Patient Consent or Assent for the Assessment

Dr. Finney returned to Mr. Svendsen's room and presented him with the scenario as she understood it. She did not take a stand regarding the twins' motivation but told him that the tests would either help support or reject his assertion that he was both cognitively and emotionally fit to run his own life. The tests provided Mr. Svendsen the opportunity to defend himself if they turned out as he expected (i.e., supporting his capacity). Agreeing with the psychologist's reasoning, Mr. Svendsen reluctantly participated in the evaluation.

Complete Testing and Interpret Results Based on All Available Data

Dr. Finney administered measures of intellectual function, perceptual-motor function, learning and memory, language facility, and executive function, along with a measure of emotional status. She complemented this evaluation with clinically specific questions regarding his rationale for treatment refusal, his views regarding current functioning, and his perception of recovery. Mr. Svendsen showed good effort during the testing session despite being challenged when limits were tested. He commented that the tests were more interesting and difficult than he had earlier imagined.

The test results supported average cognitive functioning on the basis of the patient's age and educational level. Dr. Finney considered the behavioral difficulties in the context of his changed medical status, familial stress, and results of the emotional inventory, which were consistent with mild depression. The evaluation also revealed that the patient was hopeful regarding his recovery from hip surgery and now cardiac surgery but that he was not used to mobility or other restrictions, resulting in impulsive expressions of frustration in an environment he perceived as limiting. The way in which he regained control of this environment was to refuse specific procedures. He also felt disconnected from his home life and ability to oversee his personal affairs. Dr. Finney concluded that Mr. Svendsen had adequate capacity to make decisions but was having difficulty coping with the changes in his medical status and familial stress, which challenged his core personality of being in control. She recommended treatment for depression.

Review Findings With Referral Source and Develop Plan

After having generated her evaluation report, Dr. Finney discussed her findings with her colleague, Dr. Baron. She described Mr. Svendsen's impulsive behavior by stating that he was a grouchy, once-powerful man who resented his physical incapacity. His frustrations should not be interpreted as indicative of neurological or psychiatric impairment affecting capacity. She finished by stating that antidepressant medication might help the patient's mood and recommended a serotonin reuptake inhibitor medication, to which the physician agreed. She also recommended brief therapy to discuss changes associated with his physical status and family concerns. The medical social worker provided this service given that therapy was not part of Dr. Finney's consultative role.

Review Results and Recommendations With the Patient

Dr. Finney entered Mr. Svendsen's room to review the tests and was greeted with, "Well doc, am I a nut . . . loony . . . a dullard? What do those tests reveal?" Mr. Svendsen clearly was interested in knowing the outcome.

"Mr. Svendsen . . . Joe . . . I can tell you that your cognitive abilities are well preserved. I suspect you've continued to challenge yourself after retiring from the tire business. Not only are your basic cognitive skills intact but also your learning of and memory for new material are quite good. I will say that your ability to learn visual information is better than your ability to learn spoken material, but both are still at least average. Importantly, you demonstrated that you can use new information to reason and solve relatively abstract problems. Other skills that are well preserved are . . ."

Mr. Svendsen interrupted, smiled, and leaned back in the hospital bed, "Young lady, you're talking like I'm an old pickled codger. I'm here to tell you that I haven't lost a step on those youngsters running my company. I learn better visually because I don't want to hear stupid people go on and on. I tune them out." Leaning forward in bed, he conspiratorially whispered, "Hell, the company still calls me for advice now and then . . . even after seven years out to pasture!"

Dr. Finney interjected, "The other part of the evaluation was a little more worrisome." With that, Mr. Svendsen sat back and regarded the psychologist's concern.

"Go on; just spit it out."

"I'm concerned about how you are coping with the changes in your health and your family situation. Based on the tests and your recent behavior, I think you are depressed . . . not severely, but to a mild degree. Your anger toward the staff and your *cantankerous behavior*," looking Joe in the eye as she said those words, "seem to be how you are expressing feeling depressed and frustrated with not being in control of everything."

Mr. Svendsen looked down at his hands, lying motionless in his lap. Then he glanced at Dr. Finney and stated, "Well, I'm used to having things my way . . . but I guess I've no right to take out my frustrations on the staff here. They're not to blame for my straits." Then he smiled ruefully, "I'll hand it to you, Doc; you lay it on the line."

Dr. Finney finished, "Although depression can sometimes incapacitate people, your emotional difficulties don't appear serious enough to have affected your ability to make your own health care choices. These data, in my professional opinion, do not support a legal declaration of incompetence. I have communicated my finding to Dr. Baron. I have also recommended medication to help with your mood and that you talk with the social worker, who might be able to help you with your kids and provide more general emotional support."

Mr. Svendsen said, "Thanks for talking me into the testing. It seemed like a useless idea at first, but having gone through it, I see that you've given me some facts to back up my position." He offered his hand to Dr. Finney, and she shook it warmly. Smiling wryly, he said, "Don't come back and see me." He then paused and stated more seriously, "I might even stay around here to finish my rehab program. Figure I'd better get into shape to face my kids."

Case Disposition

Three months later, Dr. Finney received a subpoena for a deposition regarding a probate court action brought by Joe's children against him. On questioning Dr. Finney, the attorney learned that she had argued in favor of Joe's capacity to make health care decisions. Heartened by this, the attorney arranged a capacity reevaluation to document Mr. Svendsen's cognitive stability. Having discovered no observable decline in function after a detailed clinical interview and brief reevaluation, Dr. Finney was satisfied that she could present credible evidence in support of her patient. A time and place for the deposition were then scheduled.

At the deposition, the attorney for Thor and Helga argued that determining their father's ability to make decisions in his own best interests was a global concept, encompassing both cognitive and emotional factors. In the attorney's opinion, Mr. Svendsen's refusal to work with the cardiologist over the phone constituted a potentially life-threatening situation; therefore, this action was consistent with the concept of self-neglect and did not represent Joe's best interests. In addition, he stated that the patient's need for antidepressant medication was evidence that the patient's emotional disturbance had clouded his cognition. To bolster his arguments, the attorney had secured the services of a reputed internist, retired, who believed the medical record supported incapacitation by virtue of the psychiatric condition.

Dr. Finney staunchly defended her opinion that the patient had the capacity to make rational choices. She methodically explained the clinical and test data and their implications. She also pointed out that Mr. Svendsen's cognitive and emotional status had not changed since her earlier assessment. She went on to describe the effects of his frustration at being physically debilitated on his behavior, including generating some impulsive actions at times but not rendering him incapacitated. Although Mr. Svendsen made nonadaptive decisions on several occasions, she emphasized that he was aware of and could detail the risks associated with his actions.

Despite her well-presented opinions, Dr. Finney heard later through Mr. Svendsen's attorney that the court had declared him incompetent. His children assumed control of his finances and immediately placed him in a nursing home closer to his rural home counter to his wishes. Johannes Svendsen, heartbroken by what he perceived as his betrayal by his children, chose not to appeal the court's decision. He lived in that facility another three years until he died of prostate cancer, alone and angry.

Additional Commentary

American society embodies the concept of respect for autonomy, which is reflected in the constitutional right to privacy and self-determination. The practical application of this concept in health care is the right to make one's own choices without interference from others (i.e., the twins in this case). Although not evident in the outcome of this case, there has been a general evolution embedded in both law and ethics that supports the concept of autonomy as resting on a continuum from totally incapacitated to totally autonomous rather than a dichotomous variable (i.e., competent or incompetent). In addition, there is no universally agreed upon definition of competence. Beauchamp and Childress (2001) defined competence as the "ability to perform a task" (p. 70). We believe that the ability to decide or the ability to carry out appropriate actions can demonstrate competence, depending on the skills or decisions at issue (Hanson & Kerkhoff, 2004). The psychologist has the responsibility to guard against both false positives (i.e., identifying a capacitated individual as incapacitated, preventing participation in the decision) and false negatives (i.e., failing to prevent an incapacitated person from making harmful decisions). Several authors have discussed the multidimensional nature of decision-making capacity. For example, Boyle (1997b) highlights the need for decision-making capacity to relate to the patient's abilities, the task requirements, and the consequences of the decision. We also have described in detail areas requiring assessment in determining capacity in persons with cognitive compromise (Hanson & Kerkhoff, 2004). In the case presented, the court seemed to rely heavily on the behavior of the patient without enough attention to the context of the behavior and the decision-making capacity related to it.

Finally, psychologists must help teams guard against biases favoring restriction of activities in patients exhibiting what teams sometimes label as "uncooperative" behavior. Psychologists armed with both neuropsychological and clinical training can facilitate the identification of underlying contributors to behavioral manifestations of inadequate coping or misunderstanding. Intervening with both the patient and the team is critical to protecting the patient's right to self-determination, promoting the patient's welfare, and facilitating healthy, efficient team functioning. When the patient's challenging behavior is appropriately managed, the team burden is lightened and resources are directed and used more effectively.

CASE 5.3
ASSENT IN DECISION MAKING AND THE ROLE OF SAME-SEX PARTNERS

Nick Noble was a 65-year-old gentleman who had a long-standing history of Type I diabetes, which had been somewhat difficult to control. He had been out all morning in freezing temperatures, decorating his house and cleaning his driveway for a holiday party later in the day. In the furor to finish the outdoor preparations, he did not pay attention to the warning signs, numbness in his feet, burning pain in his toes, slight nausea, and light-headedness. Just as he was finishing shoveling the driveway, Mr. Noble fell over like a frozen piece of fish, unconscious from a severe hypoglycemic reaction after having forgotten to eat his morning snack.

Unfortunately, Mr. Noble's now frozen toes were beyond repair. Mr. Noble awoke in the ER being prepped for surgery to amputate three toes on his right foot. Recovery from surgery did not go well, and he ended up with a below-knee amputation. Adding insult to injury, Mr. Noble developed an infection for which no antibiotics seemed to work, resulting in multiple-systems failure.

After weeks of acute medical management, Mr. Noble finally stabilized. However, he was severely deconditioned and required ongoing medical monitoring. He exhibited significant cognitive deficits believed primarily related to hypoxia, although medication and lingering anesthesia side effects could not be completely ruled out. Mr. Noble was transferred to subacute rehabilitation with the primary goals of continuing lower limb monitoring, improving his mobility, and building endurance. He made very slow, steady gains for approximately two weeks and then hit a plateau. Because of his ongoing intensive care needs, Mr. Noble's domestic partner of 11 years, Collin Pendergrass, felt he was unable to care for Mr. Noble at home. Mr. Noble was transferred to the long-term care wing of the facility six months after his surgery.

After the transfer, Floyd Whytengill, the unit's charge nurse, immediately requested a neuropsychological screening. The speech-language pathologist's note from the acute care hospital referenced Mr. Noble's moderate to severe cognitive impairment. However, no formal neuropsychological testing had been performed in either acute or subacute settings, and Mr. Whytengill wanted a second opinion regarding Mr. Noble's capacity to make decisions for a DNR (do not resuscitate) order, particularly given the conflicting input from the providers and the patient's partner. Mr. Pendergrass thought Mr. Noble was improving, but the staff told him it was wishful thinking. They reported they had seen no real improvement in Mr. Noble's mental status since admission. In addition, an internal medicine physician in the subacute unit had already documented that Mr. Noble lacked the cognitive capacity to make a DNR decision for himself.

On the basis of prior cases, Dr. Xiu Li, the consulting psychologist, knew that the internist sometimes offered opinions of decision-making capacity with only minimal data (i.e., the Mini-Mental State Exam) and with minimal consideration of related abilities. In addition, he observed that some staff offered only cursory responses to Mr. Pendergrass's questions, and he reported that he and Mr. Noble felt their opinions were being disregarded. Nevertheless, making a formal determination of capacity inconsistent with that of an attending physician was typically done with some hesitation.

Dr. Li instructed the predoctoral intern training with him to perform the evaluation, believing it would increase the provider's understanding of Mr. Noble's cognitive function related to decision making (in this case the DNR orders). Joanna DeKalb, the intern, approached Mr. Noble and acquired his *assent* to participate in the evaluation. That is, she clarified his willingness to be interviewed and to engage in neuropsychological testing. After that initial assent was obtained, the nature and purposes of the proposed neuropsychological screening were described to him. On the basis of his consistent responses across two sessions and after consulting Dr. Li, Ms. DeKalb believed that Mr. Noble had an adequate understanding of the information provided. Therefore, Mr. Noble's ability to provide informed consent regarding the cognitive and psychological testing appeared to be intact, and Ms. DeKalb performed the evaluation. The testing results revealed mild to moderate memory deficits, mild abstract reasoning deficits, and mild adjustment-related dysphoria. When specific questions regarding the DNR order were addressed, Mr. Noble consistently demonstrated an understanding of the issues and specified a stable preference regarding his choice. Thus, the overall findings were judged to be consistent with independent decision making for the purposes of validly initiating a DNR order.

Relevant Ethical Principles and Standards

Principle A: Beneficence and Nonmaleficence

If Dr. Li determines that Mr. Noble lacks capacity to consent to a DNR order, then his reporting of these results should prevent Mr. Noble from misrepresenting his own interests. If Mr. Noble demonstrates capacity, he should be given every opportunity to demonstrate independent decision making. Dr. Li or the intern should convey findings to all staff charged with working with Mr. Noble to support the process allowing Mr. Noble's wishes to be carried out. Potential harm is significant (i.e., death of the patient) if an incorrect assessment supporting independent decision making is made. Therefore, Dr. Li and Ms. DeKalb must have confidence in the procedures they use to determine capacity. If the results of the assessment inappropriately suggest that the patient's capacity is compromised, Mr. Noble might receive life-sustaining measures that are unwanted. In addition, his partner's opinion might be inappropriately given more weight than his, placing Mr. Pendergrass in the stressful position of having to make such a decision. On the other hand, if Mr. Noble lacks capacity and Mr. Pendergrass's representation of Mr. Noble's wishes is ignored, the therapeutic alliance could be permanently damaged, with Mr. Noble being the one directly affected by the consequences of staff bias.

Principle D: Justice

Life-sustaining measures are high-cost resources that should not be used inappropriately. The determination of capacity directly influences whether resources are appropriately allocated to Mr. Noble. In addition, Dr. Li needs to guard against any bias that might exist in the facility related to Mr. Noble's alternative lifestyle that also could result in misdirected resources.

Standard 2.01, Boundaries of Competence

The psychologist needs to have experience working with individuals who have been rendered decisionally incapacitated. This experience must necessarily include direct clinical assessment experience in making capacity judgments. The psychologist also should have experience in supervising interns on such cases. Dr. Li possesses both sets of skills. He has consulted to long-term care facilities for several years and has supervised numerous interns.

Standard 3.10, Informed Consent

The psychologist and intern evaluating Mr. Noble used a hierarchical approach to informed consent, first determining assent to the interaction and then determining informed consent for testing. If Mr. Noble did not evidence the cognitive capacity necessary to give informed consent, the intern should still provide an explanation of the proposed neuropsychological screening and seek Mr. Noble's assent. She should also obtain permission from the individual holding Mr. Noble's health care power of attorney, if an individual was appointed as permitted by law. Mr. Noble appeared to comprehend that the results of the evaluation could be used to deny his autonomous decision-making ability regarding the DNR order.

Standard 9.01, Bases for Assessments

The psychologist's opinion regarding Mr. Noble's capacity to decide for himself regarding a DNR order needs to be based on information and techniques sufficient to substantiate his opinion. Although neuropsychological screening instruments may provide important information regarding functions underlying such a decision-making process, scores on such measures, unless extreme, lack predictive accuracy for many "real world" decisions. It is important to include both standardized and functional assessments containing specific questions related to DNR status.

Standard 9.02, Use of Assessments

The psychologist planning the test battery must consider the availability of measures designed specifically to assess decision-making capacity and determine whether such measures would be more appropriate to use than common neuropsychological screening measures.

Standard 9.03, Informed Consent in Assessments

Mr. Noble needs to evidence the ability to give consent for the psychological evaluation. If he does not have this demonstrated capacity, his partner, Mr. Pendergrass, would likely need to be involved. In vague circumstances, it is prudent to err on the side of patient protection and involve a surrogate or proxy.

Standard 9.10, Explaining Assessment Results

After arriving at his opinion, the psychologist needs to notify the nurse and the internist to discuss their discrepant findings in an attempt to resolve the professional conflict of opinion. Dr. Li should also inform Mr. Noble and Mr. Pendergrass of the evaluation results and conclusions regarding Mr. Noble's ability to validly sign a DNR order and address lingering questions. If indicated, additional psychological support would need to be arranged.

Institutional and Legal Concepts That May Apply

Formal determination of Mr. Noble's legal competence can only be made by a judge. However, most cases never go to court because consensual decisions regarding capacity and resolutions for decision making are reached among family members and health care teams. The practical reality is that psychologists commonly make determinations regarding decision making that carry considerable weight. Dr. Li has been given the responsibility for determining whether Mr. Noble has the cognitive and psychological ability to make his own DNR decisions. If Mr. Noble were found to be incapable of giving informed consent, state law would likely dictate what substitute consent would be permitted or required. Although Mr. Pendergrass is the likely candidate to provide proxy informed consent for the evaluation, domestic partnership is not generally recognized in state statutes prioritizing decision makers to represent the interests of incapacitated individuals. The door is left open for legal challenge if informal agreements cannot be reached regarding who speaks for the patient.

Relevant Context and Key Stakeholders

Nick Noble experienced multiple-systems failure and initially evidenced significant recovery. His physical limitations appeared greater than his cognitive limitations; however, cognitive deficits persisted to the degree that his autonomous decision making is now in question. A neuropsychological screening, including both cognitive and psychological measures, is used to assist with the determination of his decision-making capacity. No specific measure of decision-making capacity is administered, as the psychologist is confident in his ability to render a substantive opinion within his evaluative approach. An apparently competent psychology intern administers the tests. These data are integrated with interview and historical information and interpreted by the supervising psychologist. An incorrect determination by the psychologist could have devastating effects for both Mr. Noble and Mr. Pendergrass. There is already disagreement between some staff and the patient and his partner regarding the patient's presentation, which may or may not reflect bias toward same-sex partners.

The following parties were considered in ultimately rendering a capacity decision.

Patient (Nick Noble). Mr. Noble was independent with all activities and decision making prior to his surgery. Although still evidencing cognitive impairment and some difficulty coping with his poor health, he appears to understand both the nature and potential implications of the evaluation. Mr. Noble has not assigned power of attorney but has discussed his wishes with Mr. Pendergrass, his partner of 11 years.

Psychologist (Dr. Xiu Li). The psychologist's role is one of considerable responsibility in offering a second opinion about Mr. Noble's capacity for independent decision making in the context of a DNR order. The methods and procedures he uses are all vital to his ultimate determination. If Mr. Noble does not demonstrate the ability to either provide informed consent or make the DNR decision, the psychologist believes he should involve Mr. Pendergrass, who wants to make health care decisions on Mr. Noble's behalf, although his position could be legally challenged. The psychologist is aware that loved ones do not always make the same decisions the patients would make. In addition, the psychologist needs to consider the possibility that staff reports reflect bias toward Mr. Noble and Mr. Pendergrass based on pejorative comments overheard in the staff break room. Finally, the psychologist has the responsibility to make the determination of capacity in the face of a contradictory determination made by a physician colleague.

Intern (Joanna DeKalb). The psychology intern carries a great deal of responsibility. Incorrect test administration or failure to observe or accurately report test-taking behaviors could contribute to the psychologist's making an inaccurate determination of Mr. Noble's decision-making capacity. This intern, closely supervised and experienced with test administration, seems competent to perform her duties.

Patient's Partner (Collin Pendergrass). Mr. Pendergrass wants to support his partner's wishes regarding the DNR orders. Mr. Noble's situation has caused significant stress for Mr. Pendergrass. He believes his observations are being discounted because of his homosexual relationship with Mr. Noble even though he knows Mr. Noble better than anyone else does. He feels respected by the psychologist, who keeps him informed of Mr. Noble's status.

Case Resolution

Assess Ability to Provide Informed Consent

The psychologist and intern used a hierarchical approach in determining Mr. Noble's ability to consent to an evaluation. First, they obtained his assent to their interaction, then his assent to the evaluation process, and finally his consent to the evaluation. The results indicated that Mr. Noble could consent to the evaluation regarding the DNR order. Had there been reservations about Mr. Noble's ability to provide informed consent, Dr. Li would have approached Mr. Pendergrass to discuss Mr. Noble's wishes. Once consent was established, Dr. Li proceeded with the evaluation to determine Mr. Noble's capacity to understand the DNR order and its consequences. At this point, Mr. Noble requested that discussions occur independently of his partner, believing it was too emotionally difficult for Mr. Pendergrass to hear repeated reference to Mr. Noble's possible death.

Assess Decision-Making Capacity

Dr. Li put together a brief screening battery of neuropsychological variables thought to underlie decision-making capacity. Given Mr. Noble's demographics and the nature of his neuropsychological impairment, the psychologist chose not to use a specific measure of decision-making capacity. Instead, he supplemented the standardized tests with interview questions that he considered relevant to DNR decisional capacity.

Reconcile Findings With the Physician

Because Dr. Li's opinion differed from that of the attending physician, he contacted the physician to discuss potential reasons for their differing opinions. The internist acknowledged the discrepancy and, aware of the differences in assessment strategies, supported the psychologist's opinion.

Encourage the Partner's Participation and Review Results

Because of Mr. Pendergrass's role as Mr. Noble's potential proxy, Dr. Li thought it was important for Mr. Pendergrass to participate in the discussion of the evaluation results. She therefore met with Mr. Noble to encourage inclusion of Mr. Pendergrass in the discussion of the assessment findings and their implications.

Pulling a chair alongside Mr. Noble's bed, Dr. Li opened the conversation, "Mr. Noble, yesterday you told me you didn't want Mr. Pendergrass included when we reviewed your test results. I know you want to protect Mr. Pendergrass, but I think it will help him to hear the results at the same time you do. I would really like to discuss the results with both of you."

Looking sheepishly at the psychologist, face shaded by fatigue, Mr. Noble answered slowly and with great effort, "Collin doesn't do well in stressful situations. I don't want him to suffer needlessly on my account; he's been through so much." Mr. Noble's wheezing gravelly voice underscored a profound sadness.

Pausing for a moment's reflection, Dr. Li responded, "I don't think your approach will accomplish what you intend." Letting the point of disagreement settle in for a few seconds, "Mr. Noble, in my experience, excluding partners from life and death matters can increase, not decrease, their stress. Imagination can create terrible possibilities in the absence of balanced information."

Dr. Li paused again and then continued, "I can tailor the information to meet the needs of each of you." He then added, leaning forward and smiling encouragingly, "If you would like, I'll make myself available to Mr. Pendergrass for any questions he may have later on . . . to allay any fears."

Mr. Noble silently concurred, looking simultaneously grim and relieved. He knew that the burden of secrecy would soon be lifted from his shoulders. The psychologist then held a feedback session with the patient and his partner to discuss the test results and answer their questions.

Address Staff Biases

Dr. Li gathered the unit staff with the help of Mr. Whytengill for a lengthy discussion of diversity and attitudinal accommodation. Those in attendance were surprised by the emotional power behind the negative attitudes held by some regarding homosexual lifestyles. Dr. Li deftly directed the discussion toward Mr. Noble and his partner. He told the staff that both Mr. Noble and Mr. Pendergrass had cooperated with care but that some staff negativity was evident, as such biases could not help but be expressed, even if indirectly. Finally, Dr. Li implored the staff to remain open-minded and respect their residents in the context of professional interactions. This position was echoed by Floyd Whytengill.

Case Disposition

The staff observed that Mr. Noble was different after the psychologist's feedback session. He became more involved in decision making regarding his daily activities and seemed to receive more meaningful interaction during nursing care. Although he remained a resident of the skilled nursing facility (because of continuing intensive care needs), Mr. Noble reported an improved quality of life. During his daily visits, Mr. Pendergrass also appeared more confident, having had his initial impressions of Mr. Noble's cognitive status validated by the psychologist's assessment.

Additional Commentary

This case highlights the need to determine both Mr. Noble's decision-making capacity, as discussed in the previous case, and his ability to provide informed consent for the specific DNR orders at issue (once capacity was established). The "process" of informed consent was addressed in this case through multiple interviews. Braaten and Handelsman (1997) argued in favor of this dynamic approach to consent over the *single-"event"* concept. The variability in performance observed in patients who are medically ill and who have neurological impairments warrants the pursuit of serial assessment of consent. (MacDonald et al., 2003). In addition to the evolutionary process of consent, informed consent involves the assessment of specific areas of understanding. Scott (1998) summarized five components of disclosure that almost all states require for consent to be legally recognized (diagnosis, nature of any treatment, risks of harm, expected benefits, and alternatives). These are the types of categories the psychologist should include in determining whether Mr. Noble has made an informed decision regarding the DNR order. In addition, the APA Ethics Code offers suggestions regarding informed consent coverage (Bush & Sandberg, 2001; Swiercinsky, 2002). By being sensitive to the complexities of assessment and by being both comprehensive and flexible in approach (especially toward a goal of such significance as the determination of the right to make DNR decisions), psychologists' actions are consistent with the principles of nonmaleficence and respect for autonomy, in particular.

This case becomes more complex if Mr. Noble is found to lack capacity to make the decision regarding the DNR order. As mentioned in other cases in this volume, the identified surrogate typically makes decisions on behalf of incapacitated patients. Unfortunately, like many other people, Mr. Noble never set up a health care power of attorney, living will, or surrogate. (See Cohen-Mansfield, Libin, & Lipson, 2003, for a summary of research documenting the percentage of older adults with advanced directives.) This case highlights the importance of familial advance planning for end-of-life decisions on behalf of nursing home residents. It is interesting that Allen, et al. (2003) found that a patient's possession of advanced directives was only marginally associated with a DNR order in the patient's medical record. Therefore, even if Mr. Noble had advanced directives, these may not have been readily accessible to the staff members who would need to act on them. Therefore, the role of the surrogate or proxy who may be aware of these directives becomes even more significant. In fact, Allen et al. found that proxies with advanced directives can influence their loved one to develop directives. However, state statutes recognizing a spouse as the first identified proxy do not necessarily extend to domestic partners. If other family members had come forward contesting Mr. Pendergrass's position, coupled with staff bias regarding homosexuality, Mr. Pendergrass's position may have been marginalized, and he may have required legal intervention to try to represent Mr. Noble's interests. Psychologists may be able to provide critical balance to emotionally charged viewpoints to prevent escalation and possibly avoid painful and sometimes lengthy legal battles.

CASE 5.4
QUALITY OF LIFE AND THE RIGHT TO DIE

Ravaged by the effects of amyotrophic lateral sclerosis (ALS or Lou Gehrig's Disease) for almost 11 months, Renee LeDeux lay paralyzed in her bed, surrounded by portable stainless steel and plastic life-support machines. She struggled to swallow a few ice chips. Before the facility's consulting psychologist, Dr. Beaufort Sumlin, finished introducing himself, Ms. LeDeux weakly mouthed the words, "Doc, please take me off this infernal machine. I'd like to go quietly with no fanfare." There was little emotion evident on Renee's face, as the paralysis induced by the ALS had progressed. Yet the expression of her emotion was deafening; a single tear slid down her cheek as she made the effort to communicate.

Briefly taken aback by his new patient's request, Dr. Sumlin took steps to ensure that Ms. LeDeux understood the implications of her request. A necessarily prolonged bedside cognitive evaluation established Renee's capacity to make and understand the consequences of decisions regarding her person and resources. Ms. LeDeux cooperated fully and was consistent in her communication across several episodes of detailed questioning and mental status assessment adapted for both her ALS and tetraplegia she had sustained years earlier. Therefore, Dr Sumlin contacted Dr. Myron Saunders, the medical director of the facility, to alert him to the situation. Other than the comment that such an action was "out of the question," the physician offered little guidance.

With Ms. LeDeux's consent, Dr. Sumlin phoned Ms. LeDeux's son and requested a meeting. Michel LeDeux responded quickly, arriving at the Ratatouille Rest Home within half an hour of the call. After the psychologist explained his findings, Michel's initial distress was replaced by anger at what he perceived was his mother's "selfish" plan. He could not imagine his mother giving up after having adaptively endured the loss of most of her family and fighting for as much independence as possible after sustaining her tetraplegia. Michel had to leave the room to recompose himself, telling Dr. Sumlin he was going to take a walk and think things over before confronting his mother. Dr. Sumlin set up a time for them to reconvene. Michel promptly left and shared his distress with a few residents. The news of Ms. LeDeux's plan spread like wildfire, and within a short timeframe, her request was common knowledge. Dr. Sumlin and Ms. LeDeux were discussing her plan for a family conference when Michel returned to the room. He was not alone. A score of residents accompanied him, obviously distressed about the request Ms. LeDeux had made.

The agitated crowd squeezed into Ms. LeDeux's room, most with walkers, a few with portable oxygen, and some in wheelchairs. Several confronted Ms. LeDeux with concerned queries, others with angry accusations. "Have you lost your mind? . . . What about us? . . . No way you're gonna check out on us, Renee. We just won't let you . . . We're here to help, like it or not!"

Ms. LeDeux's son stood in front of the gathering of extended-care residents. Hands on hips, face flaming an angry red, he said, "Mom, I can't just stand by and watch you give up. You've been a fighter all these years. You've given all of us," gesturing broadly to the residents behind him, "reasons to go on living when everything seemed hopeless." Tears welled up in his weary-looking eyes, "You can't leave us until your time is up, and you *don't* have a say in that."

Dr. Sumlin found himself between Ms. LeDeux and a concerned and angry group of seniors. He had been taken off guard when the crowd arrived during a private conversation with his patient. He shouted over the noise of the crowd, trying to calm the potentially volatile situation, "Please listen . . . everyone, please listen." When those gathered had silenced somewhat, he went on, "This is a time of great personal pain for Ms. LeDeux." Sympathetic nods from some in the gathering spurred the psychologist on, "I urge you to give her space to make decisions for herself. Ms. LeDeux has heard your concerns, and I feel certain that she respects them."

Ms. LeDeux simply sighed and closed her eyes. She successfully shut out the world with her silence. No comments by her son or any of the assembled residents moved her to respond. Soon, the residents drifted out of the room, finally leaving only Dr. Sumlin and Michel LeDeux. He then turned some of his ire toward the psychologist.

"How can you stand by and agree with my mother's desire to end her own life? How can you call yourself a health professional?"

Relevant Ethical Principles and Standards

Principle A: Beneficence and Nonmaleficence

The psychologist and physicians attending this case are bound to provide beneficial treatment for the patient with whom they have a professional relationship. The challenge is one of defining benefit in positive language, rather than resolving an unacceptable quality of life. Dr. Sumlin must consider whether there is significantly reduced harm to the patient's quality of life in taking actions that support the patient's quest to have the ventilator removed. Alternatively, this action could reasonably be construed as producing an irreversible and harmful effect (death). Is Ms. LeDeux's willingness to accept death as a consequence of treatment withdrawal justification for removing the ventilator? This case example highlights the complexities of adhering to this ethical principle by honoring the patient's right to make choices. The psychologist's challenge is to determine whether advocating for the patient supports the principle of nonmaleficence.

Principle E: Respect for People's Rights and Dignity

The health professionals are responsible for respecting the patient's right to make health care and personal resource decisions on her own behalf. If the psychologist determines that Ms. LeDeux has the capacity to make such decisions, then he must also ensure that the patient understands the implications of such decisions, as consequences of personal choices are sometimes ethically and legally complex. In addition, if an inappropriate decision is made regarding supporting the patient's right to die, the outcome is irreversible; therefore close scrutiny of all alternatives is critical.

Standard 1.02, Conflicts Between Ethics and Law, Regulations, or Other Governing Legal Authority

In addition to federal and state laws governing hastening a patient's death, the psychologist needs to be aware of organizational policies regarding withdrawal of treatment, which could potentially be in conflict. The professionals involved must weigh relative benefits and harms before assisting Ms. LeDeux in realizing her choice even if policies permit such as choice.

Standard 1.06, Cooperating With Ethics Committees

Dr. Sumlin needs to consider the potential role of an ethics committee or other consulting body in clarifying the complex factors affecting Ms. LeDeux's decision regarding treatment withdrawal.

Standard 2.01, Boundaries of Competence

Dr. Sumlin must evaluate his level of competence related to such issues as (a) working with individuals with a terminal illness; (b) the physical, cognitive, and emotional changes associated with ALS; and (c) the rights of patients to determine their quality of life and hasten their death. He must be careful not to engage in medical decision making regarding care.

Standard 3.04, Avoiding Harm

Psychologists, by the very nature of the discipline, value patients' quality of life. However, Dr. Sumlin must thoroughly evaluate the patient's emotional competence prior to supporting an action that is irreversible. Depression, for example, could be a prominent feature in Ms. LeDeux's request.

Standard 4.01, Maintaining Confidentiality

Despite the violation of privacy caused by the patient's son, the psychologist must endeavor to protect patient privacy and confidentiality in all interactions with other professionals and nursing home residents. Sharing only information that has been released by the patient, and the minimum necessary to accomplish the designated purpose, is required.

Standard 4.04, Minimizing Intrusions on Privacy

Following Michel's violation of the patient's privacy, the psychologist should endeavor to counsel him and offer emotional support resources to minimize the likelihood of future occurrences.

Standard 4.06, Consultations

The patient has endorsed consultation between the physician and psychologist. However, Ms. LeDeux must be apprised during the consent process that the consultation may not produce the patient's desired outcome. That is, the psychologist and physician are obligated to recommend what they believe is supported by their evaluations, which may be counter to the patient's wish for treatment withdrawal.

Standards 9.01–9.03, Bases for, Use of, and Informed Consent in Assessments

Given the patient's ALS, the psychologist must significantly adapt his personality and cognitive assessment procedures. These adaptations must be reasonable for an individual with paralysis and slow verbal output secondary to motoric weakness. Dr. Sumlin must be proficient in his adapted administration by virtue of his training and experience. Finally, he must obtain the informed consent of the patient to perform such an evaluation, stating the intent, method, and potential implications related to the patient's wish to terminate life support.

Standard 9.10, Explaining Assessment Results

The implications of the evaluative data must be explained in terms of applicability to Ms. LeDeux's life and death circumstances.

Institutional and Legal Concepts That May Apply

A legal distinction is made between physician-assisted suicide, in which providers give patients the means to end their own lives, and palliative care (e.g., relief of suffering through pain control even if hastening death) or the right to withdraw or withhold treatment, especially when treatment is considered futile. The Council on Ethical and Judicial Affairs of the American Medical Association (Plows et al., 1999) suggests use of a fair-process approach in determining futile treatment and recommends that health care institutions create policies on defining medical futility. Oregon is the only state that gives providers legal authority to engage in assisted suicide (Sullivan, Hedberg, & Fleming, 2000), and the U.S. Attorney General John Ashcroft unsuccessfully challenged this stance. On the other hand, the courts have upheld both palliative care and the individual's right to terminate life-sustaining measures (Gostin, 1997). The state's primary interest is in preserving life. However, this interest becomes less compelling as the burdens created by poor quality of life outweigh the benefits gained by prolonging life. In addition, the courts have fairly consistently recognized that an individual has the right to end his or her own life (Banja, 1999).

Relevant Context and Key Stakeholders

Renee LeDeux, a colorful woman of Cajun ancestry, has been a resident of the Ratatouille Rest Home for almost a decade. This deep bayou facility originated in the 1950s from the efforts of the local secular and religious communities to provide shelter for the homeless. Over the years, the Ratatouille has morphed into an accredited, not-for-profit extended-care facility with oversight provided by state and federal agencies. Most residents of the facility are from the local area and consider each other extended family. Ms. LeDeux, who grew up just 20 miles from Ratatouille, never paid much attention to the place during the majority of her life. Then tragedy struck. When most of her family perished in the same hurricane that caused her tetraplegia a dozen years earlier, Ms. LeDeux began to call "the Rat" home.

At first, Ms. LeDeux resented the reality of care that her diagnosis demanded; it was more than her surviving son Michel and his wife were prepared to manage. She let her anger push many potential caregivers away until her only option was living in the Rat, where she was initially socially isolated. Thanks to the efforts of the chaplain and her son, Ms. LeDeux gradually emerged from her angry shell and began reaching out to other residents whose fates were no less dire and no less open to life's opportunities. Ms. LeDeux gradually gained the trust of both residents and staff, becoming a peer leader in the facility. When obstacles were faced, all the residents had to do was get Renee LeDeux interested in their cause. Eventually, after much verbal wrangling and subtle application of charm, the problems were usually swept aside to everyone's satisfaction. Ms. LeDeux had even served on the local community council, with her son Michel providing transportation and assistance. This constructive social milieu persisted for almost 10 years until Ms. LeDeux was diagnosed with ALS.

The debilitating effects of the disease quickly took their toll; within three months, Ms. LeDeux required a ventilator and was totally dependent on staff for her physical needs. As her ability to provide for others in the extended-care facility diminished, Ms. LeDeux became more pensive and withdrawn. It was at that point that Dr. Beaufort Sumlin, psychologist consultant to the Ratatouille, was called.

Unfortunately, given that Ms. LeDeux's wish had attained the status of common knowledge, privacy was practically impossible to recoup. The situation had turned into the worst kind of soap opera. Everyone went fishing for gossip, not maliciously, but because each resident identified on an intimate level with the issue and their friend. Very little could now occur in Ms. LeDeux's room without the residents knowing about it.

The following people were critical in determining Ms. LeDeux's fate.

Patient (Renee LeDeux). The patient's wish to have life support withdrawn has stirred controversy in the extended-care facility. Ms. LeDeux has been found to be of sound mind and is fully aware of the consequences of her actions. Yet she does not possess the motor control to interrupt the life-support equipment. Her condition is terminal, and she has judged her quality of life to be without dignity. The very serious problem Ms. LeDeux has is that she needs external complicity to fulfill her wish.

Son (Michel LeDeux). The patient's adult son has been guided and supported by his mother throughout his whole life. He has come to rely on her emotional strength and personal resilience to weather the storms of his life. He deeply resents the choice she has made, seeing it as a significant departure from her basic philosophy of life to persevere no matter the odds. His own feelings have prevented him from accepting that his mother has the right to make and express her life's choices.

Psychologist (Dr. Beaufort Sumlin). The psychologist performs a bedside cognitive screening assessment and believes his patient has the capacity to make decisions on her own behalf. Empathetic to the patient's wish, the psychologist has endeavored to pave the way for her to be withdrawn from life support. He has not received support from the facility's medical director. Similarly, he has found no support from Michel or the residents of the Ratatouille.

Medical Director (Dr. Myron Saunders). The physician does not support the patient's wish for several reasons. First and foremost, although he believes that making the patient comfortable is part of his job, he believes taking action to assist any patient to die is against his medical code of ethics. Second, he is not convinced that Ms. LeDeux's emotional state is such that she can make a clear judgment; a patient who wishes to die must be severely depressed. Third, such a request has never been made in the history of the facility, and the medical director is uncomfortable changing that tradition. Finally, he strongly believes that such decisions are appropriately made in the confines of an acute care hospital.

Residents of the Extended-Care Facility. The social milieu of congregate living encourages activity and life enhancement. It is typical for the residents to mourn the death of one of their peers as they would a member of their own family. Ms. LeDeux represents the spirit of this life-must-go-on mindset in her role as informal "advisor" to the residents. With her change of heart, she calls into question both the concept of that life-enhancing tradition and the role she has played for so many years. This is deeply disturbing to the residents, some of whom may question their own purpose should Ms. LeDeux choose to die.

Internist (Dr. David Roi). The sensitivity of this physician allows the issue to be resolved without contravening any state legal statutes, as is shown in the Case Resolution.

Case Resolution

Immediate Intervention Supporting Both the Patient and Her Son

Dr. Sumlin offered to speak with Michel but required that they do so in Renee's room so that the patient could participate if she so chose. He agreed and took a seat near the head of his mother's bed. Dr. Sumlin began, "I can only imagine the hurt you felt when you realized that your mother wanted assistance to die." Seeing tears well in Michel's eyes, he added, "For all these years, she's been the strength within your family and for her 'adopted' family here in the Rat. Renee was the 'go-to' person no matter how hopeless anyone's problem seemed. She managed to find a solution for everyone who approached her."

Michel broke in, "Yes, that's exactly how she's lived her life . . . up until today. I've never seen her admit defeat. She always chipped away at a problem until it broke into manageable pieces." Crying more freely, "She's been the person whom I've turned to for inspiration. And now . . . all that seems to be gone . . . like a fantasy that was never real. I feel betrayed."

From her bed Renee coughed, gaining their attention, and mouthed, "I'm that same woman, my dear Michel. What I want now doesn't change the past. I've just come to see that all this equipment is keeping me from heaven. Without it, I'd have died naturally a month or two ago." Exhausted from the effort, Renee rested a few moments, then continued, "This isn't life; it's imposed artificial existence. I don't want this."

Michel sat for a long time, staring at the floor, before he spoke, "I guess I'm just not ready to say goodbye yet." Slowly rising from his chair, Michel bent over his mother and hugged her gently for a long time . . . whispering his love for a woman who was his real-life heroine.

Advocate on Behalf of Ms. LeDeux

The psychologist was directly asked to assist the patient in ending her life. Although Dr. Sumlin could not ethically disconnect the respirator, he felt a moral responsibility to approach Dr. Saunders regarding the patient's competently expressed wishes. In the company of Michel, Dr. Sumlin approached Dr. Saunders several days after Ms. LeDeux's request for assistance. Seeing that the family was supportive of this wish, Dr. Saunders agreed to discuss the issue. He again expressed his reservations. The precedent it would set might be devastating for the residents and might also harm the reputation of the facility within the community. The facility had been known as a place that both dignified and optimized life for its residents. He reiterated his position that he personally would not actively assist the patient in what he believed was active killing but that he would provide comfort care. He believed death was acknowledged, but in a spirit of natural passing, an expected but never planned occurrence.

Consult Additional Sources for Guidance

Given Dr. Saunders's response, Dr. Sumlin believed that Dr. Saunders could not adequately represent the patient's interests. This, of course, was a very delicate issue to approach. Dr. Sumlin took a cue from the physician's earlier comments and suggested that they consult the ethics committee linked to the medical center and an internist friend based in the local hospital to explore potential transfer options. Dr. Saunders finally agreed to this plan, believing the Rat would be relieved of the responsibility for any elected action and its image within the community would remain untarnished.

With the permission of the patient, Dr. Saunders and Dr. Sumlin participated in a lengthy conference call with the internist, Dr. David Roi. The internist was reluctant to admit a medically complex but stable patient to his service. However, he agreed to admit Ms. LeDeux if her condition destabilized.

Case Disposition

Several days after the conference call, Ms. LeDeux developed a pneumonia that required acute medical treatment. This had become almost commonplace for her since the ALS had worsened. After a send-off by a long line of resident well-wishers, she was transferred from the Rat to the internist's service. Upon arrival at the hospital, Ms. LeDeux gave permission for a DNR order. She had been aware of and had exercised this option during several of her previous hospital admissions. She also requested that she receive no antibiotic treatment for her pneumonia. Instead, Ms. LeDeux requested palliative care, the attendance of her son and his spouse, and the supportive services of a hospice nurse. The physician agreed with this request, and Renee

LeDeux peacefully passed away three days later in her sleep in no discomfort with the respirator still functioning.

At the memorial service for Ms. LeDeux held at the Ratatouille, many of the residents shared their stories. Ms. LeDeux's selfless deeds and priceless advice were held in great esteem almost legendary in their grandeur as each speaker embellished a bit further. The service was capped by Michel LeDeux's heart-warming story of his mother's heroic struggles to salvage what was left of the family after the great hurricane. He challenged the residents of the Rat to keep that spirit alive in their daily lives. Renee LeDeux was fondly remembered for her life of giving to others. Her death gave testimony to her independent spirit.

Additional Commentary

Capacitated patients have a broad ethical and legal right to refuse any medical treatment. The patient in this case could have refused the ventilator when it was first introduced. However, because the treatment was begun, she found herself in a more complex treatment withdrawal situation. Although the courts have long upheld the right to terminate life-sustaining measures, decisions regarding withdrawing treatment become murkier when family members disagree, even in the context of an identified surrogate. The legally complex Terri Schiavo case (in which a nutrition tube was reinserted by legislative mandate six days after removal by court order) dramatically illustrates the complexities of treatment withdrawal when patients cannot represent themselves ("Judge Names Guardian," 2003; "Terri's Law," 2003).

However, in Ms. LeDeux's case, her wishes were clearly known. The challenge here was how to respect the patient's right to self-determination when she did not have the physical capacity to exercise such a right. Dr. Sumlin had to directly confront the patient's request for assistance in terminating life support. Embodied in the tradition of psychology is respect for the person's right to choose and the importance of quality of life. Therefore, the psychologist was pressed to decide the level of advocacy he was willing to undertake on behalf of his patient.

Consistent with his professional responsibility, he had already determined the patient was capable of making her own choices. However, the amount of responsibility for implementing this determined right of choice rests with the psychologist's own sense of morality. In this case, Dr. Sumlin advocated for Ms. LeDeux to the boundaries of his professional competence. Additional commentary and debate on physician-assisted suicide are provided by several authors (Foley & Headin, 1999; Lee, 2003; Meier et al., 1998; Miller et al., 1994; Schwartz, Curry, Blank, & Gruman, 2001; Welie, 2002). An extensive discussion of the evolving model of hospice care is also provided by Jennings, Ryndes, D'Onofrio, and Bailey (2003).

Finally, this case highlights the multiple and sometimes unexpected roles in which we find ourselves as psychologists practicing in health care. If we flexibly and creatively approach our responsibilities, we have the opportunity not only to make a difference within our own profession but also to touch the professions of others toward the common goal of maximizing service to our patients and society. This behavioral aspiration embraces sound ethical practice, the roots of which run deep in the practice of psychology across the health care continuum.

REFERENCES

Allen, R. S., DeLaine, S. R., Chaplin, W. F., Marson, D. C., Bourgeois, M. S., Dijkstra, K., et al. (2003). Advance care planning in nursing homes: Correlates of capacity and possession of advance directives. *The Gerontologist, 43,* 309–317.

American Academy of Clinical Neuropsychology. (2001). Policy statement on the presence of third party observers in neuropsychological assessments. *The Clinical Neuropsychologist, 15,* 433–439.

American Educational Research Association, American Psychological Association, & National Council on Measurement in Education. (1999). *Standards for educational and psychological testing.* Washington, DC: American Educational Research Association.

American Medical Association. (1997). *Code of medical ethics.* Chicago: Author.

American Psychological Association. (2002). Ethical principles of psychologists and code of conduct. *American Psychologist, 57,* 1060–1073.

American Psychological Association. (2003). Guidelines on multicultural education, training, research, practice, and organizational change for psychologists. *American Psychologist, 58,* 377–402.

American Psychological Association, Practice Directorate. (2003). *HIPAA transaction rule guide now available.* Retrieved November 5, 2003, from http://www.apapractice.org/

Americans With Disabilities Act of 1990, Pub. L. No. 101–336, §2, 104 Stat. 328 (1991).

Andersen, R. M., Rice, T. H., & Kominski, G. F. (2001). *Changing the U.S. health care system: Key issues in health services, policy, and management* (2nd ed.). San Francisco: Jossey-Bass.

Annas, G. J. (1994). Legal issues in medicine: Informed consent, cancer, and truth in prognosis. *The New England Journal of Medicine, 330*(3), 223–225.

Baker, G., Hanley, J., Jackson, H., Kimmance, S., & Slade, P. (1993). Detecting the faking of amnesia performance differences between simulators and patients with memory impairment. *Journal of Clinical and Experimental Neuropsychology, 15,* 668–684.

Banja, J. D. (1994). Risk assessment and patient autonomy. *Journal of Head Trauma Rehabilitation, 9*(4), 70–72.

Banja, J. D. (1999). Ethical dimensions of severe traumatic brain injury. In M. Rosenthal, J. S. Kreutzer, E. R. Griffith, & B. Pentland (Eds.), *Rehabilitation of the adult and child with traumatic brain injury* (3rd ed., pp. 413–434). Philadelphia: F. A. Davis.

Batten, S. V., & Orsillo, S. M. (2002). Therapist reactions in the context of collective trauma. *The Behavior Therapist, 25,* 36–40.

Beauchamp, T. L., & Childress, J. F. (2001). *Principles of biomedical ethics* (5th ed.). New York: Oxford University Press.

Belar, C., & Deardorff, W. (1995). *Clinical health psychology in medical settings: A practitioner's guidebook.* Washington, DC: American Psychological Association.

Benson, E. (2003, June). Beyond "urbancentrism." *Monitor on Psychology, 34,* 54–55.

Berrol, S. (1992). Terminology of post-concussion syndrome: Rehabilitation of post-concussive disorders. In L. J. Horn & N. D. Zasler (Eds.), *Physical medicine and rehabilitation state of the art reviews* (pp. 1–8). Philadelphia: Hanley & Belfus.

Blair, K. L., & Gorman, P. W. (2003). Survival tips for the neuropsychologist in an inpatient rehabilitaton setting. *Rehabilitation Psychology, 48,* 310–313.

Bordini, E. J., Chaknis, M. M., Ekman-Turner, R. M., & Perna, R. B. (2002). Advances and issues in the diagnostic differential of malingering versus brain injury. *Neurorehabilitation, 17*(2), 93–104.

Boyle, R. J. (1997a). Communication, truthtelling, and disclosure. In J. C. Fletcher, P. A. Lombardo, M. F. Marshall, & F. G. Miller (Eds.), *Introduction to clinical ethics* (2nd ed., pp. 55–70). Hagerstown, MD: University Publishing Group.

Boyle, R. J. (1997b). Determining patients' capacity to share in decision-making. In J. C. Fletcher, P. A. Lombardo, M. F. Marshall, & F. G. Miller (Eds.), *Introduction to clinical ethics* (2nd ed., pp. 71–88). Hagerstown, MD: University Publishing Group.

Braaten, E., & Handelsman, M. (1997). Preferences for informed consent information. *Ethics and Behavior, 7,* 311–328.

Bray, J. H., Enright, M. F., & Easling, I. (2004). Psychological practice in rural primary care. In R. G. Frank, S. H. McDaniel, J. H. Bray, & M. Heldring (Eds.), *Primary care psychology* (pp. 243–257). Washington, DC: American Psychological Association.

Bray, J. H., Frank, R. G., McDaniel, S. H., & Heldring, M. (2004). Education, practice, and research opportunities for psychologists in primary care. In R. G. Frank, S. H. McDaniel, J. H. Bray, & M. Heldring (Eds.), *Primary care psychology* (pp. 3–21). Washington, DC: American Psychological Association.

Bruyere, S., & O'Keeffe, J. (Eds.). (1994). *Implications of the Americans With Disabilities Act for psychology.* New York: Springer Publishing Company; and Washington, DC: American Psychological Association.

Bush, S. S., Barth, J. T., Pliskin, N. H., Arffa, S., Axelrod, B. N., Blackburn, L. A., et al. (in press). Independent and court-ordered forensic neuropsychological examinations: Official statement of the National Academy of Neuropsychology. *Archives of Clinical Neuropsychology.*

Bush, S., & Sandberg, M. (2001). Utilizing "assent" to determine "consent": Proposed ethical revisions and their implications for TBI rehabilitation. *Archives of Clinical Neuropsychology, 16,* 807.

Call, J. B., & Pfefferbaum, B. (1999). Lessons from the first two years of project heartland, Oklahoma's mental health response to the 1995 bombing. *Psychiatric Services, 50,* 953–955.

Callahan, C. D., & Hagglund, K. J. (1995). Comparing neuropsychological and psychiatric evaluation of competency in rehabilitation: A case example. *Archives of Physical Medicine and Rehabilitation, 76,* 909–912.

Caplan, B., & Shechter, J. (1995). The role of nonstandard neuropsychological assessment in rehabilitation: History, rationale, and examples. In L. A. Cushman & M. Scherer (Eds.), *Psychological assessment in medical rehabilitation* (pp. 359–391). Washington, DC: American Psychological Association.

Carrese, J. A., & Rhodes, L. A. (1995). Western bioethics on the Navajo Reservation: Benefit or harm? *Journal of the American Medical Association, 274,* 826–829.

Chiu, V. W. Y., & Lee, T. M. C. (2002). Detection of malingering behavior at different levels of task difficulty in Hong Kong Chinese. *Rehabilitation Psychology, 47,* 194–203.

Cohen-Mansfield, J., Libin, A., & Lipson, S. (2003). Differences in presenting advance directives in the chart, in the minimum data set, and through the staff's perceptions. *The Gerontologist, 43,* 302–308.

Colby, F. (2001). Using the binomial distribution to assess effort: Forced-choice testing in neuropsychological settings. *Rehabilitation Psychology, 16,* 253–265.

Committee on Ethical Guidelines for Forensic Psychologists. (1991). Specialty guidelines for forensic psychologists. *Law and Human Behavior, 15,* 655–665.

Connell, M., & Koocher, G. P. (2003). HIPAA & forensic practice. *American Psychology Law Society News, 23*(2), 16–19.

Connor, S., & Adams, J. (2003). Caregiving at the end of life. *Hastings Center Report Special Supplement, 33*(2), S8–S9.

Constantinou, M., Ashendorf, L., & McCaffrey, R. J. (2002). When the third party observer of a neuropsychological evaluation is an audio-recorder. *The Clinical Neuropsychologist, 16,* 407–412.

Conway, T., & Crosson, B. (2000). Neuropsychological assessment. In R. G. Frank & T. R. Elliott (Eds.), *Handbook of rehabilitation psychology* (pp. 327–343). Washington, DC: American Psychological Association.

Council on Ethical and Judicial Affairs, American Medical Association. (1999). Medical futility in end-of-life care: Report of the Council on Ethical and Judicial Affairs. *Journal of the American Medical Association, 281,* 937–941.

Cowart, D., & Burt, R. (1998). Confronting death: Who chooses, who controls? *Hastings Center Report, 28*(1), 14–24.

Cox, D. R. (in press). Ethical challenges in the determination of response validity in neuropsychology. In S. Bush (Ed.), *A casebook of ethical challenges in neuropsychology.* Lisse, The Netherlands: Royal Swets & Zeitlinger.

Cranford, R. E. (1988). The persistent vegetative state: The medical reality (getting the facts straight). *Hastings Center Report, 18*(1), 27–32.

Crewe, N. M., & Dijkers, M. (1995). Functional assessment. In L. A. Cushman & M. Scherer (Eds.), *Psychological assessment in medical rehabilitation* (pp. 101–144). Washington, DC: American Psychological Association.

Cruzan, N., by her parent and co-guardians Cruzan, L. L., et ux. 497 US 261, 110 S. Ct. 2841 (1990).

Cullum, C., Heaton, R., & Grant, I. (1991). Psychogenic factors influencing neuropsychological performance: Somatoform disorders, factitious disorders, and malingering. In H. O. Doerr & A. S. Carling (Eds.), *Forensic neuropsychology: Legal and scientific bases* (pp. 141–171). New York: Guilford Press.

DeAngelis, T. (2002, March). More psychologists needed in end-of-life care. *Monitor on Psychology*, *33*, 52–55.

Deiden, C., & Bush, S. (2002). Addressing perceived ethical violations in clinical neuropsychology. In S. Bush & M. Drexler (Eds.), *Ethical issues in clinical neuropsychology* (pp. 281–305). Lisse, The Netherlands: Royal Swets & Zeitlinger.

DeLeon, P. H., & VandenBos, G. R. (2000). Reflecting, and leading, progress in professional practice in psychology. *Professional Psychology: Research and Practice*, *31*, 595–597.

DeWolfe, D. J. (2000). *Training manual for mental health and human service workers in major disasters* (2nd ed., DHHS Publication No. ADM 90-538). Washington, DC: U.S. Government Printing Office.

Disaster Response Network of the North Carolina Psychological Foundation. (n.d.). Retrieved November 26, 2003, from http://www.ncpsychology.com/html/Disaster Response Information.htm

Dovey, S. M. (2002). A preliminary taxonomy of medical errors in family practice. *Quality and Safety in Health Care*, *11*, 233–238.

Dresser, R. S., & Robertson, J. A. (1989). Quality of life and non-treatment decisions for incompetent patients: A critique of the orthodox approach. *Law, Medicine, and Health Care*, *17*(3), 234–244.

Driscoll, W. D., & McCabe, E. P. (2004). Primary care psychology in independent practice. In R. G. Frank, S. H. McDaniel, J. H. Bray, & M. Heldring (Eds.), *Primary care psychology* (pp. 133–148). Washington, DC: American Psychological Association.

Elliott, T. R., & Frank, R. G. (2000). Afterword: Drawing new horizons. In R. G. Frank & T. R. Elliott (Eds.), *Handbook of rehabilitation psychology* (pp. 645–653). Washington, DC: American Psychological Association.

Elliott, T. R., & Rivera, P. (2003). The experience of families and their careers in health care. In S. Llewelyn & P. Kennedy (Eds.), *Handbook of clinical health psychology* (pp. 61–77). West Sussex, England: Wiley.

Emanuel, E. J., & Emanuel, L. L. (1992). Proxy decision making for incompetent patients: An ethical and empirical analysis. *Journal of the American Medical Association*, *267*, 2067–2071.

Etcoff, L., & Kampfer, K. (1996). Practical guidelines in the use of symptom validity and other psychological tests to measure malingering and symptom exaggerations in traumatic brain injury cases. *Neuropsychology Review*, *6*, 171–201.

Ettner, S. L. (2001). Mental health services and policy issues. In R. M. Andersen, T. H. Rice, & G. F. Kominski (Eds.), *Changing the U.S. health services, policy, and management* (2nd ed., pp. 291–319). San Francisco: Jossey-Bass.

Fallowfield, L. (1993). Giving sad and bad news. *Lancet*, *341*, 476–478.

Foley, K., & Hendin, H. (1999). The Oregon report: Don't ask, don't tell. *Hastings Center Report*, *29*(3), 37–42.

Frank, R. G., & Elliott, T. R. (2000a). *Handbook of rehabilitation psychology*. Washington, DC: American Psychological Association.

Frank, R. G., & Elliott, T. R. (2000b). Rehabilitation psychology: Hope for a psychology of chronic conditions. In R. G. Frank & T. R. Elliott (Eds.), *Handbook of rehabilitation psychology* (pp. 3–8). Washington, DC: American Psychological Association.

Frank, R. G., Hagglund, K. J., & Farmer, J. E. (2004). Chronic illness management in primary care: The cardinal symptoms model. In R. G. Frank, S. H. McDaniel, J. H. Bray, & M. Heldring (Eds.), *Primary care psychology* (pp. 259–275). Washington, DC: American Psychological Association.

Frank, R. G., McDaniel, S. H., Bray, J. H., & Heldring, M. (2004). Preface. In R. G. Frank, S. H. McDaniel, J. H. Bray, & M. Heldring (Eds.), *Primary care psychology* (pp. xiii–xvii). Washington, DC: American Psychological Association.

Frankel, R., & Beckman, H. (2004). The physician–patient relationship. In R. G. Frank, S. H. McDaniel, J. H. Bray, & M. Heldring (Eds.), *Primary care psychology* (pp. 45–61). Washington, DC: American Psychological Association.

Fulmer, T. (2003). Elder abuse and neglect assessment. *Journal of Gerontological Nursing, 29*(1), 8–9.

Gatchel, R. J., & Oordt, M. S. (2003). *Clinical health psychology and primary care: Practical advice and clinical guidance for successful collaboration*. Washington, DC: American Psychological Association.

Gerety, M. B., Chiodo, L. K., Kanten, D. N., Tuley, M. R., & Cornell, J. E. (1993). Medical treatment preferences of nursing home residents: Relationship to function and concordance with surrogate decision-makers. *Journal of the American Geriatrics Society, 41*, 953–960.

Girgis, A., & Sanson-Fisher, R. W. (1995). Breaking bad news: Consensus guidelines for medical practitioners. *Journal of Clinical Oncology, 13*, 2449–2456.

Glueckauf, R. L., Pickett, T. C., Ketterson, T. U., Loomis, J. S., & Nickelson, D. W. (2003). Telehealth and chronic illness: Emerging issues and developments in research and practice. In S. Llewelyn & P. Kennedy (Eds.), *Handbook of clinical health psychology* (pp. 519–545). West Sussex, England: Wiley.

Gostin, L. O. (1997). Deciding life and death in the courtroom: From Quinlan to Cruzan, Glucksberg, and Vacco—A brief history and analysis of constitutional protection of the "Right to die." *Journal of the American Medical Association, 278*, 1523–1528.

Gostin, L. O. (2001). National health information privacy: Regulations under the Health Insurance Portability and Accountability Act. *Journal of the American Medical Association, 285*, 3015–3021.

Gostin, L. O. (2003). The judicial dismantling of the Americans With Disabilities Act. *Hastings Center Report, 33*(2) 9–11.

Guerin, B. (1986). Mere presence effects in humans: A review. *Journal of Experimental Social Psychology, 22*, 38–77.

Hagglund, K. J., Kewman, D. G., & Ashkanazi, G. S. (2000). Medicare and prospective payment systems. In R. Frank & T. Elliot (Eds.), *Handbook of rehabili-*

tation psychology (pp. 603–614). Washington, DC: American Psychological Association.

Haley, W. E. (2004). Serving older adults: Clinical geropsychology in primary care. In R. G. Frank, S. H. McDaniel, J. H. Bray, & M. Heldring (Eds.), *Primary care psychology* (pp. 227–242). Washington, DC: American Psychological Association.

Haley, W. E., McDaniel, S. H., Bray, J. H., Frank, R. G., Heldring, M., Johnson, S. B., et al. (1998). Psychological practice in primary care settings: Practical tips for clinicians. *Professional Psychology: Research and Practice, 29,* 237–244.

Haley, W. E., McDaniel, S. H., Bray, J. H., Frank, R. G., Heldring, M., Johnson, S. B., et al. (2004). Psychological practice in primary care settings: Practical tips for clinicians. In R. G. Frank, S. H. McDaniel, J. H. Bray, & M. Heldring (Eds.), *Primary care psychology* (pp. 95–112). Washington, DC: American Psychological Association.

Hansen, N. D., Pepitone-Arreola-Rockwell, F., & Greene, A. F. (2000). Multicultural competence: Criteria and case examples. *Professional Psychology: Research and Practice, 31,* 652–660.

Hanson, S. L., Guenther, R., Kerkhoff, T. R., & Liss, M. (2000). Ethics: Historical foundations, basic principles, and contemporary issues. In R. G. Frank & T. R. Elliott (Eds.), *Handbook of rehabilitation psychology* (pp. 629–643). Washington, DC: American Psychological Association.

Hanson, S. L., & Kerkhoff, T. R. (2004). The implications of bioethical principles in traumatic brain injury rehabilitation. In M. J. Ashley (Ed.), *Traumatic brain injury rehabilitation: Rehabilitative treatment and case managaement.* (2nd ed., pp. 685–726). Boca Raton, FL: CRC Press.

Harrington, A. (Ed.). (1997). *The placebo effect: An interdisciplinary exploration.* Cambridge, MA: Harvard University Press.

Health Insurance Portability and Accountability Act of 1996. Retrieved November 24, 2003, from http://www.hhs.gov/ocr/hipaa/

Hernandez, B., Keys, C., & Balcazar, F. (2003). The Americans with Disabilities Act knowledge survey: Strong psychometrics and weak knowledge. *Rehabilitation Psychology, 48,* 93–99.

Holloway, J. D. (2003, January). What takes precedence: HIPAA or state law? *Monitor on Psychology, 34,* 28.

Holzer, J., Gansler, D., Moczynski, N., & Folstein, M. (1997). Cognitive functions in the informed consent evaluation process: A pilot study. *Journal of the American Academy of Psychiatry and Law, 25,* 531–540.

Jennings, B., Ryndes, T., D'Onofrio, C., & Bailey, M. A. (2003). Toward new models of hospice. *Hastings Center Report, 33*(2), S44–S52.

Johnstone, B., Schopp, L., & Shigaki, C. (2000). Forensic psychological evaluation. In R. G. Frank & T. R. Elliott (Eds.), *Handbook of rehabilitation psychology* (pp. 345–358). Washington, DC: American Psychological Association.

Jonsen, A. R., Siegler, M., & Winslade, W. J. (1998). *Clinical ethics: A practical approach to ethical decisions in clinical medicine* (4th ed.). New York: McGraw-Hill.

Judge names guardian for Terri Schiavo. (2003, November 1). *The Gainesville Sun*, pp. 1B, 5B.

Karel, M. J., & Gatz, M. (1996). Factors influencing life-sustaining treatment decisions in a community sample of families. *Psychology and Aging, 11*, 226–234.

Kirsch, I. (1997). Specifying nonspecifics: Psychological mechanisms. In A. Harrington (Ed.), *The placebo effect: An interdisciplinary exploration* (pp. 166–186). Cambridge, MA: Harvard University Press.

Kline, T. J. B. (2001). Team members' and supervisors' ratings of team performance: A case of inconsistency. *Psychological Reports, 88*, 1015–1022.

Kohn, L. T., Corrigan, J. M., & Donaldson, M. S. (Eds.). (2000). *To err is human: Building a safer health system.* Washington, DC: National Academy Press.

Kreutzer, J. S., & Kolakowsky-Hayner, S. A. (2000). Laws of the house of rehab II: Practice fundamentals for improving therapeutic relationships and outcomes. *Neurorehabilitation, 14*(1), 41–51.

La Greca, A. M., Silverman, W. K., Vernberg, E. M., & Roberts, M. C. (Eds.). (2002). *Helping children cope with disasters and terrorism.* Washington, DC: American Psychological Association.

Lee, D. E. (2003). Physician-assisted suicide: Conservative critique on intervention. *Hastings Center Report, 33*(1), 17–19.

Levine, J. M. (2003). Elder neglect and abuse: Primer for primary care physicians. *Geriatrics, 58*(10), 37–44.

MacDonald, S., Hultsch, D., & Dixon, R. (2003). Performance variability is related to changes in cognition: Evidence from the Victoria Longitudinal Study. *Psychology and Aging, 18*, 510–523.

MacLeod, F. K., LaChapelle, D. L., Hadjistavropoulos, T., & Pfeifer, J. E. (2001). The effect of disability claimants' coping styles on judgments of pain, disability, and compensation: A vignette study. *Rehabilitation Psychology, 46*, 417–435.

Martelli, M. F., Bush, S. S., & Zasler, N. D. (2003). Identifying, avoiding, and addressing ethical misconduct in neuropsychological medicolegal practice. *International Journal of Forensic Psychology, 1*(1), 26–44.

Medical Reserve Corps—A guide for local leaders. Appendix C: Good Samaritan laws. Retrieved November 26, 2003, from http://www.medicalreservcorps.gov/appendixc.htm

Meier, D. E., Emmons, C. A., Wallenstein, S., Quill, T., Morrison, R. S., & Cassel, C. K. (1998). A national survey of physician-assisted suicide and euthanasia in the United States. *The New England Journal of Medicine, 338*, 1193–1201.

Miller, F. G., Quill, T. E., Brody, H., Fletcher, J. C., Gostin, L. O., & Meier, D. E. (1994). Regulating physician-assisted death. *The New England Journal of Medicine, 331*(2), 119–123.

Morris, D. B. (1997). Placebo, pain, and belief: A biocultural model. In A. Harrington (Ed.), *The placebo effect: An interdisciplinary exploration* (pp.187–207). Cambridge, MA: Harvard University Press.

Moseley, R. (2000). *Key terms in medical ethics and law: Definitions, distinctions and resources*. Unpublished manuscript, University of Florida College of Medicine.

Myers, D. G. (1989). Mental health and disaster: Preventive approaches to intervention. In R. Gist & B. Lubin (Eds.), *Psychosocial aspects of disaster* (pp. 190–228). New York: Wiley.

Myers, D. G. (1994). Psychological recovery from disaster: Key concepts for delivery of mental health services [Electronic version]. National Center for Post-Traumatic Stress Disorder, Department of Veterans Affairs. *NCP Clinical Quarterly*, *4(2)*. Retrieved April 2, 2004, from http://www.ncptsd.org/publications/cq/v4/n2/myers.html

National Academy of Neuropsychology. (2000). Test security: Official statement of the National Academy of Neuropsychology. *Archives of Clinical Neuropsychology*, *15*(5), 383–386.

National Academy of Neuropsychology, Policy and Planning Committee. (2000). Presence of third party observers during neuropsychological testing: Official statement of the National Academy of Neuropsychology. *Archives of Clinical Neuropsychology*, *15*(5), 379–380.

National Rural Behavioral Health Center. (n.d.). Retrieved November 26, 2003, from http://www.nrbhc.org

Nelson, P. A., Dial, J. G., & Joyce, A. (2002). Validation of the cognitive test for the blind as an assessment of intellectual functioning. *Rehabilitation Psychology*, *47*, 184–193.

Nicholson, K., Martelli, M. F., & Zasler, N. D. (2001). Does pain confound interpretation of neuropsychological test results? *Rehabilitation Psychology*, *16*, 225–230.

Palmer, S., & Glass, T. A. (2003). Family function and stroke recovery: A review. *Rehabilitation Psychology*, *48*, 255–265.

Patterson, D. R., & Ford, G. R. (2000). Burn injuries. In R. Frank & T. Elliot (Eds.), *Handbook of rehabilitation psychology* (pp. 145–162). Washington, DC: American Psychological Association.

Patterson, D. R., & Jensen, M. P. (2003). Hypnosis and clinical pain. *Psychological Bulletin*, *129*, 495–521.

Petersen, S., Schwartz, R. C., Sherman-Slate, E., Frost, H., Straub, J. L., & Damjanov, N. (2003). Relationship of depression and anxiety to cancer patients' medical decision-making. *Psychology Reports*, *93*, 323–334.

Phelps, R., & Reed, G. M. (2004). The integration and consolidation of health care: Implications for psychology in primary care. In R. G. Frank, S. H. McDaniel, J. H. Bray, & M. Heldring (Eds.), *Primary care psychology* (pp. 23–43). Washington, DC: American Psychological Association.

Plows, C. W., Tenery, Jr., R. M., Hartford, A., Miller, D., Morse, L., Rakatansky, H., et al. (1999). Medical futility in end-of-life care: Report of the Council on Ethical and Judicial Affairs. *Journal of the American Medical Association*, *281*, 937–941.

Ptacek, J. T., & Eberhardt, T. L. (1996). Breaking bad news: A review of the literature. *Journal of the American Medical Association*, *276*, 496–502.

Rogers, R. (Ed.). (1997). *Clinical assessment of malingering and deception* (2nd ed.). New York: Guilford Press.

Rosner, F., Berger, J. T., Kark, P., Potash, J., & Bennett, A. J. (2000). Disclosure and prevention of medical errors. *Archives of Internal Medicine, 160,* 2089–2092.

Rozensky, R. H., Sweet, J. J., & Tovian, S. M. (1997). *Psychological assessment in medical settings.* New York: Plenum Press.

Ruchinskas, R. A., & Curyto, K. J. (2003). Cognitive screening in geriatric rehabilitation: *Rehabilitation Psychology, 48,* 14–22.

Ruddy, N. B., & Schroeder, C. S. (2004). Making it in the real world: Diverse models of collaboration in primary care. In R. G. Frank, S. H. McDaniel, J. H. Bray, & M. Heldring (Eds.), *Primary care psychology* (pp. 149–168). Washington, DC: American Psychological Association.

Ruzek, J. I. (2002). Dissemination of information and early intervention practices in the context of mass violence or large-scale disaster. *Behavior Therapist, 25,* 32–36.

Sammons, M. T., Gorny, S. W., Zinner, E. S., & Allen, R. P. (2000). Prescriptive authority for psychologists: A consensus of support. *Professional Psychology: Research and Practice, 31,* 604–609.

Sbordone, R. J. (2001). Limitations of neuropsychological testing to predict the cognitive and behavioral functioning of persons with brain injury in real-world settings. *Neurorehabilitation, 16*(4), 199–201.

Schultheis, M. T., Hillary, F., & Chute, D. L. (2003). The neurocognitive driving test: Applying technology to the assessment of driving ability following brain injury. *Rehabilitation Psychology, 48,* 275–280.

Schwartz, H. I., Curry, L., Blank, K., & Gruman, C. (2001). Physician-assisted suicide or voluntary euthanasia: A meaningless distinction for practicing physicians? *The Journal of Clinical Ethics, 12*(1), 51–63.

Scott, R. (1998). *Professional ethics: A guide for rehabilitation professionals.* St. Louis, MO: Mosby.

Sears, S., Evans, G. D., & Kuper, B. D. (2003). Rural social service systems as behavioral health delivery systems. In B. Stamm & E. Hudnall (Eds.), *Rural behavioral health care: An interdisciplinary guide* (pp. 109–120). Washington, DC: American Psychological Association.

Sharma, P., & Kerl, S. B. (2002). Suggestions for psychologists working with Mexican American individuals and families in health care settings. *Rehabilitation Psychology, 47,* 230–239.

Social Security Administration Final Regulations for Ticket to Work and Self Sufficiency Program, Sections 411.100–411.730.66 Fed. Reg. 67,420 (Dec. 28, 2001).

Souder, E., & O'Sullivan, P. (2003). Disruptive behaviors of older adults in an institutional setting: Staff time required to manage disruptions. *Journal of Gerontological Nursing, 29*(8), 31–36.

Spiro, H. (1997). The placebo: Is it much ado about nothing? In A. Harrington (Ed.), *The placebo effect: An interdisciplinary exploration* (pp. 12–36). Cambridge, MA: Harvard University Press.

Stensland, J., Moscovice, I., & Christianson, J. (2002). Future financial viability of rural hospitals. *Health Care Financing Review*, 23(4), 175–187.

Stepanski, E., Rybarczyk, B., Lopez, M., & Stevens, S. (2002). Assessment and treatment of sleep disorders in older adults: A review for rehabilitation psychologists. *Rehabilitation Psychology*, 48, 23–36.

Strasser, D. C., Falconer, J. A., & Martino-Saltmann, D. (1994). The rehabilitation team: Staff perceptions of the hospital environment, the interdisciplinary team environment, and interprofessional relations. *Archives of Physical Medicine and Rehabilitation*, 75, 177–182.

Stutts, M., Kreutzer, J. S., Barth, J. T., Ryan, T., Hickman II, J., Devany, C. W., & Marwitz, J. H. (1991). Cognitive impairment in persons with recent spinal cord injury: Findings and implications for clinical practice. *Neurorehabilitation*, 1(3), 79–85.

Sullivan, A. D., Hedberg, K., & Fleming, D. W. (2000). Legalized physician-assisted suicide in Oregon: The second year. *The New England Journal of Medicine*, 342, 598–604.

Sweet, J. J., Grote, C., & van Gorp, W. G. (2002). Ethical issues in forensic neuropsychology. In S. Bush & M. Drexler (Eds.), *Ethical issues in clinical neuropsychology* (pp. 103–133). Lisse, The Netherlands: Royal Swets & Zeitlinger.

Sweet, J., & Moulthrop, M. (1999). Self-examination questions as a means of identifying bias in adversarial assessments. *Journal of Forensic Neuropsychology*, 1, 73–88.

Swiercinsky, D. P. (2002). Ethical issues in neuropsychological rehabilitation. In S. Bush & M. Drexler (Eds.), *Ethical issues in clinical neuropsychology* (pp. 135–163). Lisse, The Netherlands: Royal Swets & Zeitlinger.

Terri's law is challenged. (2003, October 30). *The Gainesville Sun*, pp. 1A, 4A.

Thomsen, O. O., Wulff, H. R., Martin, A., & Singer, P. A. (1993). What do gastroenterologists in Europe tell cancer patients? *Lancet*, 341, 473–476.

Turner, J. A., Deyo, R. A., Loeser, J. D., Von Korff, M., & Fordyce, W. E. (1994). The importance of placebo effects in pain treatment and research. *Journal of the American Medical Association*, 271, 1609–1614.

VandenBos, G., & Williams, S. (2000). The internet versus the telephone: What is telehealth, anyway? *Professional Psychology: Research and Practice*, 31, 490–492.

Vanderploeg, R. D., & Curtiss, G. (2001). Malingering assessment: Evaluation of validity of performance. *Rehabilitation Psychology*, 16, 245–251.

Van Servellen, G. (1997). *Communication skills for the health care professional: Concepts and techniques*. Gaithersburg, MD: Aspen Publishers.

Vincent, C., Taylor-Adams, S., & Stanhope, N. M. (1998). Framework for analyzing risk and safety in clinical medicine. *British Medical Journal*, 316, 1154–1157.

Wagenfield, M. O., Murray, J. D., Mohatt, D. F., & DeBruyn, J. C. (1993). *Mental health and rural America: 1980–1993*. Washington, DC: Health Resources and Services Administration, Office of Rural Health Policy.

Wallace, S. P., Abel, E. K., Stefanowicz, P., & Pourat, N. (2001). Long-term care and the elderly population. In R. M. Andersen, T. H. Rice, & G. F. Kominski

(Eds.), *Changing the U.S. health services, policy, and management* (2nd ed., pp. 205–223). San Francisco: Jossey-Bass.

Weijer, C. (2002). Placebo trials and tribulations. *Canadian Medical Association Journal, 166,* 603–604.

Welie, J. V. M. (2002). Why physicians? Reflections on the Netherlands' new euthanasia law. *Hastings Center Report, 32*(1), 42–44.

Wilde, E., Bush, S., & Zeifert, P. (2002). Ethical neuropsychological practice in medical settings. In S. Bush & M. Drexler (Eds.), *Ethical issues in clinical neuropsychology* (pp. 195–221). Lisse, The Netherlands: Royal Swets & Zeitlinger.

Young, B. H. (2002). Navigating and brief screening guidelines for working in large group settings following catastrophic events [Electronic version]. *National Center for Post-Traumatic Stress Disorder Clinical Quarterly, 11*(1), 1–7.

AUTHOR INDEX

Dial, J. G., 92
Dijkers, M., 91
Dijkstra, K., 212
Disaster Response Network of the North Carolina Psychological Foundation, 20
Dixon, R., 147
Donaldson, M. S., 169
D'Onofrio, C., 220
Dovey, S. M., 169
Dresser, R. S., 188
Driscoll, W. D., 139

Easling, I., 9
Eberhardt, T. L., 59
Ekman-Turner, R. M., 169
Elliott, T. R., 5, 84, 117, 140
Emanuel, E. J., 137
Emanuel, L. L., 137
Enright, M. F., 9
Etcoff, L., 69
Ettner, S. L., 181
Evans, G. D., 139

Falconer, J. A., 117
Fallowfield, L., 59
Farmer, J. E., 5
Fleming, D. W., 216
Foley, K., 220
Folstein, M., 73
Ford, G. R., 173, 179
Fordyce, W. E., 108
Frank, R. G., 5, 84, 139, 140
Frankel, R., 59
Frost, H., 59
Fulmer, T., 182

Gansler, D., 73
Gatchel, R. J., 37, 40
Gatz, M., 137, 192
Gerety, M. B., 137
Girgis, A., 59
Glass, T. A., 151
Glueckauf, R. L., 99
Gorman, P. W., 83
Gorny, S. W., 140
Gostin, L. O., 45, 50, 179, 193, 216
Grant, I., 69
Greene, A. F., 81
Grote, C., 160
Gruman, C., 220
Guenther, R., 4

Guerin, B., 157

Hadjistavropoulos, T., 169
Hagglund, K. J., 5, 137, 182
Haley, W. E., 5, 9, 139
Handelsman, M., 211
Hanley, J., 69
Hansen, N. D., 81
Hanson, S. L., 4, 203
Harrington, A., 108
Health Insurance Portability and Accountability Act of 1996, 45
Heaton, R., 69
Hedberg, K., 216
Heldring, M., 5, 139, 140
Hendin, H., 220
Hernandez, B., 179
Hickman, H. J., 31
Hillary, F., 147
Holloway, J. D., 45
Holzer, J., 73
Hultsch, D., 147

Jackson, H., 69
Jennings, B., 220
Jensen, M. P., 81
Johnstone, B., 69
Jonsen, A. R., 108
Joyce, A., 92
Judge Names Guardian, 220

Kampfer, K., 69
Kanten, D. N., 137
Karel, M. J., 137, 192
Kark, P., 169
Kerkhoff, T. R., 4, 203
Kerl, S. B., 117
Ketterson, T. K., 99
Kewman, D. G., 182
Keys, C., 179
Kimmance, S., 69
Kirsch, I., 108
Kline, T. J., B., 99
Kohn, L. T., 169
Kolakowsky-Hayner, S. A., 126
Koocher, G. P., 45
Kreutzer, J. S., 31, 126
Kupner, B. D., 139

LaChapelle, D. L., 169
La Greca, A. M., 20
Lee, D. E., 220

Sweet, J., 9, 160, 169
Swiercinsky, D. P., 211

Taylor-Adams, S., 170
Terri's Law, 220
Thomsen, O. O., 59
Tovian, S. M., 9
Tuley, M. R., 137
Turner, J. A., 108

VandenBos, G., 99, 140
Vanderploeg, R. D., 69, 169
van Gorp, W. G., 160
Van Servellen, G., 55
Vernberg, E. M., 20
Vincent, C., 170

Von Korff, M., 108

Wagenfield, M. O., 139
Wallace, S. P., 181, 182
Weijer, C., 108
Welie, J. V. M., 220
Wilde, E., 91, 161
Williams, S., 99
Winslade, W. J., 108
Wulff, H. R., 59

Young, B. H., 20

Zasler, N. D., 166, 169
Zeifert, P., 91
Zinner, E. S., 140

SUBJECT INDEX

Other Harassment standard, 186
Outpatient services, 139–179
Outreach volunteers, burn trauma, 134–135, 171–172, 177
Overwhelmed psychologist, 92–100
  APA Ethics Code applicability, 94–95
  case description, 92–94
  context and stakeholders, 96–97
  and institutional practices, 95–97

Pain
  and disability evaluation, 169
  and malingering, 60–69, 161–170
Palliative care, 216
Paternalistic approach
  risk-taking in outpatient post-stroke, 151–152
  totally incapacitated patient, 187, 191
Persistent vegetative state, 183–192
  APA Ethics Code, 185–187
  commentary on, 191–192
  legal concepts, 187–188
Personal Problems and Conflicts standard, 72
Physician-assisted suicide
  commentary on, 220
  legal concepts, 216
  and treatment refusal, 74–75
  and treatment withdrawal, 216
Placebo-based therapy, 100–109
  APA Ethics Code applicability, 102–105
  case description, 100–101
  case disposition, 108
  case resolution, 107–108
  commentary on, 108–109
  context and stakeholders, 106–107
  conversion disorder, 100–109
  legal concepts, 105–106
Power of attorney
  decision making, 208
  end-of-life decisions, 208, 211
Prejudice, accommodation, 117–126
Prescription privileges, rationale, 139–140
Primary care settings, 139–179
Privacy rules
  medical records, HIPAA, 45, 49–50
  and observation of assessment, 156
Professional boundary conflicts
  intensive care unit consultation, 28–37
  mild traumatic brain injury, 20–28
Professional competence. See Boundaries of Competence standard; Maintaining Competence standard

Professional cooperation. See Cooperation With Other Professionals standard
Protecting patients' welfare. See Beneficence
Provider conflicts
  mild traumatic brain injury, 20–28
  and professional boundaries, ICU, 28–37
Proxies
  domestic partners, 208, 210
  totally incapacitated patient, 183–193
  and treatment refusal, 137

Quality of care, and provider conflicts, 26
Quality of life, and right to die, 212–221

Racial bias, accommodation of, 117–126
Record keeping. See Documentation of Professional and Scientific Work and Maintenance of Records
Recording standard
  case description, 152–154
  commentary on, 160–161
  third party observation of assessment, 155
Recusal from care, 80–81
Referrals and Fees standard, placebo therapy, 104–105
Refusal to treat, rights, 124
Reimbursement restriction practices, 99
Release of Test Data standard
  placebo therapy, conversion disorder, 105
  risk-taking in outpatient post-stroke, 146
  third party observation of testing, 156
Respect for autonomy
  boundaries of, 125–126
  and difficult behavior, 122
  risk-taking in outpatient post-stroke, 141–152
  and treatment refusal, 71, 80–81
  and truth telling, 54
Respect for People's Rights and Dignity principle
  and difficult behavior, 120
  family-health care team disagreements, 111
  and incompetence perceptions, 195, 203–204
  malingering, 62
  medical record documentation, 42–43
  nonstandardized testing, stroke, 86–87

placebo therapy, conversion disorder, 102–103

and professional boundary conflicts, ICU, 31

and provider conflicts, 23, 31

return-to-work issues, patient with burns, 173

and right to die, 214

risk-taking in outpatient post-stroke, 144

totally incapacitated patient, 185

truth telling, cancer, 52

Response validity measures, malingering, 163, 169

Responsibility principle. *See* Fidelity and Responsibility principle

Return-to-work issues, 170–179

case description, 170–173

and catastrophic injury, 170–179

Reverse discrimination, inpatient, 120

Right not to know/right to know, truth telling, 54, 59

Right to die, 212–221

APA Code of Ethics, 214–215

case description, 212–213

context and stakeholders, 216–218

and quality of life, 212–221

Right to refuse treatment. *See* Treatment refusal

Risk-taking behavior, 141–152

APA Ethics Code applicability, 144–146

case description, 141–143

functional assessment, 149–150, 152

legal concepts, patient post-stroke, 146–147

neuropsychological testing, 148–149

outpatient post-stroke, 141–152

respect for autonomy, 141–152

Same-sex partners, 204–212

assent in decision making, 204–212

case description, 204–205

do-not-resuscitate decisions, 204–212

health care staff bias, 206, 210

as proxies, 208, 212

Secondary gain. *See* Malingering

Self-determination right

and capacity determinations, 203–204

and right to die, 220

and truth telling, cancer, 52

September 11 attack, 10–20

Skilled nursing facilities, payment system, 182

Speech difficulties, nonstandardized testing, 84–92

Spinal cord injury

family-health care team disagreements, 109–117

professional boundary conflicts, ICU, 28–37

State law

domestic partner decision making, 208

elder abuse, 182

Stroke

nonstandardized testing, inpatient, 84–92

risk-taking behavior, outpatient, 141–152

Subacute care, 181–221

Substituted judgment standard

domestic partners, 208

proxy decision-making, 191

totally incapacitated patient, 187–188, 191

Suicidal ideation

burn trauma, 74–76, 175–176

medical record documentation, HIPAA, 40–50

Surrogate decision makers

do-not-resuscitate orders, 211–212

totally incapacitated patient, 183–193

Telehealth, 99

Terminal illness

right to die, 212–221

truth telling, 50–60

Terminating Therapy standard

burn trauma, 174

family-health care team disagreements, 112

inpatient rehabilitation, 130

placebo therapy, conversion disorder, 105

truth telling, cancer, 54

Terri Schiavo case, 220

Test Construction standard, patient post-stroke, 146

Testing. *See* Assessment standards

Tetraplegia, family-health care team disagreements, 109–117

Therapy standards. *See specific standards*

Therapy Involving Couples or Families standard

ABOUT THE AUTHORS

Stephanie L. Hanson, PhD, ABPP (Rp), received PhDs in developmental and clinical psychology from Vanderbilt University. From 1986 to 1991 she was a clinical assistant professor at the University of Missouri School of Medicine, during which time she directed inpatient psychology services at Rusk Rehabilitation Center and helped establish their first postdoctoral psychology training program. She also established psychological services at the University's Women's Health Center. In 1991, she moved to North Carolina, where she led the development of the first comprehensive outpatient brain injury program at Charlotte Institute of Rehabilitation. She subsequently worked as the neuro program development coordinator for Whitaker Rehabilitation Center in Winston-Salem. Since 1996, Dr. Hanson has held the position of associate dean of the University of Florida's College of Public Health and Health Professions. Dr. Hanson chaired the Ethics Committee for the American Psychological Association (APA) Division 22 (Rehabilitation Psychology) for seven years (1993–2000) and served as a Division 22 Executive Committee member (1998–2001). She was one of the first women board certified in rehabilitation psychology by the American Board of Professional Psychology and was on the board of directors of the American Board of Rehabilitation Psychology from 1999 to 2002. She has chaired multiple APA-sponsored continuing education workshops and symposia, published, and taught on health care ethics.

Thomas R. Kerkhoff, PhD, ABPP (Rp), completed his undergraduate education at Xavier University in Cincinnati and was granted both a master's degree and doctorate in clinical psychology from Virginia Commonwealth University. He has served on the American Psychological Association Division 22 (Rehabilitation Psychology) Social and Ethical Responsibility Committee since 1996, and has presented numerous workshops and lectures focused on the clinical case study approach to applied ethics. Dr. Kerkhoff is currently a clinical associate professor in the Department of Clinical and Health Psychology, University of Florida. He teaches undergraduate health science applied ethics and graduate rehabilitation psychology, and he provides clinical rehabilitation psychology services to the Shands Health Care system.

Shane Bush, PhD, ABPP, ABPN, is in independent practice in Smithtown, New York, and is director of neuropsychological services at the St. Johnland Head Injury Rehabilitation Center in Kings Park, New York. He is board certified in rehabilitation psychology by the American Board of Professional Psychology and board certified in neuropsychology by the American Board of Professional Neuropsychology. He is chair of the Social and Ethical Responsibility Committee of Division 22 (Rehabilitation Psychology) and a member of the Ethics Committee of Division 22 (Clinical Neuropsychology) of the American Psychological Association. He is a member of New York State Psychological Association's Committee on Ethical Practice. He is coeditor of the textbook *Ethical Issues in Clinical Neuropsychology*. He is an editorial board member of *The Clinical Neuropsychologist*, coediting the Ethical and Professional Issues section. He is the coordinator of the Grand Rounds section of the *National Academy of Neuropsychology Bulletin*. He has presented on ethical issues in rehabilitation psychology and neuropsychology at national conferences and has authored or coauthored chapters and articles related to health care ethics. He is a veteran of both the U.S. Marine Corps and the Navy.